CHRISTIAN RELIEF AND DEVELOPMENT

CHRISTIAN RELIEF AND DEVELOPMENT

DEVELOPING WORKERS FOR EFFECTIVE MINISTRY

Edgar J. Elliston
EDITOR

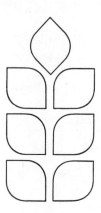

WORD PUBLISHING
Dallas · London · Sydney · Singapore

CHRISTIAN RELIEF AND DEVELOPMENT

Diligent effort has been made to locate sources and obtain permission for quotations used in this book. In the event of any unintended omission, modifications will gladly be incorporated in future editions.

Unless indicated otherwise, all Scripture quotations in this volume are from the New International Version of the Bible, copyright © 1983 by the New York International Bible Society. Used by permission of Zondervan Bible Publishers. Quotations indicated NEB are from The New English Bible, © The Delegates of The Oxford University Press and the Syndics of The Cambridge University Press, 1961, 1970. Reprinted by permission. Those indicated TEV are from Today's English Version, © American Bible Society 1966, 1971, 1976. Used by permission. Those indicated RSV are from the Revised Standard Version, © 1946, 1952, 1971 by the Division of Christian Education of the National Council of the Churches of Christ in the USA. Used by permission.

"Comparison of Forms of Education" is an adaptation of "Ideal Type Models of Formal and Non-Formal Education" in Non-Formal Education and Development, © 1977 by T. J. Simkins.

The poem *Conclusion* by Steven Turner, © 1985, is reprinted with permission of Hodder & Stoughton and Lion Publishing.

Library of Congress Cataloging-in-Publication Data

Christian relief and development.

  Bibliography: p.
  Includes index.
  1. Missions—Developing countries. 2. Community development—Religious aspects—Christianity. 3. Church charities—Developing countries. 4. Rural development personnel—Training of. 5. Missionaries—Training of.
I. Elliston, Edgar J., 1943–
BV2750.C47   1989   261.8'09172'4   89-5746
ISBN 0-8499-3155-X

Printed in the United States of America

9 8 0 1 2 3 9 BKC 9 8 7 6 5 4 3 2 1

To
Donna
Jack
Dona Dea
David

Contents

List of Figures, Tables

Foreword

CHRISTIAN RELIEF is never complete in itself. It must, biblically, eventuate in a ministry of development on behalf of the peoples being assisted. This volume carefully develops that theme.

The theme and concept of Christian development is fairly new in the Christian church in the latter part of this century, but the idea is as old as the Scriptures themselves. Scripture clearly enunciates our Christian responsibility to the poor, the displaced, the widowed, and the fatherless; and this book aids us immeasurably in being able to respond redemptively and creatively to those injunctions.

Edgar Elliston has done the cause of Christ—particularly in what we call the "First World," in contrast to the "Third World"—a great service in the presentation of this most helpful and practical analysis of an oft-neglected scriptural mandate. As one who has been involved in relief and development ministries all over the world for a quarter of a century, I know of no work in this subject area as complete and comprehensive as this volume. He and his colleagues in the School of World Mission at Fuller Theological Seminary and elsewhere have produced a fascinating amalgam of practical applications for relief and development techniques, together with the implications from a theological understanding. The basic issues addressed are relevant and practical, and call for application anywhere in today's "global village."

Dr. Elliston leads us through this study from a background of years of ministry among the peoples of the hurting, ancient nation of Ethiopia, as well as elsewhere in East Africa. With his family, he worked with farmers in various types of development projects and thereby is able to guide the chapters of this book from a hands-on knowledge and from personal interaction with those receiving this type of ministry. In the programs he directed, he helped establish schools and clinics, and build roads, and he saw how this development affected local commerce. Through years of work, as a direct result, thousands of Ethiopians came to faith in Christ, churches were planted, and the Lord was honored. Relief and development became the key to unlocking this door.

I am deeply grateful for this well-documented work and commend it most heartily. Not everyone will agree with every idea and concept represented here, yet all of us will be challenged to understand why we may disagree. Anyone involved in this terribly important field of endeavor, in behalf of neglected, hurting people in the name of our Blessed Lord and Savior, will be encouraged by this presentation.

Ted W. Engstrom
President Emeritus
World Vision

Introduction

IN 1969, I WENT WITH my family to Ethiopia to join in a ministry of evangelism and church planting. The Oromo people with whom we were to serve were subsistence farmers in an isolated mountainous area. As we began to work among them, we found that a number of development-related commitments were expected by the government and needed by the people. We established schools, literacy programs, clinics, veterinary-assistance programs, and other community-related programs. We found ourselves assisting in various ways with road maintenance and bridge building. Our economic contributions to the area were at one point in time larger than the district tax receipts! We were, after the government, the largest employer in the region. Over a period of less than ten years, we began to see many effects. The local market structures had changed. The population growth rate had begun to rise sharply as the infant mortality rate dropped from nearly 60 percent to 15 percent. The educational level had changed, and some of the more able students began moving out of the area to obtain more schooling.

Those of us involved in the ministry there didn't know how to analyze these changes. We debated the relationship between our evangelism and other programs at various levels. We were concerned about our budgets. We were alarmed at the dependencies which appeared to be growing. We wondered about the ethical issues of being responsible for changes which were sure to be disruptive for the local people. On the other hand, we saw serious needs being met. We saw the health of the people improve. We saw many new churches being formed and thousands of people accepting Christ as Lord even in the midst of persecution.

As I have reflected on our experience at that time and some parallel experiences I had while serving in Kenya, I have often thought, *If I or we had only known. . . .* Much of what I would like to have known before starting out on that path through Ethiopia is contained in this book. It is our hope that this collection of information will help others as they are walking on similar paths.

OVERVIEW OF THE BOOK

The purpose of the book is to describe contemporary foundational issues which undergird the equipping of Christians to serve in relief and development ministries. These foundational concerns and constraints come from a broad range of disciplines: history, theology, ethics, anthropology, economics, sociology and missiology. Educational priorities emerge from these perspectives for program planning, implementation, evaluation and/or program selection.

This book serves as an introduction to evangelical thinking about relief and development. Beginning with a historical perspective, the authors place social ministries in a holistic picture whose hues and depth emerge from a broad disciplinary base. Building on this base the authors develop the issues of equipping Christian workers for effective service in relief and development.

Relief and development activities generally occur in a cross-cultural context. The "haves" want to help the "have nots." Whether one works in the inner-city slums of Dallas, Denver or Detroit, or among the people who live in the plastic bag "shelters" in Mathare Valley in Nairobi, Kenya, the ministry will always take the church worker across some sort of cultural barriers.

Christians who work with development and relief will benefit from this book. It addresses issues of interest both to workers in compassionate ministries and to Christian workers whose ministries are primarily in evangelism and church planting but who face some developmental questions. The same holistic perspective fits both because each may contribute to the effectiveness or frustration of the other and both expect to bring a lasting impact on the same communities they serve in the name of Christ. These workers may go to serve among the rural poor of Appalachia or the urban poor of Chicago; they may go to work with the *favela* dwellers in São Paulo or the pastoral Gabbra people of the Gobi Desert in northern Kenya. The basic principles are the same.

The evangelist continues to proclaim the message of the gospel among the poor, hopeless, oppressed, alienated, and "needy" peoples. Similarly, the evangelist also announces the Good News of the kingdom of God, calling the rich and powerful to obedient submission to the lordship of Christ. On the other hand, the development worker works with the same peoples to establish "right" relationships with one's neighbors, with God, and with the environment in which all live. Both Christian workers serve the same Lord whose purposes remain the same for all of his servants. The wide range of Christian roles should all not only complement each other, but serve to fulfill the whole purpose of God.

The book serves Christians who are seriously interested in relief and development early in their career paths at the pre-field orientation stage. It is beneficial to the mid-career workers who are seeking to broaden their awareness of this growing concern. It serves educational planners who are seeking to design the appropriate training for Christian workers in relief and development. This book also has significance for those who seek to understand how the evangelical community approaches relief and development.

Within the evangelical community is a growing commitment to social ministries. Also emerging is an uncritical approach, which leads counter to effective development and away from the primary purposes of the church. This book can provide an evangelical Christian perspective of development. It takes social issues seriously, but does not see the goal for development in just limited, materialistic, economic, or political terms. The importance of relating development to the whole field of missiology continues to be an important issue in the equipping of missionaries and other people who plan to work in relief and development ministries.

The primary significance of this book is its importance for the orientation and reorientation of Christians who are working in relief and development. This information provides an evangelical missiological perspective to equip Christians for such ministries.

Its scope is limited in two important ways. First, training for specific technical areas in which Christians may serve in relief and development is not addressed beyond a general overview of training levels (such as well drilling, medicine, literacy, and so forth). Second, this book does not describe the curricular activities or prescribe curriculum decisions. However, it does seek to provide a curricular foundation for equipping Christian workers.

The bibliography at the end of the book serves the whole book. To find a given reference simply look for the author and date of publication. While many other useful references about development-related subjects could be cited, the bibliography in this book only includes references which are cited in the text.

THEORETICAL MODEL

Rodney McKean's curricular research model (1977) provides a way to view how the foundational disciplines serve to undergird the process of curricular decision-making for Christian relief and development

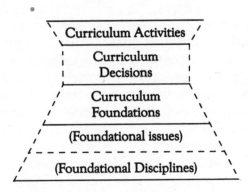

Figure 1: Theoretical Model (McKean 1977:3)

workers. The curriculum foundations emerge from the basic disciplinary perspectives and issues.

The design of curricula for equipping Christians to work with either relief or development is a growing challenge. Developmental curricula include more than just the books and teaching materials used in training courses. They include all of the processes used both to help the learners identify learning needs and to meet those needs. Such curriculum concerns are envisioned broadly in this book.

McKean suggests that curriculum development should be based on the relevant foundational disciplines. In the case of this book, these disciplines include at least the following: missiology, anthropology, sociology, history, theology, ethics, and economics. From these foundational disciplines, the foundational issues arise. The issues relate to needs and how to meet these needs in the context of values, which also emerge from these foundational disciplines.

As illustrated by figure 1, the book is divided into two major sections: foundational perspectives and issues, and curriculum foundations for equipping Christian workers.

ACKNOWLEDGMENTS

I want to express my appreciation to several people who encouraged and advised through the development of this project. The many participants in the Lake Wales series of conferences who came both from Christian institutions of higher education and from development agencies provided the initial encouragement for this text. I appreciate Paul E. Pierson, dean of the School of World Mission, Fuller Theological Seminary, who permitted time away from teaching responsibilities to edit this manuscript. I owe debts of gratitude to several colleagues including C. Peter Wagner and Paul E. Hiebert who encouraged me and advised me with the development of this project. Mo Whitworth tirelessly helped with the manuscript. Sheri Livingston provided very helpful editorial assistance. Finally, I thank the contributors to this volume.

E. J. Elliston
Editor

1

Missions and Community Development: A Historical Perspective

Paul E. Pierson

THE CHURCH OF JESUS CHRIST, especially its missionary arm, has normally understood the transformation of society to be an essential part of its task. While the focal point of missions has been to communicate the Good News of Christ, to call men and women to repentance and faith, and to baptize them into the church, it has also involved a process of teaching them to "observe all things" that Jesus commanded.

Christians have assumed that this obedience would lead to the transformation of their physical and social as well as their spiritual lives. Sometimes this has been well done, sometimes poorly done. But missionaries—whether they were Celts moving from Ireland to Great Britain and Central Europe, orthodox monks going from Kiev to Moscow and further east, American Baptists among the Nagas in Northeast India, or congregationalists in Hawaii—have always implicitly assumed that the reception and the living out of the gospel would begin to transform both individual and community life. And more often than not, specific steps were taken and institutions were established to aid this process.

Missionaries often moved by the providence of God into areas experiencing great change. They helped produce that change, often channeling it positively, and at times they helped reform some of its

PAUL E. PIERSON serves as dean and professor of the history of missions in the School of World Mission at Fuller Theological Seminary. He served from 1956 to 1973 in Brazil and Portugal.

most harsh aspects. Thus, what we would call community develop-ment has frequently, if not always, accompanied Christian missions as either an explicit part of the missionary task or an intended by-product of mission. While we recognize today that the missionaries often envi-sioned a model of the transformed community that looked suspi-ciously like the ones they knew in their own cultures, there is no doubt that this transforming dimension was an essential aspect of mission. Nor can there be any doubt that much was accomplished which was highly beneficial (see Hutchinson, 1987).

Furthermore, Christian missions have always been a result of renewal movements in the church. Such movements, more often than not, attempted to transform their own societies, or at least to focus on both evangelization and service to the poor, the marginal-ized, and the oppressed. Thus, it is natural that the missions coming out of such movements took the same concerns for the poor and oppressed to their fields of labor. The basic theological foundation for these missions was the command of Jesus Christ to go into all the world with the Good News, to call people to faith in him, and to plant the church. Additionally, there was the desire to especially manifest the love of Christ to the needy, the hungry, and the poor. This desire was seen as a valid ministry in itself, but it was also seen as a witness to the greater gift of God—the forgiveness and eternal life which came in Christ.

MONASTICISM

Nearly all Christian missionaries from the fourth to the eigh-teenth centuries were monks. There were four main traditions at that time: the *Benedictines* in the western church and the numerous move-ments which proceeded from them; the *Nestorians*, who moved east and south from Asia Minor into Arabia, India, across central Asia and into China; the *Orthodox*, who went north into the Balkan states and eventually into what is now Russia and further east; and the *Celts*, who arose in Ireland, then moved into Scotland and England, and across central Europe.

While the original purpose of monasticism was not missionary, some of the movements became missionary in spite of themselves. Others—primarily the Nestorians and Celts, and later the Francis-cans, Dominicans, and Jesuits—were ardently and purposefully mis-sionary. But in any case, these communities of monks functioned as ambassadors of the faith, moving into areas where the Christian faith had not yet penetrated, forming their communities and establishing alternative societies in areas which were either victims of constant warfare or chaos as older societies broke down.

The original intent of monasticism was to encourage men to develop lives of discipline and prayer away from the concerns of normal life. But the monasteries, and the soon-to-follow women's houses which arose, became self-sustaining communities organized around rules for daily life, rules which pertained to work as well as prayer. This concept was revolutionary in the ancient world, where manual work was seen as fit only for slaves. This concept would be emphasized again by Puritanism and have a powerful effect on the western world.

In addition, the monks were encouraged to become scholars. Thus, for the first time the practical and theoretical were embodied in the same individuals. The monks were the first intellectuals to get dirt under their fingernails. This combination helped create an atmosphere favorable to scientific development, including both workshops and libraries. The monasteries became centers of Christian faith, learning and technical progress as they expanded into northern Europe.

The contribution of monasticism to learning is well known, but its great effect on agricultural development has not been as widely recognized. Hannah writes that in the seventh century, it was the monks who possessed the

> skill, capital, organization, and faith in the future to undertake large projects of reclamation over fields long desolated by the slave system of villa life . . . and the barbarian hordes. . . . Some might have hesitated to sow crops whose fruit they might never see, but if all the founders of a monastery died others would take their place. . . . Immense tracts of barren heath and water-soaked fen were by monasteries hands turned into excellent agricultural land (1924:90–91).

In the twelfth century, the Cistercians, led by Bernard of Clairvaux, adopted great austerity, withdrew from society, and cultivated new lands in deserted places. In so doing they worked out new methods of agricultural administration and became the greatest wool producers of Europe, furnishing the raw material for the textile industry. Even today tourists visit Alcobaça, the site of the largest church in Portugal, built by the Cistercians. It is no coincidence that in that lovely town at the confluence of two small rivers, the finest fruit in Portugal is grown. The Cistercians provided this heritage by innovations introduced in the thirteenth century. Monks often found new ways of serving the world. Rome had built up roads and systems of communication, but these had fallen into disrepair. These monks, interested in keeping travel and communication open and serving travelers, founded organizations such as the hospice of St. Bernard on the road through the Alps to Italy.

The Nestorian movement, which flourished for several centuries, moved across central Asia and into India. Yet Christians in the West know little about it, primarily because most of the fruits of its labor have been lost. Still, one scholar notes:

> Nestorian missionaries introduced letters and learning among peoples who were previously illiterate, such as Turks, Vigurs, Mongols and Manchus, all of whom are said to have derived their alphabets from the Syriac, the language of the Nestorians (Stewart, 1928:36).

Monks from the Eastern church engaged in similar pursuits. Ulfilas moved north of the Danube in the fourth century and became the first person to reduce a northern European language to writing. He did so, of course, in order to translate the Scriptures. According to tradition, the Armenians were the first national group to accept Christianity as a people, late in the third century. Soon afterward, the language was reduced to writing in order that the Scriptures and other Christian literature might be made available.

Constantine, later known as Cyril, and his brother, Methodius, went as missionaries from Constantinople into the Balkan area. There they devised two alphabets in order to translate the Scriptures and establish the church. Nearly a millennium ago, monks went north and east from Kiev to Moscow and beyond. Establishing their monasteries, they were a major force in civilizing unruly tribes, bringing in better agriculture and other technology.

The Celts carried on one of the most remarkable missionary movements of any century after Patrick moved from England into Ireland in the fifth century. His spiritual descendants moved from Ireland to Scotland into England, and finally across the channel into the low countries, finally reaching into central Germany. Later, spiritual descendants moved north and became the instrument of the conversion of the Scandinavian peoples. They combined a deep love of learning along with intense spiritual discipline. "Ireland became literate for the first time in Patrick's generation" (Stimpson, 1979:147) as a result. The great monastery at Fulda founded by St. Boniface from this tradition in the eighth century became the main center of learning for much of Germany (Latourette, 1953:349). During the Carolingian Renaissance under Charlemange, the monasteries from the Celtic tradition were again the major centers of education and change. To quote Hannah again:

> On the whole they were able to achieve their destiny as Christian leaven in a rude society, to implant and preserve a Christian culture like a cultivated garden amid a wilderness of disorder (1924:86).

Thus in the West, the monasteries became "the highway of civilization, itself" (Cannon, 1960:16).

FORERUNNERS OF THE PROTESTANT MISSIONARY MOVEMENT

For nearly two centuries after the Reformation, Protestants engaged in very little missionary activity outside of Europe. However, beginning in the late sixteenth century, four movements arose which sought to renew the church according to various models. These renewal movements would construct the launching pad of the Protestant missionary movement. They were *Puritanism, Pietism, Moravianism,* and the *Wesleyan/Evangelical Revivals.*

Puritanism

The Puritans sought to "purify" the English church following a more Calvinistic model, and it was among them that the earliest Protestant missionary theology began to develop. Among the two greatest Puritan advocates of mission were Richard Baxter and John Eliot. Baxter, a pastor in England, was primarily a thinker and writer. Eliot, a pastor in New England, became an effective missionary to the Native Americans. Rooy indicates Eliot's understanding of the missionary:

> He traveled on foot and horseback, taxing his strength to the utmost, sometimes drenched for days at a time, all to bring the gospel to the natives. He brought cases to court to prevent defrauding of Indian land, pleaded clemency for convicted Indian prisoners, fought the selling of Indians into slavery, sought to secure lands and streams for Indian use, established schools for Indian children and adults, translated books, and attempted to show a deep humanitarianism that accompanied their concern for salvation (Rooy, 1965:316–317).

Pietism

Late in the seventeenth century, the Thirty Years' War had devastated Germany. The country was then subject to an unprecedented class-consciousness and saw the church totally dominated by the state.

> The truth of faith was seen in terms of propositions rather than experiential or ethical event or demand. . . Thus, between the irrelevance of the Church and the widespread despair and atheism brought about by the Thirty Years' War, Christianity soon lost its healing and transforming power (Sattler, 1982:9).

In this context, Philip Jacob Spener, who had been influenced by reading Puritan authors such as Baxter, initiated the movement which would be derisively called *Pietism*. After initiating private meetings for edification with a few parishioners, Spener published *Pia Desideria* in 1675 with suggestions for the renewal of the church. These included a more extensive use of the Word of God among the people, the establishment and diligent exercise of the spiritual priesthood, and the recognition that it was not enough to have *knowledge* of the Christian faith because Christianity consists rather of *practice*. Thus, Christians were to demonstrate to non-believers that they were considered to be their neighbors, as the Samaritan was a neighbor in Luke 10. Christians were called to love all others as they loved themselves (Spener, 1964:87–88). Spener introduced an emphasis on prayer and small-group Bible study along with the necessity of rebirth, but in addition to these emphases he included a great concern for the needy. His successor as leader of the movement was August H. Francke, who dedicated himself to the glory of God and service to his neighbor. His goal was on rebirth leading to transformed individuals then to a reformed society and world. For him, faith and action were absolutely inseparable. He demonstrated this over and over again in his ministry at the University of Halle and in his parish at Glaucha. Piety meant genuine concern for one's neighbors in terms of his or her spiritual and physical well being. Despite their zealous intolerance of worldly desires and coarse sins, it was the Pietists who fed, clothed, and educated their poorer neighbors. The education of girls of the lower classes was one of the novelties introduced by Francke. The provision of education for poor children in general was another. His orphanage, sustained only by faith, was a well-known model for that of George Mueller in Bristol. Ministry for Francke encompassed care for the physical and spiritual needs of people who, in turn, were to be involved in the restructuring of the world.

> Francke's vision encompassed the world and radiated out from Halle to the local authorities, national governments and eventually the entire

planet. The earth itself would ultimately be transformed through godly men and women serving God and neighbor, proclaiming Christ and relieving poverty and oppression. If the members of the ruling class could be converted and led into the Pietist understanding of the Christian life, the Kingdom of God could be manifested on earth in concern for the poor, an end to war, education for, in practical and spiritual matters, employment, joy and the like (Sattler, 1982:70).

The importance of understanding the goal of early Pietism becomes clear when we realize that the first Protestant missionaries to Asia came from that movement.

When Fredrick IV of Denmark wished to send missionaries to the native population in his colony in Tranquebar, India, he and his court preacher turned to Spener and Francke. In 1706, Bartholomew Ziegenbalg and Heinrich Plutschau, the first two of about sixty eighteenth-century Pietists missionaries, arrived in India. Ziegenbalg, who remained until his death in 1719, studied the religious beliefs and practices of the Hindus, translated Scripture, planted a church, set up a printing press, and established two schools, one industrial and the other a more advanced institution to prepare catechists. He stands as a prototype of Protestant missionaries to Asia. The greatest of his successors, C. S. Schwartz, not only built up the church but also stressed work with orphans and became an ambassador of peace between Muslim rulers and the British-controlled provinces in southern India. Schwartz arrived in India in 1750 and remained there until his death in 1798, never returning to Germany. Thus, the greatest of German missiologists, Gustav Warneck, wrote that Pietism

> . . . is the parent as of missions to the heathen, so also of all those saving agencies which have arisen within Christendom for the healing of religious, moral and social evils . . . a combination which was already typically exemplified in A. H. Francke (Dubose, 1979:76).

Moravianism

The Moravians who grew out of German Pietism and pre-Reformation movements constituted one of the most remarkable missionary movements in all history. Known for their one-hundred-year prayer watch in which members of the community were praying around the clock for that period, they were a highly disciplined, monastic-like community of married men and women devoted to world mission. During their early years, one in every fourteen members became a missionary to some far corner of the world. They were intensely evangelistic with "souls for the Lamb" their primary goal, but their work among the Indian tribes along the western frontier of North America is an indication of their holistic approach to mission. The work of David Zeisberger led to the community described below:

> Friedenshuetten . . . was like a garden in the wilderness. . . . It embraced twenty-nine log houses with windows and chimneys like the homesteads of the settlers and thirteen huts forming one street in the center of which stood the chapel . . . roofed with shingles and having a school house as its wing. Immediately opposite on the left side of the street was the mission house . . . back of the houses were gardens and orchards stocked with vegetables and fruit trees. The entire town was surrounded by a post and rail fence and kept scrupulously clean . . . stretching down to the river lay 250 acres of plantations and meadows with two miles of fences, and moored to the bank was found a canoe for each household of the community. The converts had large herds of cattle and hogs and poultry of every kind in abundance. They devoted more time to tilling the ground than to hunting and raised plentiful crops. Their trade was considerable in corn, maple, sugar, butter, and port which they sold to the Indians, as also in canoes made of white pine and bought by the settlers living among the Susquehanna (Schuh, 70:72).

Wesleyan Movement

The fourth stream leading into the Protestant missionary movement consisted of the Wesleyan movement in England and the Great Awakenings in North America. These were two sides of one movement, but since the Great Awakenings were, in many respects, an outgrowth of Puritanism, we will examine only the Wesleyan movement here.

Even before they experienced the assurance of salvation, the Wesleys and the Holy Club at Oxford showed concern for the poor and prisoners along with the spiritual disciplines that earned them the name "Methodists." Influenced by Pietistic Anglican praying societies and Moravians, John Wesley began to preach immediately after his heartwarming experience in 1734. While the clear focus was on evangelism and Christian nurture, especially among the neglected poor, Wesley wrote, "Christianity is essentially a social religion, to turn it into a solitary religion is indeed to destroy it" (Bready, 1942:113).

The impact of the Wesleyan movement on various movements for social reform in England is well known. Robert Raikes started

Sunday schools in order to give moral and religious instruction to the poor children on the one day of the week they were not working. This involved teaching many of them to read. He organized schools among neglected miners and colliers. John Howard tirelessly worked for the reform of the appalling conditions in prisons locally, then moved Parliament to act to improve prison conditions throughout the nation. Evangelicals in general worked to regulate child labor in the newly emerging factories and promoted the education of the masses. At Clapham, a suburb of London, several wealthy people strongly influenced by the revivals came to be known derisively as the Clapham Sect. They gave themselves to a wide variety of religious and social projects, including the long and successful effort of William Wilberforce and others to end slavery in the British Empire. The greatest of the Anglican missionary societies, the Church Missionary Society, came from the same group in 1799. It was only one of a number of missionary societies established in England in the last decade of the eighteenth century, all influenced by the revivals.

THE PROTESTANT MISSIONARY MOVEMENT

The first of these missionary societies was established through the efforts of William Carey who as a young man had been influenced by the Wesleyan movement. He had finally left the established church and became a Baptist. As a result of his challenge in 1792, the Baptist Missionary Society was formed. The following year, Carey sailed for India to initiate the first work of that society. Even though he was not the first Protestant missionary from Europe to a far corner of the earth, he has rightly been called the father of the Protestant missionary movement, primarily because his writing and career proved to be the catalyst that precipitated a host of new mission societies in Europe and soon after in North America. Thus, Carey is something of a prototype of the Protestant missionary.

No doubt his primary goal was to bring people to personal faith in Jesus Christ and thus to eternal salvation. However, he saw no conflict between that goal and the other activities for which he became well known. His two best known colleagues were Marshman, a schoolmaster, and Ward, a printer. He was deeply interested in agriculture and botany and was responsible for the founding of a horticultural and agricultural society. He hoped to make "the investment of vegetables more valuable" (Drewery, 1979:99) and lectured to the Asiatic society on the state of agriculture in one area of India.

In 1799, Carey was returning from Calcutta when he passed a village where a woman was about to be burned on the funeral pyre of her deceased husband. Unsuccessful in his attempt to persuade the woman and her relatives to desist, he never ceased to campaign against this inhuman practice.

Similarly, he campaigned against infanticide, the inhuman treatment of lepers, who were often buried or burned alive, and the needless deaths at the great religious pilgrimages. In 1802, infanticide was prohibited, but it was not until twenty-seven years later that the burning of widows was declared illegal and criminal.

His best known educational project was the establishment of the Serampore College. It was primarily to train pastors and teachers, but it also provided for the education of other youth in Christian literature and European science. This college would become one of the causes of the rift between Carey and his colleagues on the field on the one hand, and the Baptist Missionary Society in England on the other.

I will add only a few examples of the nineteenth-century concern for social transformation, but the numbers are almost unlimited.

Samuel Mills and his student colleagues took the initiative and established the first foreign missionary society in the United States, the American Board of Commissioners for Foreign Missions, in 1810 at Andover Seminary. One of its best-known early fields was Hawaii, then known as the Sandwich Islands. While those early congregationalist missionaries have been much maligned by James Michener, the reality is quite different from that which he has portrayed. The major focus of the missionaries was conversion of men and women to Christ and the gathering of converts into churches. However, they showed great concern to protect the native peoples from the economic and sexual exploitation of the traders, sailors, and business people who came to the islands. Indeed, much of the enmity shown to the missionaries by their contemporaries was due to this fact. After a few decades, the islands were dotted not only with congregational churches, but with schoolhouses in which Hawaiian youngsters were taught to read and write by Hawaiian teachers.

A pioneer named Hiram Bingham and his colleagues were told in 1819 to "obtain adequate knowledge of the language of the people to make them acquainted with letters and to give them the Bible with the skill to read it." They invented a system of writing the language using Roman characters which they used to translate the Bible and various textbooks. Eventually, they published a wide range of literature. By 1873, they had printed one hundred and fifty-three different works and thirteen magazines, plus an almanac in the Hawaiian language (Tate, 1962:182-202).

It is well known that David Livingston wished to evangelize Africa, but his concern for economic development was also strong. He hoped to open Africa to commerce and trade, primarily because he thought that would be the quickest way to end the slave trade. Nevertheless, his concern for the transformation of African society was very clear. However, Willis Banks, an obscure Presbyterian evangelist who worked in a backward area of Southern Brazil, showed the same concern. He built the first brickyard in the area, brought children to live with his family, taught them to read and sent them out to teach others. Using a home medical guide, he treated infections, tuberculosis, malaria, worms, and malnutrition. He introduced better methods of agriculture and care of livestock. He built the first sawmill in the area and constructed machinery to cut silage. An anthropologist visiting the area twenty years after Banks's death recounted a striking illustration of the community development which resulted. He visited two isolated villages, both situated in virtually identical circumstances with inhabitants of the same racial and cultural backgrounds. One was Presbyterian and had benefited from Banks's evangelism and leadership in community development. The other continued to follow the traditional folk Catholicism. The people of Volta Grande were Presbyterians. They lived in brick and wooden houses. They used water filters and in some cases had home-produced electricity. They owned canoes and motor launches for travel to a nearby city. They cultivated vegetables along with the traditional rice, beans, corn, manioc, and bananas. They had two small herds of dairy cattle and produced and consumed milk, cheese and butter. They received and read newspapers, had the Bible and other books readily available, and all were literate. The community had pooled its resources to build a school and donated it to the state with the stipulation that a teacher be provided and paid. Consequently, there was an excellent primary school there, and many of its graduates continued their studies in the city. Religious services were held three times a week even though the pastor visited only once a month.

On the other hand, the inhabitants of Jiporura lived in daub and wattle houses with no furniture. They engaged only in marginal agriculture. They did not boil or filter their water. They had no canoes, used tiny kerosene lamps for light, and were mostly illiterate. There was a school which had been donated to the community by a few Japanese families who had once lived in the area, but the people showed no interest in maintaining it and had ruined the building by stealing its doors and windows. Leisure time was filled by playing cards and drinking *Cachaç,* a kind of cheap sugarcane rum. Alcoholism was common (Williams, 1967:181–185).

In a few cases, missionaries went beyond traditional social service and attacked the political and economic injustices of colonialism. A celebrated example took place in the Belgian Congo at the turn of the century. Two missionaries from the Southern Presbyterian Church in the United States, William Sheppard and William Morrison, observed the forced labor of the Africans in the rubber-making industry and published articles calling the monopolistic economic exploitation of the people "twentieth-century slavery." They asserted, "There are armed sentries of the chartered trading companies who force the men and women to spend most of their nights making rubber and the price they are paid for it is so meager they cannot live upon it" (Sholoff, 1969:192). This brought international attention, and the missionaries were sued for libel. The suit was finally dismissed, but it created tensions between the governments of the United States and Belgium.

In summary, virtually all missionary movements during the history of the church have been concerned about and involved in what is called "community development." They have seen it as a part of their ministry of communicating the gospel. Furthermore, they demonstrated a remarkable degree of consistency through history with their focus on education, health care, agriculture, and various kinds of social uplift for neglected or oppressed members of society.

There were usually three common goals of educational institutions: to prepare leadership for the church, to be an instrument to improve society, and to evangelize non-Christian students. Degrees of success varied, but literacy rates among Protestants, especially, rose. Although the cultures of northeast India were very traditional well into this century, that part of the country, now heavily Christian, has the second-highest literacy rate in the nation.

According to a Brazilian Presbyterian paper, in 1915 the illiteracy rate among Roman Catholics in that country was between 60 and 80 percent, while that of Protestants was only one-fourth of that figure (Pierson, 1974:107–108). The work of Scottish missionary Alexander Duff, who introduced western education into India, was well known. Missions also established the great majority of schools established in Africa during the colonial period. Protestant missionaries initiated many of the most outstanding universities in Asia, including Yonsei University and Ehwa Women's University in Seoul.

Reporting on the educational work of the Basel Mission in the Gold Coast (Ghana), the Phelps-Stokes Commission reported in 1921:

> The educational effort of the Basel Mission in the Gold Coast has produced one of the most interesting and effective systems of schools observed in Africa. . . . First of all their mechanical shops trained and employed a large number of natives as journeymen. . . . Secondly, the commercial activities reached the economic life of the people, influencing their agricultural activities, their expenditures for food and clothing (Aberle, 1945:223).

Just as many of the pioneering monasteries had done in Europe, and the Puritans and Moravians in North America, many Protestant missions introduced new crops and agricultural techniques in Asia, Africa, and elsewhere. C. W. Abel of the London Missionary Society did outstanding agricultural work in Melanesia. Members of the Basel Mission introduced the cultivation of cacao, now a major crop in Ghana. And, the work of a Presbyterian named Sam Higgenbottom in Allahabad, India, is legendary.

Early in the nineteenth century, a limited amount of medical knowledge was often regarded as necessary even for evangelistic missionaries. However, prior to the middle of the century, fully trained physicians were sent. The first was Dr. John Scudder, sent by the American Board to India. His granddaughter, Dr. Ida Scudder, later established perhaps the greatest of all missionary medical centers at Vellore, India. Dr. Peter Parker introduced eye surgery into China. His successor, Dr. John Kerr, published twelve medical works in Chinese, built up a large hospital, and was the first missionary in China to open an institution for the mentally ill. Presbyterians in Thailand established no fewer than thirteen hospitals and twelve dispensaries.

However, along with educational, medical, and agricultural ministries, others focused on some of the most neglected and depressed members of society. Half of the tuberculosis work in India was done by missions, and Christian institutions took the lead in the treatment and training of workers for people afflicted with that disease. In a similar manner, missions took the lead in working with lepers in a number of Asian countries and established orphanages for abandoned children. There were pioneers in establishing teacher training schools, thus not only establishing schools, but multiplying them by the training of more teachers, many of whom were Christians.

However, one of the most significant results of Christian missions on society as a whole came through their role in ministering to and raising the status of women. In societies where women often had very low status or no rights, missions often affected their situation. They would first evangelize them and teach them to see themselves as children of God. Then they would encourage them to study, develop their gifts, and in some cases to enter professions, primarily in education and medicine.

An excellent work by R. Pierce Beaver, *American Protestant Women in Mission: A History of the First Feminist Movement in North America*, gives many evidences of the impact of women missionaries on the status of women in many countries. Focusing primarily on the evangelization of women in areas where men normally could not have had contact with them, they soon branched out into educational and medical work with women. From there the movement progressed to the point where women were frequently employed as lay evangelists, called "Bible women," especially in Korea and China. Even though they were not given equal status with men, these faithful workers had a very powerful impact not only on the growth of the church but on the status of other women in their societies. When the first Protestant missionaries arrived in Korea in 1884 and 1885, a woman had no status in society other than as the daughter of her father, the wife of her husband, or the mother of her son. By the middle of the following century, as a result of the work of Christian missions, not only had the largest women's university in the world been established in Seoul, Korea, but the president of that university, Dr. Helen Kim, was widely recognized as one of the greatest educators of Korea and as a great leader of evangelization in the church.

Women missionaries from the United States not only initiated the first medical work for women in India and China. They also established the first schools for women at various levels, eventually establishing nursing and medical schools for women. They had a powerful impact on the medical care of women in those societies, and on their status, as well. One result is that medicine today is the most prestigious profession open to women in India, and there are thousands of women doctors in that country.

Dr. Clara Swain, the first woman medical missionary appointed to any field by any society or board, arrived in India in 1870. Beaver makes it clear that the people saw no separation between their work as medical missionaries and evangelists.

Their manifestation of loving concern for their patients as individuals and their mediation of the love of God in Christ for persons were as important as their scientific knowledge and technical skill. Their writings and speeches of the women medical missionaries make it clear that they consider themselves evangelists (Beaver, 1980:135).

We conclude our brief survey of the first nineteen centuries of Christian missions with a brief examination of the series of lectures by James S. Dennis. He gave these lectures at Princeton Theological Seminary beginning in 1896. In them he expounded what he called the sociological aspects of foreign missions (Dennis, 1897, 1899, 1906). They were delivered at staunchly orthodox Princeton at a time when the social gospel movement was gaining momentum in the United States. Dennis argued that the historical focus of Christian missions was to communicate the gospel, call men and women to faith in Jesus Christ, and gather them into the church with the belief that social change would come as a result. His lectures presented massive evidence as a vindication of his point of view that missions introduced a social dynamic which changed persons *and* their communities and societies.

Dennis demonstrated that no contradiction existed between the task of evangelism and social transformation. Indeed, they were two sides of one coin. He also documented the contribution of Christian missions to social progress in several areas discussed in this book and many others. Among them were the establishment and promotion of education, contributions to the intellectual life, deliverance from the opium habit, motivation of habits of industry, elevation of women, restraint of polygamy, abolishment of child marriage, improvement of domestic life and family training, protection of children, diminishing of infanticide, diminishing of the slave trade and inhumane labor, abolishment of cannibalism and the diminishing of human sacrifice, crusades against foot binding, promotion of prison reform and famine relief and better care of the poor, introduction of modern medical science, and the establishment of orphanages, leprosaria, industrial training, and universities.

Dennis probably exaggerated the effect of Christian mission in many of these areas, but his lectures do indicate that the missionary movement at that time did not see evangelism as antithetical to community development and social transformation. It was assumed that one would accompany the other. Dennis no doubt reflected the naivete of his time in his understanding of culture and what might constitute progress. Nevertheless, we cannot fail to recognize both the massive investment by Christian missions in projects designed to bring about social transformation and their significant contributions—not only in the last two centuries, but through much of Christian history. The rejection of such concerns by evangelical missions earlier in this century was thus a reversal of the practice of missions through most of history. Today's tendency to reverse this "great reversal" while maintaining a focus on evangelism and church planting is long overdue.

2

Recent Historical Perspective of the Evangelical Tradition

Linda Smith

INTEREST IN INTERNATIONAL development as a focus of study and legitimate area of government activity arose relatively recently, dating from the mid-1940s and post-World War II reconstruction efforts. However, private voluntary groups, especially the Christian church, have been undertaking development activities and structural changes for generations.

Over the past two and a half centuries, the church has emerged as a significant initiator of development and reforms, particularly in non-European lands, including the United States, where it began missions, opened up the first schools and medical facilities, and initiated many new tasks in other sectors. Statistical yearbooks from the early twentieth century show the extensive contributions of European and North American Protestant and Catholic churches in starting hospitals, health clinics, dispensaries, leprosaria, schools for all educational levels, industrial training centers, publishing facilities, orphanages, and other enterprises.[1] Written accounts are given for other contributions that cannot be reduced to numbers: pervasive social reforms—such as providing the critical impetus to bring the slave trade, slavery, infanticide, cannibalism, and widow-burning to a halt in many parts of the world—introduction of the plow, modern agriculture methods, new industries, better living conditions, sanitation, improved nutrition,

LINDA SMITH serves as the director of extended education at Dubuque Theological Seminary. Her Ph.D. studies focused on the history of evangelical relief and development at Washington University.

roads, and countless other improvements for millions of people living at the subsistence level or worse (see Dennis, 1899).

EVANGELICAL HERITAGE

Evangelicals have historically played an important role in Third World development, though they retreated during the first half of this century and have only recently re-emerged as a significant and growing force in Third World development activities. Their involvement in development work has depended on their overall view of the validity of social concern for Christians.

Prior to the early 1900s, evangelicals took an active role in helping to reduce the poverty conditions in foreign countries. Modern evangelicals look back to the nineteenth century as in effect a "golden era" of evangelical missions and consider themselves inheritors of those traditions. However, they often overlook the extensive roles those missions played in fostering programs to meet the basic human needs of deeply impoverished peoples.

Among evangelical missions, social welfare projects and programs abounded which targeted particular underprivileged segments of the population, such as orphanages and leprosaria (Dennis, 1899). Great strides were made in building up social services, the "soft" infrastructures of developing countries. Many educational and medical facilities were planned, constructed, equipped, staffed, operated, and financially supported on a continuing basis decades before "development planning" began its formal existence after World War II (Dennis, 1899).

American missions groups were also heavily involved in the "hard" economic development sectors. By the turn of the century, theologically conservative missions agencies operated at least thirty-five industrial training institutions, most of which had been founded during the previous decade. Training courses for skilled labor and practical experience at these mission work facilities were offered for men and women in the main trades of the day, such as engineering, iron-working, blacksmithing, carpentry, sawmilling, road construction, masonry, printing, textile production, and sewing.

Missionaries made an impact on agricultural development and food production wherever they went. They introduced more modern agricultural techniques, new farm implements such as the plow, and diverse varieties of grains, fruits, and vegetables. They also shared their knowledge of animal husbandry and state-of-the-art food processing methods. All of these were used to develop and improve the agricultural sector.

THE "GREAT REVERSAL"

The early 1900s brought great upheaval among Christians in America. Kantian philosophy, Darwinism, the rise of sociology and psychology, new understandings of science, and new ways of examining the Bible based on analyses of historical and literary contexts were perceived as threatening basic beliefs about the nature of reality, human nature, God's role in creation, the nature of the Bible, and the historicity of Jesus and his miracles.[2]

A major controversy among American Protestants broke out. The climax of the Fundamentalist-Modernist debates came in 1925 with the Scopes "Monkey Trial" challenging a Tennessee law against teaching evolution in a public school. Though the fundamentalists won the court case, they lost public credibility and became equated with adamant rural ignorance.

As a backlash against liberalism, the inheritors of the evangelical tradition went into a period of retreat and separatism which had a profound impact on their social concern. It resulted in what has been called the "Great Reversal." All progressive social concern, private as well as political, was nearly eliminated among evangelicals by the end of the 1900–1930 period. George Marsden, one of the foremost historians of evangelicalism, attributes the decline of private social concern to the increasing stigma caused by the Social Gospel, which was in its zenith during this same period and was strongly identified with theological liberalism. The Social Gospel emphasized Christian obligation to respond to physical need and oppression, the priority of social action, and the task of establishing the kingdom of God on earth now through human efforts. The fundamentalists rejected these and emphasized spiritual need, evangelism, and the future heavenly aspects of the kingdom of God. Theological conservatives began to rigidly dichotomize evangelism and social concern, word and deed.

Historically, word and deed had been tightly fused together in evangelicalism. Now the strong negative reaction against liberal theology, particularly the Social Gospel, had a critical effect on the fundamentalists' view of social action. The fundamentalists rejected an integral part of their own historical beliefs in an attempt to avoid the greater perceived threat of liberalism (Marsden, 1980:90–91).

However, traditional evangelical social concern had been *different* from the actions of the Social Gospel. Among evangelicals, both social programs and individual assistance were natural outgrowths of the regenerating work of Christ and salvation. In contrast, the Social Gospel overlooked sin, underplayed the need for repentance and salvation, and exalted the role of doing good works. In respect to evangelical social concern, the critical fact is that evangelicals did not retain their own traditional emphasis on social action while rejecting the distortions of Social Gospel theology.

It is hard to evaluate what the impact of the "Great Reversal" was on international programs. Shifts were made in the types of missions programs planned from the home offices. In the field, however, the division between evangelism and social action was never as clear-cut. Missionaries, ostensibly abroad to meet spiritual needs, found themselves responding to other physical and material needs, but not necessarily according to any planned program. Schools and hospitals were maintained, though many of the social or economic programs were discontinued. However, some of the reductions may also have been due to decreased funding as a result of the depression. Short-term, spontaneous "Good Samaritan" actions were never eliminated. They were legitimized by the prominence of mercy as a theological tenet. Programs of social reform and planned, intentional aid toward human physical need, however, were no longer seen as appropriate areas of involvement.

THE RISE OF DISCONTENT

After World War II, many theological conservatives began to take a second look at the strict subculture in which they lived. While adhering to the "fundamentals" of Christian doctrine, they objected to the rigid mindset of fundamentalism which ignored current science and culture. The National Association of Evangelicals (NAE) and Fuller Theological Seminary were formed in the 1940s as two of several new groups trying to offer a positive alternative to this negative image. The most significant early critique of the retreat from the general culture, social responsibility, and political action was *The Uneasy Conscience of Modern Fundamentalism*. It was written by Carl

F. H. Henry, who would become one of evangelicalism's leading theologians, the book began with the following observation:

> Those who read with competence will know that the 'uneasy con-
> science' of which I write is not one troubled about the great biblical
> verities, which I consider the outlook capable of resolving our prob-
> lems, but rather one distressed by the frequent failure to apply them
> effectively to crucial problems confronting the modern mind. It is an
> application of, not a revolt against, fundamentals of the faith, for which
> I plead (1947:ii).

Carl F. H. Henry was later joined by growing numbers of others
who voiced similar criticisms of the abdication of Christian social
responsibility. These people retained their belief in the doctrinal fundamentals, but wanted to avoid the stigmatized connotation which by
then surrounded the label "fundamentalist." They chose to be called
"neo-evangelicals," a term coined by Harold J. Ockenga. It referred
back to the pre-1900 American evangelical tradition, but also entailed
a new acceptance of modernity. This name was soon shortened to
"evangelical."

Despite the questions raised, it would take years before a significant shift in actions occurred. Meanwhile, the fifties saw a great surge
in American evangelical missions activities. Programs and personnel
grew at an unprecedented rate. However, most of the new efforts
were evangelistic rather than the historically typical mixture of evangelism and activities which contributed to the physical, social, and
economic welfare of the nationals. World Vision, which was initially
founded in 1950 to assist Korean orphans and then expanded into
child care and relief programs, was criticized in the early days for
nearly every new area of need it tackled. Among most American
evangelicals, word and deed remained separated.

The sixties brought great social discontent in America. Many
young evangelicals were disillusioned by the apathy and sometimes
opposition of evangelicals and fundamentalists with the Civil Rights
Movement. Many began to question the lack of evangelical involvement in justice causes. They also questioned whether theological conservatism necessarily had to be tied to socio-political conservatism,
especially if the latter reinforced a *status quo* of racism or exploitation.
This era had a profound effect on evangelicals such as Fred and John F.
Alexander and Jim Wallis, who have since spoken out through the
founding and growth of *The Other Side* and *Sojourners*, two magazines
which focus on social issues from a Christian activist perspective.

RESURGENCE OF EVANGELICAL
DEVELOPMENT WORK

The seventies brought more calls for evangelical involvement in social concern, politics, and Third World poverty issues. Finally, actions began to catch up with words.

A whole series of disasters occurred during the seventies which drew nationwide concern. The Sahelian drought prompted one of the first prolonged media coverages of desperate poverty conditions. The devastating cyclone of 1977 in Andhra Pradesh, India, the Vietnamese boat people from 1978 onward, the aftermath of the overthrow of Idi Amin in 1979, the growing plight of Indochinese refugees in 1979, and the terror left by Pol Pot until his overthrow in 1979 all received substantial news coverage. They evoked increased response from donors to agencies which were offering relief assistance for the victims. This immeasurably aided the flow of funds to evangelical agencies, such as World Vision, which were involved in relief and development assistance. It resulted in major increases in evangelical attention toward social concern and Third World needs (Smith, 1987:347-349).

Vietnam drew major attention away from ethnocentric America and forced Americans to look at a war-torn and impoverished part of the world. The retreat from Vietnam also changed America's sense of its place in the world to a humbler, less patronizing view. Furthermore, the political disruption of both Vietnam and Watergate freed many evangelicals, especially the younger ones, from automatic acceptance of prevailing socio-political presuppositions and left them open to explore a wider range of alternatives.

Pressure was also growing from Third World countries. Third World leaders were asking for assistance that would not increase the dependency of the poor, but would foster self-help, indigenous decision-making, and cultural sensitivity.

Meanwhile, within evangelicalism, various other developments helped to heighten social concern. The improved social science education in evangelical colleges, beginning in the mid-sixties, resulted in more socially conscious young evangelicals entering into the workforce of Christian churches and agencies. According to Richard J. Mouw, an astute observer of evangelicalism who is professor of philosophy and social ethics at Fuller Theological Seminary, the seventies brought a broadening of evangelicalism (Smith, 1987:365-367). Young evangelicals, who had been shaped in the sixties by the civil rights and anti-war movements, began to move into positions of lower- and middle-level leadership. This movement resulted in growing visibility of black evangelicalism, evangelical feminism, and concern about lifestyle, hunger, and nuclear arms. It caused a breakthrough "in the older, narrower understanding of the ethnic-geographic-gender zone of evangelicalism" (Smith, 1987:366).

Perhaps the most significant of the many evangelical books in the seventies for Third World attention was Ronald J. Sider's book, *Rich Christians in an Age of Hunger* (1977). It highlighted the plight of the world's poor, led readers through a study of biblical materials on poverty and injustice, and offered ideas for action for concerned Christians.

Significant evangelical conferences began to give more attention to social concern and Third World issues. In 1973, fifty key evangelical leaders gathered and drafted the "Chicago Declaration," which contained statements against racism, sexism, militarism, and materialism. The 1974 International Congress on World Evangelism in Lausanne, Switzerland, directly addressed the relationship of evangelism and social concern. The resulting *Lausanne Covenant* was a major breakthrough. In a specific section on Christian social responsibility, it affirms, "We therefore should share [God's] concern for justice and reconciliation throughout human society for the liberation of men from every kind of oppression."[3]

By the end of the seventies, the momentum had increased within evangelicalism to the point that two conferences specifically focusing on lifestyle and development issues were planned for March 1980 in Hoddesdon, England, and co-chaired by John R. W. Stott and Ronald J. Sider. The International Consultation on the Theology of Development agreed:

> The goal of Christian involvement in development should be not only the provision of basic human needs, but also social change which secures just relationships in societies. It was also agreed that a partnership of equal relationships should . . . [characterize] the link between givers and receivers of aid (International Consultation on a Theology of Development, 1980:1-2).

The consultation on lifestyle most significantly resulted in a statement, "An Evangelical Commitment to Simple Lifestyle," which had major articles on stewardship, poverty and wealth, personal lifestyle, international development, and justice and wealth. It called for development rather than aid, but also for justice actions because "change can come, although not through commitment to simple lifestyle or development projects alone" (International Consultation on Simple Lifestyle, 1980).

Vietnam, media coverage of disasters and poverty conditions, pressure for change from the Third World, and the leadership of concerned evangelicals through writings and conferences all contributed to changing evangelical perspective in the seventies. But did changed views lead to changed actions? What was the impact on actual outreach toward the Third World poor?

EVANGELICAL AID

A study of eighty-five evangelical agencies involved in relief and development, specialized programs such as child care, or missions and evangelism shows substantial increases in Third World assistance over the seventies (Smith, 1987). Annual expenditures for Third World programs increased from $124 million in 1969–70 to $515 million in 1981–82. The estimated amount directed toward relief, development, and refugee activities quadrupled from $62 million to $238 million. The relief and development agencies, such as World Vision, World Relief, and Food for the Hungry, provided the bulk of this, $190 million. Since most of this money came from small donations averaging $26 each, this means about 7.3 million individual donations!

The breadth of evangelical development activities also increased. Traditional areas of heavy involvement for American Christian groups in Third World countries, particularly missionaries, have been the medical, educational, and social welfare sectors. Biblical injunctions have prompted them to heal the sick, teach the uneducated, protect the orphan, and feed the starving. Missionaries have established major health programs, hospitals, educational systems, alphabetization and literacy programs, orphanages, leprosaria, and famine relief programs in nearly every country where they have settled. Though many of these programs are legitimately development activities, they have usually been undergirded by a "Good Samaritan" charity and relief approach to poverty assistance. However, in the seventies, the focus shifted toward development programs.

During the period of 1969–70 to 1981–82, a significant number of new involvements in development activities were initiated. Table 1 summarizes the increases by sectors. Food production and agriculture, enterprise development and management (small industries),

	1969/70	1976/77	1981/82	Net Change 1969/70 to 1981/82
Medicine & Public Health	57	71	69	+12
Education	48	59	61	+13
Social Welfare	31	37	35	+ 4
Communications	21	17	18	− 3
Food Production & Agriculture	20	45	49	+29
Material Aid	10	26	30	+20
Community Development	6	19	18	+12
Cooperatives & Credit Loans	5	10	18	+13
Enterprise Development & Management	1	13	23	+22
Population & Family Services	0	8	7	+ 7
Economic Policy & Planning	0	3	2	+ 2
Totals:	201	325	351	+150
Average Number Sectors Per Agency:	3.4	4.2	4.6	+1.2

TABLE 1: EVANGELICAL AGENCIES: NUMBER INVOLVED IN EACH DEVELOPMENT ASSISTANCE SECTOR BY YEAR.
Source: Derived from TAICH, *U.S. Non-Profit Organizations in Development Assistance Abroad* (New York: TAICH, 1971, 1978, 1983).

and construction and housing lead the field of new undertakings. Material aid is also a leader because it includes new agencies using relief assistance as a beginning point and other agencies starting new refugee and resettlement programs, which are significantly different than traditional relief programs.

Interestingly enough, it was not just relief and development organizations that added new development sectors. The missions and evangelism agencies added an average of one new development assistance sector each.

During the seventies, evangelical assistance in relief and "soft" infrastructure sectors, such as medicine and education, was augmented with new programs in economic development sectors. Relief work has not been abandoned where appropriate, but evangelical agencies have moved into development work for a more enduring assault on poverty conditions. The rapid expansion during the seventies of many aid programs to combat poverty is unprecedented.

THEOLOGICAL SHIFTS

Underlying the increased attention toward poverty issues are some significant theological shifts among evangelicals. These shifts include a renewed acknowledgment of the humanity of Christ, a rejoining of word and deed, a re-interpretation and re-emphasis on the kingdom of God, and a Christ-and-culture paradigm shift.

Renewed Acknowledgment of the Humanity of Christ

Traditionally, Christians have acknowledged that Jesus Christ is fully God and fully human. During the early part of this century, the divinity of Christ was under attack. In strenuously attempting to preserve the divinity of Christ, theological conservatives lost the balance between the human and divine natures of Jesus. This situation worsened the age-old tendency to dichotomize body and spirit.

This imbalance had a significant negative effect on evangelical social concern. Limited focus on Christ's divinity leads to such vertical emphases as divine holiness and judgment. Taken alone, it can result in the highest values being ascribed to inner piety and righteousness, to the exclusion of considerations of physical needs and the horizontal relationships between humans. This focus must be balanced with emphasis on Jesus Christ's humanity, which underscores his total identification with humans (except that he did not sin). As a physical human being, he knew hunger and poverty, suffered pain and death, and had compassion for his fellow humans which included concern for both bodily and spiritual needs. Through comprehension of the humanity of Jesus, the Christian church gets its motivation for humanitarian actions and service toward others. Because the humanity of Jesus was overlooked, the whole area of service toward the physical needs of others was also devalued.

In recent years, prominent aspects of the humanity of Christ are being re-emphasized, though not necessarily as a direct rectification of the central theological imbalance. Most of the efforts appear to be piecemeal rediscoveries of old truths. For example, evangelicals have appropriated and widely applied the content of The Wounded Healer, written by Henri J. M. Nouwen, a Roman Catholic priest (1972). In a key passage, Nouwen points out that Jesus has made "his own broken body the way to health, to liberation and new life" (1972:82). Christians are to follow this example. "Thus, like Jesus, he who proclaims liberation is called not only to care for his own wounds and the wounds of others, but also to make his wounds into a major source of his healing power" (Nouwen, 1972:82–83). The personal experiencing of pain can become an invaluable source of deepened comprehension of others' pain and compassion-turned-action to help them.

Rejoining of Word and Deed: A Wholistic Gospel

Another related theological change contributing to the shift in attention toward world poverty is the rejoining of word and deed. The renewed recognition of Christ's humanity opened the way for the once stigmatized physical and social concerns leading to a more wholistic gospel.

Re-Interpretation and Re-Emphasis of "Kingdom of God"

The conservative-liberal conflict also resulted in the use of the term "kingdom of God." Liberals used it as a major buzz-word, believing that Christ would not return and that they were to bring in the kingdom of God by their own social and political actions. Conservatives, in contrast, preoccupied with Christ's return, emphasized only the spiritual aspects of the kingdom of God leading to an "otherworldliness." Three significant corrections have occurred in this view.

Both Present and Future

First, the kingdom of God entails present and future elements. The question of whether the kingdom of God is wholly in the present or the future has been clarified. Instead of either of these options, "eschatological dualism" is now widely maintained by evangelicals. The kingdom of God is "already but not yet." Jesus brought in the beginnings of the kingdom, a new redemptive order which continues to slowly grow and develop in this age. However, the kingdom will not be fully realized until Christ returns.

The effects of this shift minimize the previous overemphasis on "other-worldliness" which contributed to the neglect of matters in this world. It legitimizes focus on the redemptive elements of the kingdom of God unfolding in this world. It allows a dual emphasis retaining the promise of Christ's future return while not abdicating social responsibility here and now.

The new message is clear: Christ's kingdom work has already begun on earth and Christians should participate in it now, even before it is fully attained at Christ's return.

Socio-Political Content

Second, the kingdom of God has socio-political content. Key writers have countered the idea of an ephemeral, spiritual-only kingdom and have begun to emphasize the socio-political content of the kingdom of God. Perhaps most significant among them is Mennonite John Howard Yoder, the author of *The Politics of Jesus*. Written in 1972 and widely circulated, his book carefully examines passage after passage to highlight the socio-political content of Jesus' actions and message, especially related to the kingdom of God. It serves as one of the major legtimizations of political participation for Christians. It is also important because it speaks to the separatist tendencies of Mennonites and other Christians who feel they should withdraw from involvement in culture, especially socio-political institutions.

Jesus' proclamation of the kingdom of God and participation in political relationships serve as a legitimization of socio-political activity and an example for Christians to follow.

Transformational

Third, the kingdom of God is transformational. The transformational nature of the work of Christ in bringing about the kingdom of God has been emphasized in recent years.

Seeing the kingdom of God as transformational legitimizes Christian participation in the process of change. Efforts to improve living conditions, plan development projects, institute reforms, champion justice causes, foster reconciliation, and build human community all become valid evangelical endeavors.

The re-emphasis on the kingdom of God has undergirded social involvement for evangelicals. Key re-interpretations of kingdom-of-God theology have reinforced the ideas that the kingdom is being built now as well as in the ultimate future, that it has socio-political content, and that it is transformational. Thus, the message from the kingdom-of-God theology is that actions should be taken *now* toward socio-political issues, such as world poverty, to help change the oppressive conditions to ones which reflect divine justice, reconciliation, and love.

Christ, Culture, and Paradigm Shift

At the heart of the issue of Christian involvement in social concern is the perennial debate about the relationship of Christ to culture (which includes economics, politics, and other social institutions), and thus about what role Christians should play in relation to their society. After the liberal-conservative controversies early in this century, conservatives retreated with a Christ-against-culture attitude. They felt they had to be separatist, setting themselves apart from sinful society.

In recent years, many of the leaders and writings have implicitly advocated a *Christ-transforms-culture* stance.[4] For example, Ronald J. Sider considers himself a transformationalist. He places his hope for effective aid to the Third World poor in the "transforming power of Christ through the Holy Spirit" (Sider, 1980b). This, of course, ties in well with the idea that the kingdom of God is transformational— Christ is the transforming power behind it.

The transformationalist paradigm is a natural for fostering Christian involvement in development work, which even by secular advocates is intended to slowly transform society into a place where all can flourish. Though evangelicals do not believe that "the good society" (in their terms, "the kingdom of God") will be fully realized until Christ's return, they nonetheless have now legitimized ongoing persistent efforts to change society. Most still think in terms of gradual change, rather than abrupt and pervasive changes in societal structures. A theological value shift to a Christ-transforms-culture stance serves to legitimize and promote development work.

Taken together, these four main theological shifts open the way for and support poverty assistance that goes beyond simple, spontaneous acts of compassion. They undergird intentional involvement in long-term strategies for holistic development.

Reclaiming Our Heritage

Social concern and attention to the poor are part of thousands of years of Judeo-Christian heritage for American evangelicals. It is not something that originated only in the seventies. Evangelicals simply rediscovered and reactivated an integral part of their own heritage then.

Now we must hold on to what we have regained and keep word and deed united. We must reclaim the fullness of our theology and live out the words of Menno Simons, father of the Mennonite-Anabaptist movement, who proclaimed in 1539:

> . . . True evangelical faith cannot lie dormant.
> It clothes the naked,
> it feeds the hungry,
> it comforts the sorrowful,
> it shelters the destitute,
> it serves those that harm it,
> it binds up that which is wounded,
> it has become all things to all men
> (Moore, 1980:frontispiece).

---

[1]See, for example, James S. Dennis, *Centennial Survey of Foreign Missions* (New York: Fleming H. Revell Co., 1902); James S. Dennis, Harlan P. Beach, Charles H. Fahs, eds., *World Atlas of Christian Missions* (New York, NY: Student Volunteer Movement for Foreign Missions, 1911); World Missionary Conference Commission I, *Statistical Atlas of Christian Missions* (Edinburgh, World Missionary Conference, 1910).

[2]For a full treatment of this struggle over complex issues, see George Marsden, *Fundamentalism and American Culture: The Shaping of Twentieth Century Evangelicalism, 1870-1925* (New York: Oxford University Press, 1980)

[3]The Lausanne Covenant, Article 5.

[4]See, for example, Tom Sine, *The Mustard Seed Conspiracy: You Can Make a Difference in Tomorrow's Troubled World* (Waco: Word Books, 1981); Richard J. Mouw, *When the Kings Come Marching in: Isaiah and the New Jerusalem* (Grand Rapids, Eerdmans, 1983).

Planning Ministry in a
J-Curve Generation

Joe B. Webb

A TONGUE-IN-CHEEK ADAGE for our time is, "If you're not confused, you probably don't know what's happening!"

I recently read an astronaut's account of the awesome experience of liftoff, and the journey to earth's orbit. Incredibly, the space shuttle is traveling over one hundred miles per hour by the time the bottom clears the tower. At midway, the g-pressure leaves the pilot gasping for air.

Before the point of orbit is reached, the space craft is straining and shaking wildly before being thrust through the final grasp of gravity's grip, and into the peace and eerie quiet of outer space. Such is the stuff of small steps and giant leaps.

Spaceship Earth seems on a similar journey. The post-war generation is reaching for the pilot's stick. The computers are whirling. Many find themselves breathless from the speed and pressure. The craft is straining and shaking as the future breaks over its bow.

What facts, values, and wisdom will assist our journey into the twenty-first century? What heavenly points will provide navigational reference? This chapter attempts to identify some key issues in getting from here to the future. I seek to respond proactively to the future, preparing for it and embracing it like the father did his prodigal son. In discussing some of the theological, technological, economic, and

JOE B. WEBB was commissioned by the Lausanne Committee for World Evangelism to identify the major worldwide trends affecting the church. His ministry has been with Campus Crusade for Christ.

social challenges to come, I will focus on issues of special relevance to the ministry planner.

"FUTURE SHOCK"

It was Alvin Toffler who first alerted most of us to a fact we had experienced for some time; we are living in a *time of unprecedented change!* He called the sometimes staggering psycho-social impact of this *tsunami* of change—and the human struggle to adapt to it— "future shock."

Toffler coined the term in an article for *Horizon* magazine, and developed it further in the influential book by that title in 1970. In his book, Toffler highlighted two aspects of the change equation which produce future shock: the *rate* of change, and its *direction* (1970:5). Both are relevant variables to consider in planning ministry.

The Rate of Change

There are a number of social currents which suggest that society is still reeling under the pressure of future shock. From "punkers" on one end of the spectrum to religious fundamentalists on the other, people seem disoriented by the events of these turbulent days. To cope, increasing numbers seek refuge in caves of despair or clouds of absolute certainty.

Stress is a growth industry, peace for many an illusive commodity. Anxiety disorders, the most rapidly growing category of psychological problems, are estimated to effect 4 to 8 percent of all Americans (Weissman 1986:13). Most problems in what doctors call the General Stress Response (GSR), the primitive fight/flight mechanism central to human adaptation and survival for millennia, are rooted in anxiety related to loss, lack of control, and uncertainty. These in turn are brought on by the massive personal and social changes common in modern culture.

But the problems which plague North Americans may be even greater in the developing countries. This is because the changes which are associated with industrialization and technology have been gradually absorbed over two hundred years in western civilization, while in recently industrialized cultures the timeframe is collapsed into a decade or two.

For deep and effective ministry in such an environment, we must move away from glib verse-quoting and seek a deeper understanding of how Christian faith relates to the powerful ambivalences experienced by people in the developed and developing worlds.

The Direction of Change

If the *rate* of change is one concern, then the *direction* of change is another. In 1970 Herman Kahn, the noted futurist and encyclopedic thinker, claimed to discover thirteen "basic, long-term, multifold trends" on a global scale which he projected to continue through the end of the twentieth century. The list is of particular interest to the Christian who is planning ministry programs:

1. Increasingly sensate, empirical, this-worldly, secular, contractual, hedonistic cultures.
2. Bourgeois, bureaucratic, though "democratic" elites.
3. Accumulation of scientific and technological knowledge.
4. The "institutionalization of change" through research, development, and innovation.
5. Worldwide industrialization and modernization.
6. Increasing affluence and leisure.
7. Population growth.
8. Urbanization and the growth of megalopolises.
9. Decreasing importance of primary occupations.
10. Increased literacy and education.
11. Increasing capability for mass destruction.
12. Increased tempo of change.
13. Increased universality of these multifold trends.

Figure 2: Basic, Long-Term, Manifold Global Trends
(Adapted from Kahn, 1970:7)

Few trends are comforting, nurturing, and supportive of human spirituality. 1968 was the apex year of the social revolution of the 1960s. We now look back in a twenty-year retrospective on the sexual revolution, the human and civil rights movements, the cold war and detente, and also on a youth revival of that period that brought many into the kingdom.

What better time to take stock, to execute a mid-course correction, and to prepare ourselves for *spiritual* and *moral* leadership in the closing years of the twentieth century. To borrow a phrase from management training circles, we need to make sure that the ladder we are climbing is leaning against the right wall.

A J-CURVE GENERATION

The mathematicians call it exponential growth. The physicists call it geometric expansion. Social scientists refer to the phenomenon of massive and rapid change as "J-curve" increases, because a line describing such a change would inscribe the steep upward curve of the letter "J."

We live in a J-curve generation. Population increases, the size of cities, the proliferation of books, documents, and information, technological advances; all of these are undergoing unfathomable growth. Concludes social psychologist Warren G. Bennis, an expert on change and its effects, "No exaggeration, no hyperbole, no outrage can realistically describe the extent and pace of change. . . In fact, only the exaggerations appear to be true" (1969:438).

Perhaps, these J-curve increases are best illustrated by understanding population growth, the factor which drives many of the others. Nearly everyone has seen the sweeping graph distributed by the United Nations which shows world population soaring toward six billion by the end of the century. But consider figure 3 which focuses more precisely on the rate of population growth. From the eighteenth century to the present, the population growth rate has moved from 0.1 percent in 1700 to 2.1 percent in 1965 (Kahn 1982:30). Without discussing the projected drop in growth predicted by the graph, note that our generation is at the very apex of the population surge.

Some demographers calculate that as many as half of the people

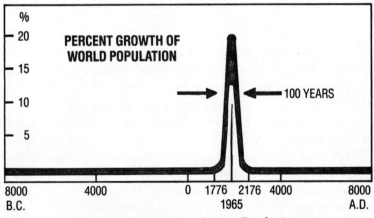

Figure 3: The Population Explosion

who have ever lived are alive today. Studying figure 3 from the point of view of world evangelization, it is fascinating to consider that the growth of the modern Protestant missions movement, which also began in the eighteenth century, parallels the population growth rate. The implication is that if we are faithful to the evangelistic task in our lifetime, the majority of people who have ever been born will also have an opportunity to be born again.

However, from the point of view of human suffering—people caught in the squeeze of urban overcrowding, and inadequate distribution systems for food, shelter, and other necessities—the graph is a stark visual aid explaining why new responses are needed. These twin insights from the graph are perhaps the best argument for the linking of evangelism and social service in Christian outreach ministries. In addition, compassion and credibility demand it.

TIME OF MAJOR TRANSITIONS

The rate of change is one reality, but additionally, we are at a clear turning point in the life of the global church. There are three major transitions which I see taking place at this time:
1. A passing of the leadership torch to the post-war generation in the western church.
2. A power shift from the western to the non-western church.
3. A shift from multi-national to "global" thinking about mission.

The first transition means that the largest, most sophisticated, best educated, most media-aware, and *most unchurched* generation in the history of western civilization is assuming the leadership mantle in society. Are we prepared in the church for the differences this might make?

They are the first "vid kids" who grew up mindful of the Power of Media. Rock music fans, they still tap their feet under the desk. Drug experimentation, now rejected, nevertheless leaves them with a somewhat altered consciousness.

Sensitive to irresponsible authority, easy answers, and social injustice, these children of Watergate, Vietnam, and Civil Rights are in an uneasy "truce" with the system. Responding to what opinion researcher Daniel Yankelovich calls "new rules" and a new "ethic of commitment," they are, according to him, challenging the unwritten social contract which has guided western culture through the Industrial Revolution (1981:8). I predict changes when they take over the reigns from the responsibility-laden children of the Depression.

The second transition means that the power center of Christian thought and mission will flow to the developing world. A wonderfully appropriate shift, I might add, because most unreached people groups and evangelistic momentum reside there. The coming era will be the era of the Two-Thirds World, "the people of color."

Likewise, missions in the twenty-first century will reflect this new reality. Christians in the West will continue to have great challenges—pioneering technology for a truly modern missions movement, dealing with nominal Christian renewal, graciously sharing power and responsibility with emerging Two-Thirds World leadership—these and other challenges will present opportunities to serve.

Finally, the third transition, the globalization of mission, is changing the way we think about the task. Unilateral decisions to "send" missionaries is being replaced by multi-lateral conferencing between the sending and receiving churches.

There is a new sensitivity to the issue of culture, and to discovering the "transcultural core" or the "supracultural truth" of the gospel as we seek to spread it cross-culturally. Soon we in the West will be confronted with new Christian theologies from the Two-Thirds World which, while true to Scripture, challenge our understandings of what it means to follow Christ. Let us prepare now for that exciting time of growth!

PLANNING MINISTRY IN AN AGE OF CHANGE

How do we plan ministry in such volatile times as these? The most important and relevant question for the church in an age of change is one that is seldom asked by evangelicals: What is God's intended future?

Ray Anderson, in his book *Minding God's Business*, highlights the difference between two Latin words: *futurum*, from which we get our English word future, and *adventus*. *Futurum*, "what will be" or "what may be," speaks of events which arise out of the possibilities of the present. Says Anderson, "In this [*futurum*] sense the future cannot be any more than the extrapolation of the present. Thus, the 'future' is already a 'future past,' because nothing can enter in which is not already present as some possibility" (1986:49).

Adventus, in contrast, "describes the arrival of persons or the occurrence of events that were anticipated but not under control or power of the present" (Anderson 1986:49). "Advent" is the choice of biblical writers (or the Greek *parousia*) to describe the arrival of God and his solutions in the human present. "Preparing the way" for the *adventus*, whether for the Advent or daily *adventi*, is a believer's consciousness regarding the future.

We, however, seem to be absorbed with the acts of God in history, a marvelous dimension of our faith, without pushing on to reflect on his intended acts for our future. We are adept at *working from history forward*—dreaming, for example, of a "New Testament church" in our own era, or the more dubious restoration of so-called "traditional values"—but what would happen in our theological thinking if we *worked back from* "God's intended future"?

When I think of working forward from history I think of the foundation laid by the apostle Paul. He was the premier theologian of the New Testament era. Under the inspiration of the Spirit, he was the architect of theological wisdom for his age, and properly understood and contextualized, for our own. Most of us feel comfortable with Paul.

However, when I think of working back from "God's intended future" I think immediately of Jesus. His radical teaching never fails to disturb me. I feel morally pushed, mentally troubled, spiritually stretched to the breaking point by his giantesque life and words.

Perhaps that is why some evangelicals have sifted Jesus through a theological screen which leaves his teaching in another dispensation, or in the world of toothless metaphor. It could be that if we re-examined and sought to apply his teaching of the kingdom, though it defies both comfort and conservatism, it would provide a glimpse of "God's *intended* future."

I am suggesting a dynamic theological method which gives life to the questions "what is God doing?" (present) and "where is he going?" (future) as well as to the more static "what has he done or promised to do?" (past/future). Biblical revelation is not so much a "seeing into the future," as it is a "breaking into the present on the part of the future" (Anderson 1986:55). In a time of radical change in a J-curve generation, we need dynamic evangelical theologizing which will guide us toward our appointment with a future *which is both here and coming to meet us.*

Trends and Forecasting

With the understanding that our theology needs to be re-examined in light of what Jesus revealed about God's intended future, we can proceed to another area of importance in planning ministry in an age of change: an understanding of the significant trends taking shape in our world. In understanding today's trends we can anticipate tomorrow's reality.

Trends research is increasingly important for all kinds of planning, including planning for ministry. The skeptical should consider mission anthropologist Paul Hiebert's warning, " . . . change is now so rapid that past experience is no longer sufficient to help us plan for the future. We need to know as best we can where the world is headed" (1987:37). If not, we may end up somewhere else. A friend of mine recently described the graduates of a midwestern Bible institute as "extremely well-prepared to face the problems of the nineteenth century!" We laughed. I hung up the phone and recommitted myself to preparing the church for the future.

There are three categories of trends which I would like to develop within the limits of the space available. These trends include: technological trends, social developments, and political and economic shifts. Each holds import for the planning of church business in the days ahead.

Technological Trends

Participants in short-term missions projects have exploded from six hundred in 1965 to sixty thousand in 1986 (Gibson 1987:3). Has anyone stopped to consider that a single technological innovation called the "jet airplane" is largely responsible? Without the ease of jet travel, this significant missions movement would not exist.

Could we have predicted this development and have been prepared for it if our "future eyes" were better developed? What other innovations lie buried in the next wave of technological advance? What current gold mines lie untouched because we fail to see them?

Communication technologies provide us the means to span the world with the gospel message. Television, videos, satellite networks, computer-generated mail, and especially the video cassette recorder (VCR) provide broad new platforms and pulpits. But where are the thoughtful young Christian media critics and writers who will insure these new technologies are used to actually *further* the gospel, rather than turn the audience off?

The current discussion of "appropriate technology" is central to organizations involved in developing countries. Since all technology is a two-edged sword with the potential to help and harm people and societies, Christian organizations must develop a theology of appropriate uses of technology within the constraints of kingdom values.

Social Developments

Dramatic social changes have taken place which will challenge nearly every aspect of Christian ministry in the years ahead. Let us hit some high points:

Population Growth

Since every other child born today is Asian, it seems that Asia ought to be a central focus for missions. If population growth is highest in areas currently unreached by the gospel, church planting in these areas—such as Pakistan, Indonesia, and India—must be emphasized.

Population trends are important components of ministry planning. Do you know them for your area of concern?

Urban Growth

Nearly all mission outreach in the twenty-first century will be in the city. People began arriving in the city about the time the church was moving to the suburbs. If the stereotype of the missionary in the last century is the khaki-clad man or woman in a bush helmet, then the cleric of the future is an educated, sophisticated, urban guerrilla.

Why, then, are most seminaries and Bible schools in the suburbs or the countryside? Are we preparing students for the future? Is evangelical theology flexible enough to grapple with the complex problems of the urban jungle? We must begin not to reposition ourselves for the urban century ahead.

Changing Families

Most of us have grown up with the "myth of the nuclear family." And most of us know it does not work. Fathers were absentee electrons who floated in orbit around the nucleus. Now mothers are gone, too.

According to the Joint Center for Urban Studies of M.I.T. and Harvard, thirteen separate types of household arrangements will eclipse the conventional family by 1990. The church was right to decry the "breakdown of the family," but wrong to assume that nuclear families are God's exclusive design.

In the years ahead we need to rediscover the notion of the extended family and the importance of providing social cohesion through Christian community and small support-group structures and networks. Old Testament witness, after all, is to the importance of the identity of *tribe* and *clan* in addition to family.

Women's Roles

The changing role of women in the latter third of the twentieth century is a revival of the way men's roles changed at the end of the nineteenth. The industrial revolution took men from the home then, and the new information and service economy is doing the same to women in our time.

How will the church respond? Will we embrace the problem with open and creative minds, or hark back to simpler times and outmoded models? Two issues emerge. First, will leadership in the church be extended equally to women? Yes, if the church is to prosper. Second, will working women be seen as a new target of compassionate concern, and their unique needs addressed? Yes, if we are to reach and minister to this new generation of women.

Political and Economic Shifts

The great moral issues of the next decade will be rooted in economic problems. In the same way that Christians, liberal and conservative, have become involved in politics in the eighties, so must we become involved in economics and wealth distribution in the nineties.

One outspoken political and religious leader, Jesse Jackson, calls the problem "the issue of economic violence." David McKenna, an evangelical scholar and president of Asbury Theological Seminary, says it bluntly: "Economics may well be the most significant social issue for the church in the Age of Information" (1987:122).

However, many barriers exist for Christian involvement in economic issues. The conflict is perhaps best summarized by the statement of Bishop Camara of Brazil when he said, "When I want to help the poor, I am called a Christian. When I answer the question, 'Why are they poor?', I am called a Communist."

Absolute poverty, which describes an increasing percentage of the world population, is a term that cries out with frustration and injustice. When the cycle of poverty is unbreakable by those within it, outside assistance is essential. How else are we to fulfill our mandate "to set free the downtrodden" which is the task of all who are anointed, as was Jesus, by the Holy Spirit?

The church of Jesus Christ, if it is to have credibility in the twenty-first century, must respond with a social and economic analysis which addresses the problem at its structural root. Compassion—in the form of hunger relief, evangelism, social service, and first aid—must be further augmented by economic "CAT scans" and structural surgery.

To do so we must forge into territory currently dominated by Marxist thinkers. We may even find points of agreement. Such volatile thoughts, unthinkable to many in the current poisoned atmosphere, must be faced. The economic conditions in the developing world are becoming *moral issues* which Christians dare not ignore.

Could it be that the Two-Thirds World will teach the First and Second how the strengths of their diverse systems are to be blended? As God raises up new leaders in the southern hemisphere, they may not share our entrenched commitment to Cold War. Perhaps human rights and political freedom can coexist with "economic rights" such as employment, housing, and medical care.

Perhaps our justification for the economic inequity in our time ("the poor will always be with us") will sound as callous a century from now as the justification for slavery a century ago sounds to us today. I, for one, would not be surprised!

PULLING THE PIECES TOGETHER

It is not surprising that new information and creative thinking is increasingly important in an information age. The brief discussion above only begins to treat issues which each deserve research and indepth thinking. My purpose here is to call attention to the radical changes and creative thinking which needs to be done.

If you are feeling pretty comfortable as a Christian in these days, you are probably not living in reality. My prayer is that we will tune into God's intended future, preparing the way for his advent, and that we will be available to him to see it enacted on our own stage.

4

Theological Reflections on Assisting the Vulnerable

Wayne G. Bragg

IN JULY OF 1988, THIRTEEN people from eight countries met for two weeks in Costa Rica for the Workshop on Rural Development and the Environment. As a group of Christian ecologists, development workers, agronomists, social scientists, and community leaders, we met to examine alternatives for ecologically sound uses of the fragile tropical resources in Latin America in view of growing human needs and ecological crisis. The need for cash and food are driving forces in the economy of Latin America, putting pressure on tropical forests and on ecological stability in the name of "development." We visited several regions of Costa Rica to observe the effects of both deforestation and conservation on the environment and on people, followed by a week of intensive reflection and the preparation of documents and a declaration to the church in Latin America (*Declaración 1988*). This workshop stimulated the following theological reflections on the role of Christian aid and development in relation to the vulnerable people in poorer countries, especially in light of the Christian's mandate to care for the earth and to love one's neighbor as one's self. Both of these concepts are involved in the current development model and the destruction of tropical resources.

WAYNE G. BRAGG is a consultant to international and indigenous development programs on socio-cultural transformation in the Two-Thirds World, where he has worked and lived for twenty-seven years. He is affiliate professor in the School of Engineering and Applied Sciences at Washington University in St. Louis, working in bioresources development for meeting basic human needs.

DEVELOPMENT AND DEFORESTATION

With the high international debts of Latin American nations, the most readily accessible source of cash is to strip forests of high-value woods since the other typical agricultural export crops are being dangerously exploited and world prices for these commodities are low. Despite laws protecting national forests and parks, the need for foreign exchange to service the debts, combined with the corruption of politicians and governing elites, accelerates the destruction of unprotected areas belonging in many cases to tribal groups (Rabben, 1988:598–599). In Honduras, for example, the Biosphere Reserve along the Rio Platano, set aside in 1980, is quickly and illegally being timbered out. The Miskitu and other Indian groups which rely on the fruits of the forest are concerned about their traditional hunting and gathering way of life.

Furthermore, population pressures and inequitable land distribution force peasants to invade the forests for subsistence farming. Land distribution is a continuing problem. In some regions of Latin America, 93 percent of the arable land is controlled by 7 percent of the population, so landless people and governments look at sparsely inhabited forest lands as the answer to overcrowding and poverty (Lee and Taylor, 1986:62). Absentee landlords are converting tropical forests into cattle *haciendas*, thus devastating extensive areas and contributing to unemployment since ranches require few cowboys for large extensions of land. The forests are being replaced with cattle production for meat export to the United States, Europe, and Japan—not primarily for local consumption. Historically, the cattle *latifundio* (large landholding) has destroyed tropical dry forests (Edelman, 1985; Gudmunson, 1983; and Barton, et al., 1988), but now with the population and economic pressures combined with modern technology, the tropical rain forests are falling under the chainsaw.

Mining and lumbering industries are also putting pressure on these forests. One of the world's largest virgin rain forests, the Amazon basin, is a current target. Brazil is notorious for its colonization and "development" policies toward the Amazon basin (Bragg, 1976). Every day in Brazil's Amazonia, two million trees are felled (Rabben, 1988:597). Such developers are rapidly deforesting vast areas that can never be recuperated due to the fragility of the soils, forcing the tribal groups into Indian reservations at best and killing them at worst. Even the tribal reservations are endangered by "progress."

The proposed Xingu Dam Complex of Brazil's Ministry of Energy which is sponsored by the World Bank would displace nine thousand people, including twelve indigeneous groups, and flood over six thousand square miles of forest (Cockburn, 1988). Davis (1977) documents the impact of modernization on the tribal peoples of Brazil. In Rondonia, a Brazilian state near Bolivia, the Polonoroeste Project which is being funded by the World Bank will deforest an area the size of Great Britain by the mid-1990s (George, 1988:604). Central America contains one of the richest reserves of biological diversity in the world, but tropical rain forests are disappearing at the rate of almost eight thousand square miles annually, mostly for cattle grazing to profit from the U.S. demand for low-cost beef and pet food (Lee and Taylor, 1986:62).

This deforestation process is part of a worldwide phenomenon in which each minute, one hundred acres of tropical forests fall under the chainsaw and bulldozer—which on a yearly basis is equivalent to an area the size of Nebraska, or seventy-seven thousand square miles (Lee and Taylor, 1986:61). The degradation of habitat means the extinction of one species of wildlife a day, and at the current rate, "by the year 2000 between 500,000 and 1 million species will become extinct, or about ⅙th of the world's organic diversity (*The New Road Bulletin*, 1987:7). Along with the loss of genetic diversity, the deforestation process is threatening the very existence of millions of tribals who live in the forests, and along with them their traditional knowledge and the usefulness of tropical plants for food and medicine which they have accrued over thousands of years. Development is a threat to indigenous people:

> The estimated 200 million tribals, hunters and gatherers, now of the receiving end of "progress" are among the world's largest and most endangered species. Hunger, disease, development, and war are their enemies . . . it is like destroying a library of information. A range of culture enriches us all. If we get rid of these people we're effectively destroying a part of ourselves (*Newsweek*, 1981:92).

With the destruction of tropical species and the people who understand their uses the potential sources of medicines for present and future diseases also disappear forever. Forty percent of the drugs prescribed in the United States contain these natural products, and there are undoubtedly many undiscovered remedies in the biological diversity of the tropical species. Unintelligent "development" is burning the library before anyone has a chance to read the books!

The catastrophic impact of ecocide also affects the industrial world. It involves climactic changes in rainfall, desertification, flooding, soil erosion and degradation, and the increase in the world's carbon dioxide. These climatic changes accelerate the Greenhouse Effect that is already modifying the climate of the world, creating a drought of enormous proportions in North America (Ramirez, 1988). The ecological impact on the future of agriculture is alarming. In Costa Rica, the site of the Workshop on Rural Development and the Environment, over 17 percent of the country is severely eroded. Soil losses reach 680 million tons a year (EPOCA, 1987:5), threatening even the traditional agricultural base. "It takes 150 to 2,000 years to form two centimeters of topsoil, but only 10 years to destroy it" (*The New Road Bulletin*, 1987:6). Desertification is accelerating worldwide; an area twice the size of Canada is in imminent danger (Lean, 1980). Another effect of deforestation is flooding. In 1988, Bangladesh was ravaged by a record flood leaving six hundred dead, twenty-five million homeless, two million tons of crops destroyed, drinking water contaminated, and hunger and water-borne disease spreading rapidly among the flood survivors. Monsoon rains that would formerly have been absorbed by the forests of the Himalayas now threaten the very basis of life in that poor agricultrual nation. The crisis continues to grow worldwide. Rensberger (1977) states that within the next twenty-five years, fully one-third of today's arable land will be lost and the world's need for food will double.

It was in this context of balancing the needs for rural development with the fragility of the ecosystem that the group of concerned professionals met in San Jose, Costa Rica, in July to look at alternatives, especially from a Christian perspective.

THE CHRISTIAN CONNECTION

This small workshop brought together Christians concerned with preserving the environment while stimulating rural development. Our concern derives from two sources: the need for a sustainable system for meeting basic human needs while preserving the environment in a world marked by growing degradation, and the need for a biblical mandate for the mission of the Christian in the world. As Christians, we were seeking a biblical perspective on the rampant destruction of irreplaceable rain forests and dry land tropics in the name of development. We were concerned with the silence and complicity of the Christian church in this process of ecocide, since Latin America is highly "Christianized," both Catholic and Protestant.

Christian relief and development agencies are increasingly important in community development programs in the continent. Those from the north (the industrial rich nations from the northern hemisphere) often unconsciously promote destruction of ecosystems in their pursuit of assistance to the economically poor and vulnerable. In the Costa Rica workshop, we sought a biblical basis for a sustainable, ecologically-sound system of production in the context of growing human need.

A Biblical Mandate

One of the primary theological themes in the Bible is creation. God first created the heavens and the earth, followed by the first man and woman, whom he placed in a special relationship with the rest of created order. Human beings are part of the whole of creation, but God gave us a unique role in continuing and caring for creation in function of the *imago Dei*, the image of God.

> Then God said, "Let us make man in our image and likeness to rule the fish in the sea, the birds of heaven, the cattle, all wild animals on earth, and all reptiles that crawl upon the earth." So God created man in his own image; in the image of God he created him; male and female he created them. God blessed them and said to them, "Be fruitful and increase, fill the earth and subdue it, rule over the fish in the sea, the birds of heaven, and every living thing that moves upon the earth." God also said, "I give you all plants that bear seed everywhere on earth, and every tree bearing fruit which yields seed: they shall be yours for food. (Genesis 1:26-29, NEB)

The Hebrew parallelism in the Genesis account links the likeness between God and humans, the *imago Dei*, with their rule over creation. The image of God in man and woman is not a physical likeness, nor even primarily spiritual or moral, but rather it is our role as caretakers of the earth, the environment, which is just as essentially part of the creative God as the human race is. The *Book of Common Prayer* (1979) outlines this role:

Q. What does it mean to be created in the image of God?
A. It means that we are free to make choices: to love, to create, to reason, and to live in harmony with creation and with God.
Q. What does this mean about our place in the universe?
A. It means that the world belongs to its creator; and that we are called

to enjoy it and to care for it in accordance with God's purposes
(*Book of Common Prayer* 1979:845).

Adam and Eve were made vice-regents over their whole habitat,
for protection, creation, enjoyment, and for sustenance. The psalmist
puts us into a unique role regarding the rest of creation:

> When I look up at thy heavens, the
>   work of thy fingers,
> the moon and the stars set in their
>   place by thee,
> what is man that thou shouldst
>   remember him,
> mortal man that thou shouldst
>   care for him?
> Yet thou has made him little less
>   than a god,
> crowning him with glory and
>   honor.
> Thou makest him master over all
>   thy creatures;
> thou has put everything under his
>   feet:
> all sheep and oxen, all the wild
>   beasts,
> the birds in the air and the fish
>   in the sea,
> and all that moves along the
>   path of the ocean.
> O Lord our sovereign,
>   how glorious is thy
>   name in all the earth!
>   (Psalm 8, NEB)

The glory of the Creator is manifested in the regency of humankind over creation. Caretaking the rest of creation, or stewardship,
is the role given humankind. However, the old English concept of
caretaker was "sty-warden," the one who took care of the pigsty for his
lord. This is an inadequate description of the role that our first coun-
terparts had as God's image-bearers. They were to take care of and
bring order into the whole of creation, in a real sense as co-creators,
increasing and filling the earth, not just predators caring for the source
of food in a selfish way. Adam's first delegated job, for example, was to
name all the animals and birds in the Garden of Eden. The giving of
names in the Hebrew context connotes deep relationships.

Creation is a continuing process in which humans have a key participation, especially after the disorder and violence that resulted from rebellion (Genesis 3:17–19 and 6:11).

Anti-Creation or a Sustainable System?

Unfortunately, instead of replenishing the earth, we have been destroying it in acts of anti-creation. The devastation has accelerated with the advent of modern technology and the scientific revolution. It is now possible, as we have noted above, to destroy in epochal seconds what has taken eons to develop. Perhaps for the first time in history, we are able to decide what kind of earth our grandchildren will inherit. The whole growth model of the Western technological society is based on an extractive and dominionistic approach to nature. We see ourselves as masters of nature. We rapaciously take from the environment without replacing. The appetite of wealthy nations for non-renewable resources is legendary. The richest 6 percent of the world's population, the United States, consumes 30 percent of the world's nonrenewable resources, as Ward and Dubos (1972) pointed out in *Only One Earth*. The U.S.A. uses one-third of the world's production of mineral resources each year and consumes 5.7 times the annual per capita energy consumption of the entire Third World.

Renewable resources are also under pressure from overconsumption. Food consumption, for example, continually exceeds needs in the U.S., which then produces 2.3 billion excessive pounds of collective body weight that we spend $10 billion a year to diet and exercise off. Our water usage is recklessly depleting reserves that took millennia to form, such as the Ogalalla aquifer, and the supply of pure water is shrinking in this country to a dangerous degree, complicated by the rapid contamination of aquifers by toxic wastes which we produce. The Environmental Protection Agency estimates that the U.S. generates more than 77 billion pounds of hazardous chemical wastes a year and only handles 10 percent of this safely, endangering ground water supplies and the environment (Magnuson, 1980:58). Insecticides, pesticides, and chemical fertilizers find their way into the fragile web of life and endanger *all* life, because life is interconnected through the whole food chain.

These consumption statistics for the United States can be multiplied by statistics from Europe and parts of Asia which are rapidly catching up to North American consumerism. Ethical questions invariably arise in a world thus polarized by wealth and poverty, where two-thirds of the planet live in abject poverty while the other third lives sumptuously, reminiscent of the parable of the Rich Man and Lazarus. Our profligate life-style has made us into the "prodigal sons" of the world, wasting in riotous living the inheritance from our forefathers, without a concern for our children and grandchildren. The prevailing economic development model is not sustainable and it negates our role as co-creators and caretakers of habitat earth. It is therefore seriously lacking an ethical dimension, especially as the model is applied worldwide (see Bragg, 1988).

The effects of the prevailing northern industrial or "modernization" model are just as dramatic on those of us in the "developed" world. When we assume that production equals development and that large-scale, capital-intensive systems are the most productive, we reduce humans to a unit of production. Humankind becomes *homo faber*, the producer, with all the alienation and anomie that goes with mass production. In the industrial states, workers suffer from psychological symptoms and socio-pathological behavior from meaningless work. The achievement of a high level of material goods does not necessarily produce a good quality of life. Indeed, there is more malaise and anomie in the industrial societies than in poorer ones. We have high rates of crime, suicide, delinquency, violence, and neuroses in spite of—or because of—the productive system that provides us with material goods in abundance. When this system is exported to traditional societies, the same symptoms of social breakdown begin to appear. And in poorer countries where labor laws are more lax, the modern productive system extracts an even more damaging social cost on people. In Hong Kong, for example, where *laissez faire* capitalism is working well, some multinational corporations are exploiting thirty-four thousand children under the age of fourteen, half of whom work ten hours a day (Hayter, 1981:106). In Thailand, children are sold to factory-owners by poor peasant parents, according to United Nations studies on child slavery. Women in Korea lose their vision at an early age working on microchips under deficient lighting for long periods of time. While high productivity has created a better life for some, the social cost of this system seems to be acutely high for ourselves and for others.

There is a qualitative aspect to development that productivity ignores. Development is more than meeting economic needs. Humans are multidimensional with physical as well as psychological needs: dignity, self-esteem, freedom, and participation. To reduce people to only producers-consumers is to assume a basic materialism as the goal of life. Capitalistic materialism is still materialism, and in some ways no better than the dialectical materialism of socialism. Obviously, meeting material human needs is necessary, but it is certainly not sufficient for human self-realization, as indicated by Maslow's "hierarchy of needs" (1954). A society that produces neurotics, latchkey kids, runaway teenagers, child-abuse, wife-beating, a large prison population, abortions, high suicide rates, and other social maladies just to remain economically strong is not a model of development. In fact, many poor societies manifest social and cultural features that are certainly more "developed" than the rich, industrial societies such as sharing, caring for the weak, protecting the land, and other traditional values.

Furthermore, the modernization economic model is not sustainable even in economic terms. The emphasis on high-technology and capital-intensive production creates more problems in the long run than it solves. Large industrial plants, situated in urban centers, tend to exacerbate the rural-urban migration and create cities with pollution and other problems. When this model is exported to the Two-Thirds World, it creates large external debts and dependency on the One-Third World. Furthermore, it worsens structural unemployment and underemployment by destroying traditional sector jobs, especially in agriculture, creating a pool of cheap labor for industry (Sunkel, 1981:98). These countries become vulnerable to the fluxes of the external market for their exports. The current trend in off-shore assembly industries, called *maquiladoras* in Mexico, in poor countries brings employment but serves as a magnet to attract peasant farmers from their subsistence agriculture—besides not leaving any real benefit to the host country since the workers cannot even purchase their own manufactured goods. These assembly plants are also very volatile, and when conditions change, these plants flee to another country, one of the serious contradictions between national interests and the multinationals' interests (Barnet and Muller, 1974). This is the social and economic cost of articulation into the international, capital-market system rather than developing an internal, decentralized, rural-based system that will keep people in the countryside. Some new models of autonomous local industries are being explored in this regard (Bragg, Martinez, and Shultz, 1988).

Christianity and Nature

Lynn White, Jr., suggested in 1968 that the primary cause of our ecological problems can be traced to the Judeo-Christian tradition (cited by Sheldon, 1984). Traditional societies and religions tend to be more harmonious with nature than western Judeo-Christian-based societies. Tribals and peasants have a world-and-life view that stresses awe and respect for their surrounding habitat, and their technology tends to be "gentler" than western technology. Harmony with nature is observable in most traditional societies. It took a visit to India for F. F. Schumacher, a British economist, to understand the relationship with nature that the Hindu culture promotes and out of this he wrote *Small is Beautiful*, the classic discovery of appropriate technology and economics. In contrast to the Hindu worldview, Schumacher realized that western technology has "created a system of production that ravishes nature and a society that mutilates man" (Schumacher, 1973).

But is ecological destruction due to the Judeo-Christian tradition, as alleged, or due rather to a deformation of the Christian perspective by the western scientific, technological, and economic worldview? The secularization that has accompanied the scientific-industrial revolution has broken down the holistic, unified view of reality that permeates more traditional societies, opening the way for the mastery of the physical world that would have been unimaginable before, such as putting a man on the moon and other scientific achievements. By divorcing the physical world from the spiritual, modern science has made it possible to conquer nature and subject it to the dictates of human manipulation through high technology. There is nothing held sacred in such an anthropocentric world. However, in view of the counterproductivity of the high-tech approach, there is a gradual, almost imperceptible awareness growing that the environment needs protecting if our world is to be habitable over time. Perhaps the Amish farmers were right in their rejection of modern technology; perhaps the tribal taboos that protect the land from abuses are more amenable to a sustainable agriculture than the scientific revolution. There is nothing inherently destructive to nature in Christianity, so perhaps Christians ought to return to their biblical roots in terms of the care of the earth, linking their belief in God to taking care of his creation.

The Silence of Evangelicals

The question remains: Why have evangelical Christians been so thunderously silent on the rapaciousness of the "development" model?[1] Why have Christians not been at the forefront of the conservation movement? Ironically, evangelical Christians, some of whom tend to be more "conservative," have not distinguished themselves for conserving the environment. Their silence can be attributed to bad exegesis of scripture, apathy born of theological ignorance an ethnocentric model of development and simple greed.

Evangelicals have been known to openly advocate the exploitation of natural reserves on biblical grounds. One notable advocate was former Secretary of the Interior James Watt, an avowed evangelical, who justified on biblical grounds the opening of national forests to lumber and mining companies, accelerating the sale of oil and gas leases, and expediting surface mining of coal: "My responsibility is to follow the Scriptures which call upon us to occupy the land until Jesus returns" (cited by Ajemian, 1981). Ironically, this is a misquote of Scriptures. "Occupy the land until Jesus returns" is a misapplication of Luke's parable of the talents, where Christ is really teaching the opposite of exploitation: good stewardship. In the parable, the wise steward multiplied rather than diminished resources. Faulty exegesis is at the heart of the problem.

According to Sheldon (1984:4), other Christians have also asserted that the Scriptures teach exploitation rather than caretaking, based on the Genesis 1:28–31 passage where the Hebrew *Kabash*, "subdue," may also mean "to tread down or bring into bondage" and the word for "rule," *redah*, can mean "to trample" or "to prevail against." But Sheldon disagrees with this justification of exploitation and points out that in Genesis 2:15, the tone changes where Adam and Eve were put into the garden to "till" it and "keep" it. *Abad* can be translated as "work" and is the root Hebrew word for "serve" or "be a slave to," and when added to *Shamar* to "keep" or "watch" or "preserve." Sheldon does not find an exegetical basis for naked exploitation of nature and concludes: "Thus our ruling should be viewed in the context of servanthood. We are to subdue the creation and rule it as good stewards. We are called to be the shepherds of God's creation."

Apathy and theological ignorance by evangelicals is another reason for silence. Sheldon cites a survey done by the U.S. Fish and Wildlife Service and Yale University in 1980 which indicated that the more frequently Americans attend religious services, the less they know about wildlife and the more utilitarian and dominionistic their attitudes are toward nature. The lack of theological teaching in the church on the *imago Dei* as caretaking is really a lack of teaching about God's vision for his people and the world. Our awareness of God himself is limited by this dangerous anthropocentrism. Bishop

John V. Taylor, in his delightful book *Enough Is Enough* (1975:53) warns that "only in his unbroken awareness of God is man's technological mastery safe. Only in his acceptance of creature-hood can his dominion be prevented from becoming raw domination."

Another reason that there is not an outcry by evangelicals against the exploitative system is that we are part of it as members of western society and as participants in the institutions that represent the modern, developmentalist perspective. We are blinded by our ethnocentrism. Wolterstorff (1983:23–41) discusses the modern world-system, showing that the structures of our society are fallen and need reform and that the modernization approach to resolving human problems is bankrupt. It is difficult for us to extract ourselves from the system that has benefited us to judge it objectively for its strengths and weaknesses. Elsewhere I have analyzed the various "development" models and found modernization to be intolerably destructive to both humankind and nature as a worldwide model, even though it benefits the world's minority immensely (Bragg, 1987). The modern technological solution to human need is seriously flawed.

Still another reason, perhaps unconscious, for our silence is greed. Christians in rich nations benefit immensely from the current arrangement. Our standard of life is very high in comparison with the Two-Thirds World. In his analytical article "Silver and Gold Have I None: Church of the Poor or Church of the Rich," Barrett (1983) discusses Christian financial resources at the global level, finding that Christ has 1.5 billion followers today who receive annual incomes totaling U.S. $6.5 trillion and who own two-thirds of the earth's entire resources. In the same study, evangelical Christians are reported to have a personal income of just under $1 trillion a year (out of a total Christian population financial income of $5.9 trillion a year, not counting net worth). However, of these Christians, 13 percent live in absolute poverty while 52 percent live in affluence and another 35 percent are relatively well-off. Barrett concludes: "It is outrageous that 750 million affluent Christians can continue to allow 195 million brethren in Christ to exist in abject poverty year after year" (1983:148).

Obviously the disparity represented in the above figures needs addressing if there is to be any equity and justice within the Christian community worldwide. It is not a new problem. The early church also had to face disparities. The apostle Paul instructed the Corinthian church on a solution to the drought-induced poverty of the church in Jerusalem:

There is no question of relieving others at the cost of hardship to yourselves; it is a question of equality. At the moment your surplus meets their need, but one day your need may be met from their surplus. The aim is equality; as Scripture has it, "The man who got much had no more than enough, and the man who got little did not go short" (2 Corinthians 8:13–15, NEB).

This sharing ethic of the early church was seen also in the Jerusalem Christian community, where economics was vitally linked to their communion in common life, and to their witness and growth.

All whose faith had drawn them together held everything in common: they would sell their property and possessions and make a general distribution as the need of each required. With one mind they kept up their daily attendance at the temple, and, breaking bread in private houses, shared their meals with unaffected joy, as they praised God and enjoyed the favour of the whole people. And day by day the Lord added to their number those whom he was saving (Acts 2:44–47, NEB).

The early church had its disparities as well. The apostle James had to admonish the brothers who claimed faith yet were unwilling to show it through sharing: "Suppose a brother or a sister is in rags with not enough food for the day, and one of you says, 'Good luck to you, keep yourselves warm, and have plenty to eat' but does nothing to supply their bodily needs, what is the good of that?" (James 2:15–16, NEB). He warned them against piling up wealth at the expense of exploited laborers and against living wantonly in luxury, "fattening yourselves like cattle" (James 5:1–5). If James were alive today, his message would be appropriately applicable to the wealthy church that benefits from an exploitative system and then gives back a miserly charity to the poor.

Until there is a fundamental, structural rearrangement of the way Christians respond to the poverty gap among themselves and in the world, all the relief and development efforts of the church and para-church organizations are only band-aids. Until we come to grips with the implications of our made-in-the-north economic development model, we are rearranging the deck chairs while the Titanic is sinking. Unless Christianity is able to separate itself from the western cultural-economic milieu, it will continue to worship the false gods of production and prosperity and perpetuate inequitable and inhumane conditions of life for the poor, including poor Christians worldwide.

THE NEW BAALISM

Production-oriented materialism is not new in this century, nor is it unique to the western world. After the Children of Israel were liberated from Egypt where they were enslaved as cheap labor for the Egyptians, Jehovah gave them a new socio-economic system upon entering Canaan. Historically, the exploited tend to become exploiters when given the chance, since that is their only model, so God gave the Hebrew nation a new government, a new way to relate to God in a theocracy, with a new way to relate to each other and to their environment. The Deuteronomical and Levitical laws were to keep them from idolatry, slavery, and exploiting or being exploited again as they were in Egypt, the most prosperous, powerful, and "scientific" nation of that day. While a review of the laws and the Jubilee principles would be instructive here, suffice it to say that the purpose of the new system was to guarantee freedom and a good life to the Hebrew children on a sustainable basis. The rules governing land use and conservation, the rules of gleaning, the prohibition of slavery, and the other socio-economic arrangements were radically different. The evil socio-economic and political injustices of Egypt were never to be repeated, and the Passover Feast as a symbol is still at the heart of Judaism.

The new land of milk and honey, however, offered some temptations. When the Hebrew spies went across to scout the land (Numbers 13), they were frightened by the fortified cities and powerful gigantic inhabitants. Only Caleb and Joshua saw them as they really were, big but vulnerable. The Lord told Moses to speak to the people:

I am the Lord your God. You shall not do as they do in Egypt where you once dwelt, nor shall you do as they do in the land of Canaan to which I am bringing you; you shall not conform to their institutions. You must keep my laws and conform to my institutions and my laws: the man who keeps them shall have life through them. I am the Lord. (Leviticus 18:1-5, NEB)

The plan of the Lord was for them to be counter-cultural, heeding a new set of socio-political norms. But the land was flowing in milk and honey and the Israelites were tempted to join the local culture and worship Baal and Ashtoreth, local deities which had apparently brought about this prosperity. Baal was a god of fertility and productivity. So they dallied with the Midianite women and offered meat sacrifices to Baal of Peor. As a result, they were punished through a plague and twenty-four thousand died (Numbers 25:3-18).

The Hebrews found it easy to join the productive system, easier than to follow the new system mandated by Jehovah. The parallel today is the ease with which Christians are drawn into the modern world system that produces material goods and pleasures, the "success" syndrome of free-market enterprise. The evangelical intrigue with the Theology of Prosperity and Yuppie Christianity are manifestations of this conformity to materialism. The staggering statistics on church building costs indicate a Baalistic narcissism in the American church. The Canaanite success syndrome is ever-present; two years ago the alumni association of a noted evangelical college in the Midwest dedicated a whole issue of its news magazine to "successful" graduates, those who have made it big in their professions, mostly business people. In the same way that God disdained and punished the Children of Israel in Canaan for assimilating into the local institutions, he will today punish the church of the rich and powerful (*not* just the handful of notorious televangelists who seem to focus on glorifying themselves). The punishment is not always as immediate, as with the Israelites; the saddest words for any church are "the Spirit has departed," while the outward forms of worship continue. True religion has an ethical basis, not mere verbal orthodoxy. God spoke through Isaiah to those who were maintaining outwardly correct worship while perpetuating an unjust system: "Is not this what I require of you as a fast: to loose the fetters of injustice, to untie the knots of the yoke . . . (Isaiah 58:5).

CHRISTIAN DEVELOPMENT AND THE KINGDOM

But what of the church or Christian agency that is indeed attempting to live out the precepts of the kingdom of God? There are hundreds of agencies or groups, large or small, with a deep concern for the vulnerable of the world. They carry out programs of relief in emergency situations, and are among the first to respond to natural and human disasters. They promote child-care, hospitals, medical teams, well-drilling, agricultural programs, small-business entrepreneurs, housing, health-care, literacy—the list goes on. Are these development programs contributing to the demise of the environment and the dependency of the Two-Thirds World on the rich countries? Are they not helping the poor communities gain a better control on their own destinies, with some modicum of dignity and autonomy? Do these Christian agencies, both international and indigenous, not promote appropriate technologies that are indigenous to the culture and situation rather than high-tech solutions that create problems? Are they not seeking a sustainable system? The answer is increasingly "yes." However, it has not always been positive because they have been shaped by their historical context.

The Roots of Development

The very concept of "development" arose in a specific historical socio-cultural context, it is hard to separate the ideas of development from the source. In the case of the northern-based development programs and organizations, they gained ascendancy following World War II in response to the critical needs of the poorer nations. The contemporary developmental movement is predicated on the western scientific and technological revolution, asserting that the ultimate goal is to increase production and economic growth which will raise the standard of living and provide a better life for as many as possible. Modern medicine, farm equipment, fertilizers, hybrid seeds, irrigation, and so on were seen as the panacea for the "backward" or underdeveloped Third World. With this transfer of technology, the economic gap would be closed. Thus, the model of development underlying the efforts of both secular and Christian groups is basically derived from the secular humanism of the Enlightenment than from Christian thought, as has been documented by Sine (1981:72).

"Development" was derived from the Cold War politics of the U.S.A. and Europe. Helping the poor nations become viable would make them less susceptible to the rising tide of communism, it was theorized, since poverty creates more revolutions than ideology. W. W. Rostow, a presidential advisor to several administrations, published *Stages of Economic Growth: A Non-Communist Manifesto* in 1960, delineating a theory of socio-economic Darwinism that charted societies according to stages of growth. According to Rostow, societies develop from the point of being backward until they reach the "take-off stage" into sustained economic growth, or the western industrial state. This was a real part of the U.S. policy and programs for assisting poor nations, Truman's Point-Four Program, Kennedy's Alliance for Progress, and now U.S. Agency in Development (AID). AID is an arm of foreign policy which creates American ethical dilemmas (Bragg, 1988).

Underlying this approach to development is an assumption that progress is basically materialistic. This assumption is one-dimensional and ignores the whole non-economic side of life, the human and cultural values that in some cases are much more advanced than those in the industrialized north. It also assumes that the capitalist monetary system is the vehicle for progress, and ignores traditional economic systems that have worked for millennia and which might be better than participating in the world monetary system. Furthermore, modernization assumes that what worked in one hemisphere and climate will work universally—such as a capital-intensive agricultural or industrial system. But it ignores the realities of the parts of the world where capital is scarce and where human labor is the main resource. To introduce tractors or mechanized factories in these situations is to create unemployment and contribute to chronic underemployment. The climates and soils are also different, as are the social structures. We have already noted the disastrous effects on the environment and on the social fabric of poorer nations of the transfer of a production-oriented technology.

Christian Development Programs

To the degree that Christian development organizations adhere to the assumptions of the western development model, they buy into its inherent problems. The effects can be just as bad on a micro level as the effects of the World Bank projects on a macro level. While fewer people will be involved, qualitatively no difference exists. For example, the highly touted Green Revolution created dependency on imported seeds, fertilizers, machinery and parts, insecticides, and fuel. When a Christian agency introduces the Green Revolution, it creates the same dependency. Again, production is emphasized in a community where there is enough to go around, if it were not monopolized by the elites, the agency is missing a chance to stress redistribution and community solidarity, which may in the long run be more culturally acceptable in that community. Or, when a small-business agency makes loans to individuals only rather than to cooperatives or extended families or community organizations, it contributes to the western individualization ideal, not the community ideal.

Furthermore, when a development program fosters export-cropping or artisan products for export only, dependency is furthered as is vulnerability to changes within the market. In some cases, child-sponsoring agencies have established orphanages where the culture does not normally have "orphans" because a relative will *always* take in an orphaned child. There are a few children's programs in operation which sponsor only one child, the worst malnourished, in a large family; that child gets letters postmarked U.S.A. and birthday and Christmas gifts, while the others do not. All these examples illustrate some practices based on the western ethnocentric model of development unconsciously assimilated by some Christian agencies.

Other Christian organizations from the west often work in isolation from local and national efforts to meet human needs in an attempt to be politically neutral. But the effectiveness of agency programs *will* be affected by political considerations, both on the national and international levels. If Christian agencies receive money from the U.S. Agency for Development, they are already politicized. Recently, the American Baptist Hospital in Nicaragua refused several hundred thousand dollars from USAID (part of $17 million authorized by the U.S. Congress for humanitarian aid to the "contras" and other victims of the war) because "the funds come from the same hands which are causing the destruction and death throughout Nicaragua," and because the funds were not to be used in any projects carried out in coordination with the Nicaraguan government. Dr. Gustavo Parajon, Baptist pastor and the chairman of CEPAD, a Christian relief and development organization, said that carrying out programs without coordination with the Ministries of Education or Health would be short-sighted and wasteful, as well as being counter to the principles of long-term community development (*CEPAD Report*, 1988). Other Christian relief and development agencies also refused to administer those funds on the grounds that their ministries would be compromised.

Even at the local level, no development is done in a vacuum. Whatever is done at the village level invariably will be linked to the greater surrounding context. Christian agencies that think they can be apolitical and only deal with "neutral" local leaders are incorrect. If a program is successful, someone in the government will notice. In some cases, it has backfired because the success attracts long-absent landlords who saw no benefits from the land as it was! To do a health program without linking it to the national health plan is to court disaster and also be ineffective in the long run. Medical aid programs that refuse to send medicine to Nicaragua while sending aid to Ethiopia are following the policy of the United States Department of State, not the Holy Spirit.

Many Christian agencies are seeking new answers to the dilemma of being part of the system while trying to carry out kingdom principles. Some lively discussions are going on, such as the Workshop on Rural Development and the Environment with which we started this discussion. And some of the small, national, indigenous agencies are doing a much better job of asking the right questions than a lot of the larger, multinational relief and development agencies. One group in Mexico has created a model based on kingdom principles that is quite exciting. This effort is paralleled by other small national groups in the Two-Thirds World. Any real contributions of Christian relief and development agencies will depend on their self-conscious departure from the accepted developmentalist models, especially the bankrupt western technological model, and their creation of truly biblical models of assisting the vulnerable. These models must be based on the principles of the kingdom of God, while adapting to and deriving from the local contexts and cultures. What are these kingdom principles?

SHALOM AND KINGDOM PRINCIPLES

A balance and holism exists in the biblical view of the Christian life, perhaps seen best in the concept "shalom" in the Old Testament and the "kingdom of God" in the New Testament. These complementary terms deal with the relationships between Creator and creature, humans with nature, and human beings with each other and themselves. They present a view of these right relationships lived out here and now, as well as a preview of the eschatological future where balance and harmony will be fully restored.

Shalom

Shalom means not only peace in the sense of an absence of strife, but also in a positive sense of health, wholeness, prosperity, justice, harmony, and general wellbeing. Wolterstorff (1983:69–72) has a short treatise on "For Justice in Shalom" in which he defines shalom as "the human dwelling at peace in all his or her relationships: with God, with self, with fellows, and with nature." He cites the Isaiah 11:6–8 passage about the wolf dwelling with the lamb as a sample of shalom. "To dwell in shalom is to enjoy living before God, to enjoy living in one's physical surroundings, to enjoy living with one's fellows, to enjoy life with oneself."

The Old Testament cosmo-vision of shalom was one of peace and prosperity for the people of God. William Temple is reported to have said that Christianity is the most materialistic of all the great religions. God's purpose for his people is "prosperity and not misfortune" (Jeremiah 29:11) Prosperity, however, has to be realized with justice, or it becomes exploitative. Justice is the basis of shalom. The Psalms remind us that the earth and all its fullness belongs to the Lord. The land itself was not to be sold outright "because the land is mine" said the Lord, to be held for the use of all the people of God (Leviticus 25:23). The Jubilee principles underlined the protection and revitalization of the land, care for the poor, freedom of the oppressed debtor, and restoration of relationships.

Kingdom of God

The Old Testament shalom is expressed in the New Testament as the kingdom of God or the kingdom of Heaven. The Sermon on the Mount gives the charter of the kingdom. Living in peaceful and rightful relationships is the heart of the message of the gospel. Christ came to heal not only the broken relationships of humans with their Creator in a redemptive way, but also to engage them in harmonious fellowship among themselves, in the community of faith. Wolterstorff (1983) insists that there can be delight in community only when justice reigns and human beings no longer oppress each other, when "justice and peace embrace" (Psalm 85). This embrace of justice and peace happens, of course, in Christ, who came to bring us reconciliation both with God and with each other. The prophetic vision of the mission of the Messiah was fulfilled in Christ, who "came and preached peace to you who were far off and peace to those who were near" (Ephesians 2:17), referring to the Gentiles and the Jews who were natural enemies. Paul's ministry to the Gentiles was a sore point to the Jews who thought they enjoyed an exclusive relationship to God. The integration of both within the early church was a sign of the peace-making mission of Jesus.

However, the reconciliation was not limited to personal or ethnic relationships. "Through him God chose to reconcile the whole universe to himself, making peace through the shedding of his blood upon the cross—to reconcile all things, whether on earth or in heaven, through him alone" (Colossians 1:20). Christ brought a cosmic salvation, not just an individualistic redemption of human souls nor just a reconciliation of enemies. "When anyone is united to Christ, there is a new world; the old order (*ta panta*) has gone, and a new order has already begun" (2 Corinthians 5:17). In these passages, *ta panta* is the totality of things, a new order that has broken into history. The lordship of Christ gives us the responsibility to make the changes in history that will predict the day when the kingdom will be fulfilled with harmony with God, with neighbor, with nature, and with one's self. This is kingdom. This is shalom, but is it only to be realized in the future, in a Christian utopia? The kingdom is both present and future, contemporary and eschatological. Jesus taught us to pray, "Thy kingdom come, Thy will be done on earth as it is in heaven." To the degree that kingdom values are implemented here and now, economic and socio-political values will be transformed, wounded relationships will be healed, and the purposes of God for humanity and for all of created order will be fulfilled. The implementation of the kingdom depends on the mission of Christ and our mission here on earth.

MISSIO DEI: CHRIST AND HIS FOLLOWERS

When Jesus sent the twelve disciples on their first mission (Matthew 10), he told them to go to the towns and villages and proclaim the message: "The kingdom of Heaven is upon you," and he instructed them to heal the sick, raise the dead, cleanse lepers, cast out devils—that is, to take care of their physical and emotional needs as a manifestation of the kingdom that has drawn near. This they were to do in a context of shalom. He sent them penniless and vulnerable to the villages and told them to look up some worthy person to live with: "Wish the house peace (*eirene* or *shalom*) as you enter it, so that, if it is worthy, your peace may descend on it; if it is not worthy, your peace can come back to you." This intriguing passage concerning shalom shows that the kingdom draws near the needy when the shalom of the Christ is brought to them in the ministry and message of his disciples.

The essence of Christ's mission is encapsulated in the passage just preceding the mission of the disciples, and the parallel is striking. Indeed, we need to see the mission of disciples as inextricably linked to the mission of Jesus on earth. Matthew 9:35–10:1 is the *modus operandi* of the kingdom:

> So Christ went round all the towns and villages teaching in all their synagogues, announcing the good news of the kingdom, and curing every kind of ailment and disease. The sight of the people moved him to pity: they were like sheep without a shepherd, harassed and helpless; and he said to his disciples, "The crop is heavy, but labourers are scarce; you must therefor beg the owner to send labourers to harvest his crop." Then he called his twelve disciples to him and gave them authority to cast out unclean spirits and to cure every kind of ailment and disease (NEB).

Jesus charged his followers: "As the Father has sent me, so send I you." Jesus was sent incarnationally; he had the power and the glory, but gave it up in order to take on human form and to identify with the poor, being born of peasant stock in a borrowed crib. "For the divine nature was his from the first; yet he did not think to snatch at equality with God but made himself nothing, assuming the nature of a slave. Bearing the humanlikeness, revealed in human shape, he humbled himself, and in obedience accepted even death—death on a cross" (Philippians 2:6–8, NEB) Christ came down the success ladder in order to comprehend the human condition and to intervene in history. It was through his humility that he challenged the powerful. As Mary in her *Magnificat* exclaimed: "He has brought down monarchs from their thrones, but the humble have been lifted high. The hungry he has satisfied with good things, the rich sent empty away" (Luke 2:52–53, NEB). Ultimately, Christ's mission was a challenge to the power structures predicated on strength through weakness. He took the weak, the nobodies, the uncouth peasant poor and formed them into followers that shook the foundations of the Roman Empire through a ministry of compassion and reconciliation.

In his ministry, Christ was moved to compassion by the sight of the harassed and helpless villagers. He compares them to shepherdless sheep. In today's world, the harassed and helpless are the poor. To be poor is to be powerless. The landlords, the absentee *hacendados*, the corrupt political system, the unfair wages, the export-oriented cropping system, the multinational corporations with their off-shore sweatshops, the dictators, the lack of education, the absence of health-care—all keep the poor powerless. Theologian Gutierrez describes the effects in *We Drink from Our Own Wells* (1984:9–10).

> Poverty means death. It means death due to hunger and sickness, or to repressive methods used by those who see their privileged position being endangered by any effort to liberate the oppressed. It means physical death to which is added cultural death, inasmuch as those in power seek to do away with everything that gives unity and strength to the dispossessed of this world. In this way those in power hope to make the dispossessed an easier prey for the machinery of oppression.

The mission of the church is to empower through a ministry to the poor, not just preach liberation in the future coming kingdom. But the power imparted has to be the power of powerlessness, the power of vulnerability, the power of Christ—not the Roman Empire nor the political power of the Sanhedrin. The method has to be different. The passages above indicate the method: proclaiming the kingdom and taking care of human needs. These are parallel and synchronous activities, as equally important as two sides of a coin. For too many years the evangelical church in America has cast social concern into a negative or, at best, a secondary function of the *missio Dei* through the church. The dichotomy between evangelism and social action has characterized America's evangelical church since the liberal-fundamentalist split at the turn of the century, and only recently has there been a rapport between evangelism and social concern resulting from serious reflection.

The villagers of Christ's day resemble the villagers in the Two-Thirds World today more than we do in the industrialized north. The conditions in rural India or Africa are closer to those of first-century Palestine than are westernized, modernized nations of today. If Christ were to walk through the towns and hamlets of the "underdeveloped" world today, he would experience the same compassion he felt for the helpless of two thousand years ago. The same conditions prevail today. Barrett (1983:46) describes the current world conditions:

> One billion one hundred million human beings without adequate shelter, landlessness and mass unemployment; 2.1 billion do not have access to adequate water supply, some 50 million are temporarily displaced or permanently unsettled refugees, 800 million adults are illiterate with no access to literature; 850 million have little or no access to schools; 1.5 billion have no access to medical care; 500 million people . . . suffer from inadequate and uncertain diet and thus from severe protein-calorie malnutrition; and some 1.5 billion human beings on earth are hungry or malnourished.

Every ten seconds, three children in the world die of starvation. The world is indeed characterized by the indifferent rich man and the ragged, diseased, hungry beggar sitting on his doorstep.

The rich north of today resembles the rich and powerful of Jesus' day—the religio-political Sanhedrin, as well as the secular rulers of the Roman Empire. Jesus' Messianic message to the powerful was repentance and restitution, but few heeded his call. The Rich Young Ruler went away sad, the cost of discipleship too high, while the disenfranchised poor received him gladly. The good news is also for the rich, but Jesus warned that attachment to their earthly wealth would make it awfully difficult to enter the kingdom—like trying to squeeze a camel through the eye of a needle!

Jesus' mandate comes to his disciples across the centuries, but remains startlingly relevant. The mission of Christian relief and development is to proclaim the Good News of the kingdom *and* minister to the needs of the weak and oppressed. To do so we must walk through their dusty roads, feel their pain, identify with their sorrows, and experience their powerlessness, just as Jesus did. It was he who had no place to lay his head. It was Jesus who confronted the corrupt religio-political system of his day and was ultimately crucified by it. It was he who said that the servant is not greater than his master and that we should take up the cross and follow him. It was his disciples who were to become vulnerable and dependent in proclamation and service to the needy.

IMAGO DEI AND MISSIO DEI IN CONTEMPORARY PERSPECTIVE

There are frontiers of activities that are crying out for Christian engagement and creativity as a manifestation of the *imago Dei* and *missio Dei*. We should be the ones on the cutting edge of formulating an alternative economic system based on kingdom principles. Christians should not be satisfied with the current system that consumes inordinately, destroys unrenewable resources, endangers life on earth, threatens the survival of people and their cultures, alienates and mutilates humankind, and perpetuates a world of extremely rich and extremely poor nations and peoples. Concretely, new models of development need to be thought out for our industrialized society as well as the traditional ones in the Two-Thirds World. Our lifestyle needs transforming to be more in line with the rest of the world and to guarantee a future life for our children and grandchildren. Those charged with the care of the earth should seek a gentle technology, an appropriate technology. The church ought to be involved with the wise conservation and use of natural resources. We also should be engaged in the cultural survival of people and their traditions, redeeming the positive values of all cultures. We should be at the forefront of peace-making and healing, not supporting wars as a means of conflict resolution. We need to set an example for a more equitable and just distribution of goods and services worldwide, as well as engage in relief and development.

Curricula on all these issues should be developed from a biblical perspective for schools, churches, relief and development agencies, and mission societies. Christian scholarship can no longer remain distant from contemporary issues in the real world. We must stop educating our youth to merely fit into the establishment in well-paying professions. Through experiential education where theory is challenged by practice, students must be fitted to change the world. Even theological reflection must be done by people who are actively involved in the struggles. There are great problems facing this generation and generations to come. It was said of David that he "served his generation." Our mission is also to serve the generations to come.

Christians must create the agenda for a more sustainable and humane way of life. It is too important to leave the agenda to politicians, economists, and scientists. When the church takes seriously its mission, there will be a qualitative difference in the way Christians and Christian agencies approach the question of assisting the vulnerable.

> When our relationship with God
>   is changed.
> our relationship with our poor neighbor
>   transformed,
> and our care of the environment
>   markedly different,
> we will begin to fulfill the *imago Dei*
>   and the *missio Dei*,
> we will together begin to realize
>   a new shalom,
> and the kingdom will draw near.

"Thy kingdom come, Thy will be done on earth as it is in heaven."

---

[1]There are some exceptions to the unconscionable silence by evangelicals. John R. Shaeffer and Raymond H. Brand wrote and appeal to ecological soundness, *Whatever Happened to Eden?* (1980), from an evangelical position. A critique of the whole development model is found in Nicholas Wolterstorff's "The Modern World-Systems" in *Until Justice and Peace Embrace* (1983). Some Catholic Christian writers on the environmental question include F. F. Shummacher, *Small is Beautiful: Economics as If People Mattered* (1973); Barbara Ward and Rene Dubos, *Only One Earth* (1972); and Mary Evelyn Jegen and Bruno Manno, *The Earth is the Lord's* (1978).

5

Anthropological Insights
for Whole Ministries

Paul E. Hiebert

CHRISTIAN MINISTRY BEGINS WITH relationships, and ends in the transformation of people and communities. This was the way of the incarnation, and it is the model for Christian development programs.

For Christians, development has two dimensions to it: theological and contextual. Theologically, our vision of the mission and motivation of development must emerge out of our fundamental understanding of the nature of God, humans, the fall, redemption, and the kingdom of God. Contextually, development must take place in twentieth-century communities such as the Maasai in Kenya, the Enga of Papua New Guinea, and the untouchables in south Indian villages. It is in understanding these that history and the social sciences, particularly anthropology, are of great help.

We will explore here some insights which anthropology offers us for development programs, particularly those in which we work in other cultures.

DEVELOPMENT IS BASED ON RELATIONSHIPS

Good relationships are essential in any development program. They are the bridge across which ideas and values are carried. Too often we try to introduce new technology and new ways of thinking

PAUL E. HIEBERT was raised in India where he later served as missionary with the Mennonite Brethren. He is now professor of anthropology and East Asian Studies in the School of World Mission at Fuller Theological Seminary.

before the bridge has been built, and we later wonder why we have failed. In fact, the bridge itself is, in many ways, more important than our developmental schemes because it links us together as humans in a fragmented world. It is important, therefore, when beginning development projects to focus *first* on relationships and *then* on the tasks to be accomplished. But building relationships is difficult, particularly with strangers and non-Christians. It is doubly difficult when the people to whom we go speak another language and live in another culture. In such settings, we need to understand how cultural differences affect us and our relationships.

Culture and Cultural Differences

Culture is the world in which we live, the language we use, the ideas we have, the feelings we emphasize, the values we share, and the way we act. Culture enables us to communicate with one another and to understand what is going on.

Often, we are not aware of our own culture until we enter another one. We soon discover that not only do people in other cultures eat different food and dress in different kinds of clothes, they also think in very different ways. For example, traditional Indian villagers take it for granted that people are not equal. They believe that in their previous lives, some people have done good and so deserve to be high-caste people honored by all. Similarly, others must suffer in this life for sins in their past lives. Many villagers believe that those who come to help the poor and needy in this life cause them to be reborn in poverty and hardship in their next life in order to suffer their just punishment. We, on the other hand, assume that every person should be a free, fulfilled individual who can make the most out of this life.

In a real sense, people in different cultures live in different worlds. Each of these worlds has its own language, eating habits, styles of dress, and patterns of human relationships. But there is more to it than that. A culture is made up of the basic categories which a community of people use to order their perceptions of reality. It is the feelings they have about music, sports, and their country. In short, it is the more or less integrated systems of ideas, feelings, values, behavior patterns, and products shared by a group of people which enable them to create a society. It is the maps the people have of their world—the maps they also use to live their lives.

How can we build mutual relationships of trust with people who are so different from us? How can we communicate to them ideas that can transform their lives and bring them together into communities of hope and reconciliation in a broken world? The task is not an easy one, but one which is both exciting and profitable if we are successful.

Adjusting to New Cultures

We are all excited, and a little fearful, when we enter a new culture. Our first response is fascination and wonder. We spend the days exploring new sights and sounds. Everything seems so strange, so exotic. At this stage, however, we are still tourists, and the day comes when we realize we cannot be tourists forever. We must either return home, or get down to the serious task of learning to live in the new culture.

Culture Shock

After our initial enthusiasm passes, other realities begin to occupy our attention: mosquitoes, strange foods, bad roads, the lack of running water, and problems with communicating with the people. Those who welcomed us so warmly have gone back to their work, appearing to ignore the problems we face. We feel alone in a strange and sometimes frightening world. The result is "culture shock," the shock that comes with being torn from all that is familiar and not knowing what is going on. This shock really strikes home when we realize that we have decided to make this place our "home"!

Our initial response is hostility and anger. We find fault with the culture and compare it unfavorably with our own. We withdraw and take refuge in a small circle of people from our own country. Above all, we wish we could "go home" to our own country and community, so we write letters of resignation. We do not realize that we are perfectly normal people experiencing the trauma of learning a whole new way of thinking and living.

But if we make the effort and commitment to stay, it isn't long until we learn to say a few words in the native tongue and can find our way around town. We make friends among the people and realize that they do not all look alike. We begin to enjoy many of the local customs. Eventually, we throw away our letters of resignation and begin the long task of adjusting to the new culture.

The return of humor often marks the beginning of adjustment. We begin to laugh at our predicaments rather than criticizing the people. We begin to sympathize with our foreign associates who we think are worse off than ourselves.

This period of adjustment is one of the most important in our whole stay abroad. How we learn to relate to the people and culture at this stage becomes the pattern for the rest of ministry. If we develop positive attitudes toward our host people, and learn to live as they do, as much as psychologically possible, we have laid the foundations for an effective ministry among them. They will listen to what we say because they learn to trust us as people like themselves. On the other hand, if we remain critical and aloof, chances are we will be seen as foreigners throughout our stay. And since we are models of the gospel for the people, it, too, will appear to them as distant and foreign.

The final stage of culture shock comes when we feel comfortable in the new culture. Some of us build western ghettos from which we sally forth to do our work. Others of us seek to live more like the people, while incorporating some of our own cultural practices. In either case, we cherish the friendship of the people and learn to like local customs. We realize that when we leave we will miss the people and their ways.

Mental Shock

Beneath culture shock is a much more profound philosophical shock. For many of us this is the first time we truly realize that there are other ways of looking at the world, and these ways make sense! Moreover, our ways are not always the best or the most civilized.

When we first go abroad, we assume that our culture is better. After all, we are going out to help these people improve their lives. In time, however, we learn to appreciate much in the new culture, and we begin to wonder whether all cultures are equally good and true. This relativism, however, disturbs us, for it ultimately denies any truth or universal good. But we realize that for us to judge other cultures by the standards of our own is ethnocentric.

Most of us, in the end, move beyond our original ethnocentrism, and beyond the relativism we first experience when we live deeply in another culture. We develop a "metacultural" perspective—the ability to stand above any one culture, and to compare and judge different cultures from a multicultural perspective. As Christians, this standard by which we evaluate all cultures is the kingdom of God—the way God intended humans to live, had there been no sin. By that standard we find both good and bad in all cultures, including our own.

As Christians, we also face theological shock when we confront other kinds of Christians, and even more so when we relate to

Hindus, Muslims, and Buddhists. We wonder why we are Christians and not Hindus or Muslims, and why we believe Christianity is the only way to salvation. Confronted with religious pluralism, others adopt a theological relativism which holds that all religions lead to God. To claim the uniqueness of Christianity, they say, is ethnocentric. Most of us move beyond this destructive relativism to a more deeply rooted faith in the gospel. Now, however, we no longer equate it with our own culture. We realize that the gospel is transcultural and belongs to all peoples, and that Christians may use different cultural ways to express the same universal message.

Building Trusting Relationships

Relationships of mutual understanding and trust are the foundation on which all Christian development ministries must be built. Without them, the gospel is alien and development programs are merely foreign imports. Culture shock helps us to adjust to a new culture, but it does not guarantee good relationships with the people. These must be carefully cultivated throughout our ministry. In doing so, there are several barriers we must surmount.

Misunderstanding

The first barrier to trusting relationships is misunderstanding. This sometimes occurs in humorous ways that have little serious consequence. Indians laugh when someone eats lefthanded. They use the left hand only for toilet purposes and what they consider dirty work. People in a remote African village thought North Americans were cannibals because they fed their babies out of tin cans with pictures of infants on them.

Sometimes, however, misunderstandings create serious problems. In one case, Americans decided to help a southeast Asian village by digging a well for it and installing a pump. When the project was finished, the villagers were angry and refused to use the water. On investigating the situation the Americans discovered they had drilled the well on a sacred site inhabited by the village ancestors. The villagers were afraid that this would anger the ancestors and bring sickness on them.

The obvious solution to misunderstanding is learning to understand. Development agents must continue to study the local culture throughout their stay. This does not mean they must spend all of their time studying. In fact, sharing their ideas while learning more about the culture is one important way of testing these ideas with the people. A second solution, as we will see, is to share the planning and implementation of a development project with the people who will be affected by it.

Ethnocentrism

A second barrier to trusting relationships is ethnocentrism. This is the feeling that somehow our cultural ways are better than those of the people among whom we serve. Intellectually, we may agree that their culture makes sense, but deep down we still think ours is preferable. When we are confronted by another culture, our own is called into question. Our defense is to avoid the issue by concluding that our own is better and other people are less civilized.

This attitude of cultural superiority is a serious hindrance to cross-cultural communications. We may identify with the people by adopting their dress, eating their food, and living in their houses. We may even make them bosses in the project and work under their direction. But the people can sense if there are any feelings of superiority and will respond by remaining distant and aloof.

To build trusting relationships, we must learn to genuinely appreciate the people and their culture. One way to achieve this is to relate closely to them, to learn to see and love them as persons like ourselves. Another is to examine our own unconscious cultural prejudices. Normally we are not aware of how deeply our own thoughts and behaviors are shaped by our culture. We "simply live our lives as normal humans do," unaware that what we think is "normal" has been defined by our culture. We are often more aware of our Christian message which we "talk about" than we are of our deep cultural assumptions, because these are what we use to "talk with."

Premature Judgments

A final barrier to good relationships is premature judgments. We are naturally inclined to judge other cultures when we encounter them. Too often, however, we do so before we have taken the time to try to understand or appreciate them. The result can destroy our work.

One example of this is the conclusion many westerners reach that Africans, Indians, and many other people "have no sense of time." Western agents often complain that the people show up late or miss appointments without informing them. The people know this and conclude that the agents are more interested in their own programs than in the people. In these societies, relationships take priority over tasks, so if friends or relatives drop in when a person is about to leave for an appointment, she or he must take time to visit before departing.

It is important that we seek to understand and appreciate a culture before we judge it. When we do, we need to test our judgments with the people, lest we have misunderstood their ways. Interestingly enough, when we come to truly understand and appreciate other cultures, we will be less judgmental of them and more judgmental of our own.

Sharing the Work

Development is not something we do for people. There are times when immediate relief is needed and we must act. But development goes beyond this, looking not only to successful projects but also to transformed communities. Success on this level requires relationships of mutual benefit and control between the people and the development worker.

Mutual Benefit

One of the hardest things for us as development agents to learn is that true development benefits us as much as it does the people. Until we realize this, we too readily go with a "savior" mentality that demeans the people, breeds arrogance in us, and destroys the community we hope to help build. We bring technology and material goods. They offer us themselves. When we finish a task we leave and move on to a new assignment. They remember us long after we are gone and write to keep contact. We place our confidence in self-reliance. The poor teach us our vulnerability and what it means to trust in God in our everyday lives.

A development program must also benefit the people. In other words, it must be something they, as well as the agent, wants. It is easy for us to define what *we* think the people need. It is important that we also take *their* needs into account. Both are important in planning the work.

Sharing Control

There is nothing harder for those of us from the West than to give up control of "our" development projects. We like to come "to help the people." By this we mean: (1) we will examine the situation, decide what is wrong, (2) we will plan what needs to be done, (3) we will provide the resources and do the work, and (4) we will evaluate the project and decide whether it was a success or failure. Unfortunately, no real mutual relationships are involved in this process. Consequently, when we leave, the project often dies. It was our project. The people often never wanted it, and never owned it.

An example of this was a water project in Laos. Western development workers decided the people needed good water, so they dug wells and put in pumps. A few years later many of the pumps were broken, and no one bothered to repair them because they had been put on public lands by outsiders. Only those pumps located on Buddhist temple lands were maintained because the priests "owned" them (Niehoff, 1966:234–245).

In recent years some development agencies have been willing to share the first step with the people. They sit down with the leaders and examine the situation. They agree on a mutual course of action. And then the development agency carries out and evaluates the work.

While this approach is a beginning step, it does not go far enough. It is important that development projects be based on mutual relationships. This means the local people must be deeply involved in the planning, resourcing, working, and evaluating of the project. The last step is often the hardest to give up. We may want to evaluate the program a success, only to find that the *people* judge it a failure. To give them control of the final assessment is to place ourselves in their hands. But this is the last and most important step in a truly mutual endeavor. If we do not take it, we are not willing to fully trust the people. If we take it, the project has a much greater chance of succeeding. World Vision, a leading Christian agency working in development, is exploring the importance of the following steps in developing mutual participation in development programs:

1. The people must take the lead in defining the needs.
2. The people must take the lead in defining the resources.
3. The people must take the lead in implementing the program.
4. The people must take the lead in evaluating the success of the program.

To give these lip-service is one thing; to put them into effective practice is another.

In the end, the greatest contribution we can make to a community is not the completion of a particular project. It is to help them discover that they can formulate, complete, and evaluate development programs on their own. It is to empower them. Only then will the transformation of the community truly begin.

Bi-cultural Brokers

Fortunately, and unfortunately, the development worker does not work only on an interpersonal level. He or she is part of larger social systems. Workers are normally sent out by an agency that has specific expectations and assignments for them. On the other hand, they work daily with a community of people who also have particular expectations of these foreigners. Often these sets of expectations differ a great deal, and the workers must make difficult decisions: do they side with the sending agency, or with the people? As development workers associate and identify with the people, the sending agency becomes suspicious. On the other hand, if the workers identify with the agency, the people mistrust them.

This tension is minor, but real, in everyday matters. The more time we spend in filling out reports and balancing accounts, the longer we are away from the people. If we spend all our time with the people, however, we do not fulfill the requirements of the agency.

The tension becomes particularly serious when strong disagreements between the agency and the people arise. In such situations, each party expects the worker to be on their side. In the end, the worker may have to choose to speak up for one side or the other, opening himself to any consequences.

It is helpful for us to know that people working between two cultures, sometimes referred to as "bi-cultural brokers," constitute some of the most important people in our modern world, but that they are almost always lonely people. Both the people in their home culture and those among whom they work distrust them to some extent. The bi-cultural broker knows both sides, and each party is suspicious when the broker is siding with the other party. In the end, bi-cultural brokers often find their most intimate friendships with other bi-cultural people.

Family Life

Finally, a word needs to be said about the family life of the development agent. Normally, he or she goes with a spouse and children. What about them?

Some agencies recognize the need for both husband and wife to be involved in the work, but many do not. Consequently the spouse, generally the wife, has no reason to be there except to accompany a partner. But life is difficult in another culture, and the spouse gets few personal rewards for being there. In rural India, for example, it takes about five and a half hours to cook meals that they could normally prepare in an hour. The reason, in part, is that chickens are still running around at the market. Normal household chores—cooking, laundry, cleaning, and shopping—take much more time and effort than expected. Moreover, there are few friends nearby. Consequently, wives often face a great deal of discouragement and loneliness. The husband feels rewarded by his work and he usually has a lot of opportunities to meet new people. But the wife bears the drudgery of keeping everyday life going and raising the children with little or no immediate reward. It is very important, therefore, for wives to have a meaningful involvement in the work.

Children raise other difficult questions. Where should they go to school—to local schools, to home school, or to a distant boarding school? Which culture should they identify with—the local culture or their home culture? Often, if they live long periods abroad in their formative years, they no longer fit back into North American culture. Their first culture, in fact, is the North-American-abroad culture, not the North American culture. When they go to North America, they are going to a strange land. They feel out of place. We need to understand this and realize that they are not really "one of us." They are bi-cultural people who will be most at home in bi-cultural settings all their lives (Hiebert, 1985:227–254).

It is important that development workers take seriously their personal and family lives, because the people around them observe and judge these closely. In cross-cultural settings there is often no distinction between public and private life as we experience it in the West. Our personal lives are closely observed, and people come for help at all times of the day or night. In building relationships, therefore, it is important that we do so as person-to-person, and not in our official roles. Only then will the trust be built that is the basis for all effective cross-cultural communication.

DEVELOPMENT AS TRANSFORMATION

Development is based on relationships, but its goal is transformation—the creation of new communities in which people live in harmony under God and enjoy the basic necessities of life. Mel Loewen of the World Bank points out that there are two types of necessity: absolute needs and relative needs. A person who is starving says, "I need food to live"—this is absolute necessity. Another person says, "I need another yacht. My friend has two and I have only one"—this is relative necessity. Our concern is with the former.

TRANSFORMATION AND
SOCIOPOLITICAL STRUCTURES

The type of transformation needed varies with the society and involves two dimensions: (1) changing the social systems, which include the distribution of power, resources, and status; and (2) changing the culture which is the systems of beliefs, feelings, and values that order the people's ways of seeing reality.

In general terms, we deal with three types of societies: tribal, peasant, and urban. Tribal societies are often characterized by strong communities based on kinship ties. Generally, there is care for the poor and the marginal within the tribe itself. In these surroundings, the greatest problems are often technological. To successfully introduce changes, we need to work *with the leaders* so that the programs we initiate will benefit the whole community.

Peasant societies raise more difficult problems. They are generally made up of more than one community. Several ethnic groups may be living together in the same village. Class differences exist as well, with rich elites wielding the controlling power, and poor marginal people who are unorganized and powerless. If we try to help the poor directly, we may bring more hardships than benefits to them, because when we leave, the powerful reassert their dominance and punish the poor for looking to outsiders for help. This is what almost happened when development agents tried to help the Indian *campesinos* in Vicos, Peru. Local businessmen fought the organization of a cooperative store in which the Indians saved much money buying basic foodstuffs. Rich landlords tried to block the sale of land to the agents, who were trying to get small plots of land for the *campesinos* (Dobyns, et al., 1966, and Lear, 1966).

On the other hand, if we try to help the poor by helping the whole community, and hope that some "trickles down" to the poor, the rich and powerful benefit the most, and that the gap between rich and poor becomes greater. This happened when new hybrid seeds and fertilizers were introduced into North India. The result was a dramatic increase in food production. The poor, however, ended up worse off than before. The rich could now afford tractors, so they drove poor renters off their lands and consolidated their farms into large holdings. The renters had nowhere to go and ended up as day laborers.

Development in the urban society is much more complex because the number of people is so large and the problems are so great. Here it is important that different development agencies work together in order to multiply their effectiveness. No one agency can begin to tackle the problems faced in even one ghetto or barrio.

Transformation and Culture Change

Transformation involves not only changing the social relationships in a community, it also involves changing the way people think and behave. In other words, it involves changing their culture.

Cultures, however, are not merely collections of different customs. These customs are linked together into larger patterns, and these patterns integrated into a single whole. While no culture is completely integrated, it is true that in most the important beliefs and behavior patterns are interrelated so that a change in one affects the others.

A classic example of such unintended side-effects was the introduction of steel axes into North Australian societies by seamen. Traditionally, the aboriginal tribesmen made stone axes. But when transient seamen gave steel axes to local women with whom they had affairs, the whole society broke down. Women controlled the new, highly valued commodity which was obviously superior to the axes their own men made. So they asserted their independence and the social order collapsed.

It is important, therefore, that we carefully watch for unintended side-effects to changes we introduce so that these do not harm the people.

A second problem arising from the fact of cultural integration is that few problems are as simple as they at first seem to be. We may think that introducing latrines is a good thing because it breaks the disease cycle and promotes rural health. Unfortunately, latrines need at least one quart of water each time they are used. In large households, this doubles the workload of the women who draw and carry the water, often great distances. If we introduce pumps to provide the water, we must find people who will maintain them, and funds for their repair. This, in turn, requires organization and added taxes.

Another case illustrating the complex nature of most socioeconomic problems is food production. The introduction of new hybrid seed and fertilizers into North India brought about the Green Revolution—a significant increase in food production. But without proper storage, much of the grain rotted in the fields. Even when storage bins were eventually constructed, there were not enough tracks and trains to transport the surplus grain to areas where the people were starving. It is essential, therefore, that we look at the problems within their broader sociocultural settings. We must realize that to achieve change in one area of life, we may need to make changes in many other areas as well.

Finally, change always involves risk. Farmers know that their old methods work—they have for centuries. But what about these new methods? These strangers promise them great increase in crops, but the methods are locally unknown and untried. Most small farmers live on the edge of subsistence and cannot afford even a small drop in their crop production. Consequently, they cannot afford to make what seems to us to be even a small risk. If the new venture fails, they die.

We who grow up with affluence do not understand this fear of risk-taking. In such situations, the gains seem potentially so great that some risk is worth it. To illustrate the peasant's dilemma, I once challenged an economist complaining about the resistance of small farmers. We were in Kansas, and he lived in California. I bet him to throw two dice: if they came up with anything except double ones I would pay him the price of a round trip air ticket from California to Kansas; if they were double ones he would have to give me his ticket and walk back to California. He refused the bet. The cost of losing was too great for him to take any risk at all. Traditional farmers often feel the same way about our new ideas. It is important, therefore, that we make sure there is no risk to the people when we first introduce new technological ideas. We need to remember, *we* are not the ones to pay the price if the project fails.

Adding and Subtracting: New Ideas and Technology

Our normal idea in development is to add new ideas and technology into the community. We believe that the people will be better off if they have latrines, or pumps, or vaccinations, or schools, or hospitals. On first appearance these seem unquestionably good, but problems often arise when we add new traits to an existing culture.

First, as we have seen, there are often unintended side-effects. Good medicines reduce infant mortality, creating a population explosion, which in turn places greater demands on the earth to produce. Exposure to the outside world causes the brightest young people to leave the village for the city, drawn by the excitement and promises of better lives—promises which for most are never fulfilled.

Second, the technology and practices we introduce do not always work in this new setting. Agriculture agents wanted to help villagers in the forests of Central Africa increase their food production. They therefore encouraged the villagers to cut down the forests so that the agents could deeply plow the soil and plant row crops using steel plows. For a few years crops were good, and then things began to go wrong. The plows wore out much faster than they do in North America because the African soil particles are angular, not rounded. The heat evaporated the ground moisture, drawing up salts from the soil which deposited on the surface, destroying the fertility of the land. And the hot sun baked the now-exposed surface of the soil, creating a hard crust that even tractors could hardly break. In the end, the farming practices imported from North America proved to be very destructive. The agents had assumed that technology that worked in one place would work equally well in other places. It does not.

Third, there is always a risk in introducing something new—a risk we must recognize and share. For instance, development workers in India encouraged the villagers to dredge out the little reservoir tanks that irrigate their fields. So, in summer when the tanks were dry, the people dug them deeper to hold more water. After the first rains the tanks filled and the people rejoiced, but a few days later their joy turned to horror. All the water was gone. The development agents discovered that the soil at the bottom of the new tanks was so porous that the water seeped into the ground. Old tanks have sediment that seals the bottom and keeps the water in. When this was removed, the water was lost.

Development agents should be aware that new things are often misunderstood. Often, the tribe members thought that white people were spirits, or their ancestors returned from the grave. In Papua New Guinea, native Christians thought that short-wave radios were a type of super prayer which white people kept for themselves, because missionaries used them to order goods which arrived out of the clouds by means of airplanes. The introduction of immunization and birth-control measures is also frequently misunderstood, and the people accuse the development workers of trying to weaken or kill them off, or to violate their women (Hanks and Hanks, 1955).

Sometimes development agents want to subtract something from the culture. For example, in Nigeria they tried to eliminate the tsetse flies that caused sleeping sickness. The Indian government has tried to eradicate the caste system that oppresses the untouchables, and African national leaders have sought to remove old tribal loyalties. Subtracting traits is often difficult, and when they are removed, they often leave a cultural vacuum that is hard to fill. The removal of traits often destabilizes the society.

Substituting Traits

The best changes generally involve substituting something new for something old. For instance, old crops can be replaced by new ones. In Bangladesh, this meant introducing soybeans and sunflowers for oil production in place of castor beans. Similarly, new medicines can be introduced as substitutes for traditional ones (see Carstairs, 1955). Introducing change by replacing old ways with new ones creates a minimum of cultural stress.

Appropriate Technology

Change is most satisfactory if it is made by increments rather than by large steps. This is often referred to as "appropriate technology." For example, the United Nations program for developing dry lentils started with the farming practices which the people use. In India this meant oxen and wooden plows. The first step was to add steel tips to the plows, the second to contour plow, the third to initiate better water management from the existing village tanks, the fourth was to outline a system of better timing in planting the crops, and so on. By these simple changes, none of which was dramatic, crop production was increased over 50 percent! One does not need to jump to tractors and costly fertilizers to make major improvements in the quality of rural life.

Creating New Solutions

One important solution to development problems commonly overlooked is that of discovering new solutions within the local setting. Ideas brought in from outside can help, but until the people begin exploring new avenues of development in their own midst, they are dependent upon others for their advance. Transformation truly begins when the local community begins to take control of its own development.

The basis of transformation is not technology. It is the reordering of the vision, values, and goals of the community, and the creating of social organizations that coordinate the community pursuit of those goals. In short, it is a transformation of the society. When a community has a new vision of what its future can be, new technological solutions will be sought within local resources. Only then will transformation be a self-sustained and locally owned process.

Adoption and Confirmation

Decision to change is a complex process. Too often we think that people simply hear a new idea, think about it and decide to adopt it. Decision-making involves both ideas and feelings. In some decisions our heads rule, in others our desires do. The same is true of the people with whom we work.

Decision-making is also a process of reaching a conclusion and re-evaluating that conclusion (see figure 4). Faced with new ways, some decide to adopt them and others to reject them. But both

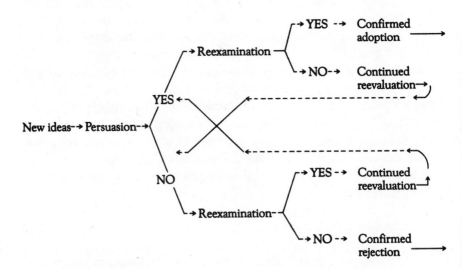

Figure 4: The Process of Decision and Confirmation

groups continue to examine their initial decisions. If the promised gains do not occur, those who have adopted the new ways often change their minds and reject them. It is very crucial, therefore, to ensure that the initial changes are as successful as possible. On the other hand, those who initially reject new ideas can be persuaded later to adopt them through demonstrations of successful innovation.

In any community, there are a few who are ready to change almost at once. These, however, are often marginal people who command little respect in the community. The next group to accept change are the innovators—those willing to look at new ways. These people are more respected, and others watch to see how they fare. Once change has been successfully introduced to these people, it generally spreads through the community as a whole. We should not expect everyone to accept development easily, or at the same time. Lasting change takes a great deal of both time and patience.

CONCLUSIONS

Development involves people and cultures, and anthropology can help us greatly in understanding both of these, as well as ourselves in new cultural settings. Cyprian Kia of West Africa has summarized a number of anthropological principles related to development.

1. People are more important than things; the person is more important than the activity.
2. Growth comes from within each person; all persons have talents waiting to be discovered and used.
3. People grow in responsibility as they are helped to accept responsibilities.
4. Learning becomes most relevant when it is built into a life-experience.
5. The most effective venue for training for the community's gain takes place within the community environment.
6. Community leaders know their problems and the solutions that may work better than others know them.
7. There are resources and skills within each community that are under-utilized and waiting to be harnessed.
8. The pace of development will be determined largely by the community; a particular change will be permanent only if that community is ready for that particular change.
9. The energy put into community action will be proportionate to the involvement of the community in the planning.

10. As communities are comprehensive social systems, they are best served by integrated development methods, rather than departmentalized units that work in isolation from one another.

11. The most effective agent to act as helper is a person who strongly identifies with the community, and who develops a relationship based on mutual trust and respect.

12. Too much help leads to dependency; people should be helped only insofar as it enables them to become more self-reliant (1987).

Our goal in development is ultimately to help people discover ways in which they can help themselves.

6

The Development Ethic:
Hope for a Culture of Poverty

Darrow L. Miller

WHY DO SOME PEOPLES and cultures become "developed" while others continue to struggle for survival? Observation of a wide range of cultures provides insights and answers. A culture's religious and philosophic underpinnings give birth to its successful development. The minds and hearts of its people play a larger role in a nation's development than its circumstances or natural resources. There is an ethic—a set of principles—which creates fertile soil for development.[1] In contrast, there is another of set of principles which stands its adherents in a quagmire of underdevelopment.

Two cultural groups in a region of the Dominican Republic illustrate this contrast in principles. The town of Constanza lies in a fertile valley, surrounded by picturesque mountains. Water is plentiful, and the climate is moderate year-round. Yet the local population suffers from physical poverty. At the end of World War II, a number of Japanese families settled near Constanza. They had the same basic opportunities as the local inhabitants, and they had the disadvantage of not knowing the language or culture. Yet, after two generations the Japanese own prosperous farms, while the Dominicans remain in poverty. Why? One factor is the difference in beliefs and values between the two people groups. The Dominicans approached the future fatalistically, while the Japanese viewed it with imagination, hope, and persistence.

DARROW L. MILLER serves as the director of training with Food for the Hungry, International.

Different life-perspectives yield different levels of development. A similar example is examined by *Washington Post* columnist William Raspberry. In a 1988 article entitled "Values," Raspberry contrasts recently arrived Asian-Americans' expectations of the United States with those of native-born American minorities. He writes:

There are two intriguing things about this group [the new Asian-Americans]. The first is that they have viewed America the way a youngster views a candy store: with nose pressed to the glass and an attitude that says: If only I could get in there!

In short, they see America, with its free education, free enterprise and manifest rewards for serious exertion, as a land of unsurpassed opportunity. They take advantage of the opportunity and succeed at a pace that eclipses that of privileged whites.

Our native-born minorities, on the other hand, tend to see America as the place that has treated them unfairly and shows no sign of changing. As a result, they tend to focus not on opportunity, but on their disadvantage. Their conclusion, too often, is: What's the point of trying when the cards are stacked against you?

The second intriguing thing about the newly arrived minorities is their notion that the key to their success is not in their special intellectual gifts, but in hard work. They seem to take as a given that anybody who works hard enough can achieve success.

How is it that this attitude has escaped our native-born minorities, particularly our low-income black and Hispanic groups? A major part of the answer, I think, is that we have, in the last quarter century, tended to view everything through the prism of civil rights. The assumption is that the absence of the good things of life is proof of discrimination (1988:A31).

EXTERNAL CRITIQUE

There is no denying the deep suffering and vast despair in much of the world. Why are people poor? Why, in a world of increasing food production, are people hungry? Two common responses are based on *external critique*—that is, the reasons for hunger and poverty are found "outside" of people and their cultures. People are hungry, external critique says, because of circumstances beyond their control.

One form of external critique blames a region's poverty on inadequate natural resources or devastation of resources by acts of nature, such as drought or flood. Somalia, in the horn of Africa, is deemed "undevelopable" by some authorities because it severely lacks natural resources. Ethiopia, with seemingly more natural resources per capita than Somalia, experienced severe drought conditions in 1985 which destroyed the nation's food supply and left seven million people at risk of starvation. The three "Z's"—Zimbabwe, Zambia, and Zaire— have abundant resources per capita; they have the agricultural poten- tial to feed the entire continent of Africa, yet they languish in poverty. In contrast, Japan—with limited natural resources per capita— prospers. A deficiency of natural resources, by itself, is an inadequate explanation of poverty.

Another form of external critique says that some people are poor because others are wealthy and some are hungry because others are well-fed. Poverty is not "nature's problem," but a human problem. For example, one hears that 6 percent of the world's population (those who reside in the United States) consumes 40 percent of the world's resources each year. The culprit, says the critique, is colonial- ism or neocolonialism (capitalism). However, nations like Thailand and Ethiopia—which were never colonized or only colonized briefly and are proud of their independence—are relatively poor, while for- mer colonies like Canada and the United States have prospered.

It must be admitted that limited resources and institutionalized human greed can be contributing factors to hunger in our world; but they are not, by any means, the root cause.

As long as poverty is blamed solely on external causes, people and cultures will remain imprisoned by it. If its origin is external, then there is nothing the impoverished can do to change it, for nature and other people control their destiny. Individuals, cultural groups, and whole nations are seen as helpless, without responsibility. Because problems are defined in external terms, solutions, by implication, are also viewed as external and imposed by well-intentioned outsiders. Problems are described in impersonal rather than personal terms. The result? Dehumanization is reinforced; paternalism is extended. The great Russian novelist and moral philosopher Leo Tolstoy summa- rized the problem clearly: "Everybody thinks of changing humanity and nobody thinks of changing himself" (Mead, 1965:400).

INTERNAL CRITIQUE

Why are people poor? Why are people hungry? *Internal critique* provides an often overlooked answer. Internal critique looks within people or their culture for an understanding of the problem. It finds poverty inside a person and culture, not outside. Internal critique says that poverty is more than material condition or circumstance: it is a way of looking at the world, humankind, and ultimate reality. It stifles life and leads to underdevelopment. This poverty is both personal and, on a wider scale, cultural. Indeed, every person and every culture is faced in some way with internal poverty.

In an internal critique of poverty, it is assumed, as Richard M. Weaver said, "ideas have consequences" (1984). There is a logical relationship between an idea or a value and its outworking in life. Ludwig von Mises, the internationally known economist, stated: "Action is always directed by ideas; it realizes what previous thinking has designed" (1963:188). For example, a culture which values human life will function very differently than a culture which does not. What is it that a woman carries in her womb? Is it a "baby" or a "product of conception?" The answer given reflects a person's or a culture's ideas concerning life, and those ideas result in distinct patterns of behavior. If a woman carries a "baby" in her womb, it is cared for and nurtured. If it is considered mere "tissue," it may be removed from her body and discarded.

A culture's belief system determines its progress—or lack thereof—in the material world. Anthropologist Oscar Lewis used the term "culture of poverty" to describe a poverty way of perceiving and integrating reality, as opposed to poverty as an economic condition (Stavers, 1983:5–6).

Personal poverty begins to be alleviated when an individual literally changes his mind and his view of reality. (Many call this change *repentance*.) Similarly, cultural poverty is alleviated in two ways; first, by a *reformation* of ideas—the gradual replacement of values that produce poverty with a new ethic of development; second, by *reclamation* of structure—the application of a development ethic to create dynamic, life-supporting structures. This process is labeled "development by discipleship" by community-development worker Alan Voelkel. A development ethic affirms that progress is possible for both an individual and a culture.

DEVELOPMENT ETHIC PRINCIPLES

Before examining the principles of this development ethic, it is important to establish several points.

First, the development ethic is not merely wishful thinking. The strength of the ethic is that it manifests itself historically and pragmatically. The ethic is *affirmed by our experience of reality*.

Second, the development ethic *transcends culture*. Truth is true, no matter where it is found. The development ethic is based on transcendent principles which have been manifested in cultures around the world. These transcendent principles can be found, to a greater or lesser extent, in any culture, even in "least developed countries" (LDC's). Two examples are seen in the priority of human relationships in many LCD's, and the strong "work ethic" in the rapidly developing Pacific Rim countries. Likewise, a lack of development principles produces underdevelopment, even in "most developed countries" (MDC's). Mother Teresa proclaimed that she had never seen such poverty in all her life as when she visited New York City. She referred to the great moral and spiritual poverty she saw in one of the most materially advanced cities of the world. Crass consumerism—that which the ancients called hedonism—is evidence of underdevelopment of the human spirit and is found in much of the western world.

Third, the development ethic is an *enhancer of culture*. It affirms those elements that are eternal and stands in contrast to those which produce death. It will not—must not—destroy a culture in order to introduce modernism or to bring change for its own sake. On the other hand, the development ethic is not value-neutral, idolizing culture or arbitrarily affirming those aspects of a culture which produce death.

The task before us at the end of the twentieth century is to *intentionally* share the values and ideals of this development ethic with those caught in cycles of poverty. The affluent consumer, the subsistence farmer, the drug addict, the university intellectual, the non-literate, the factory worker—all need the hope brought by the development ethic.

What is this ethic that leads to development? It is comprised of twelve principles, the most familiar being what the west calls the "Protestant Work Ethic." This work ethic is functionally equivalent to the Tokugawa religion of Japan (Bellah, 1985 xiii). The twelve underlying development principles may be loosely categorized into three factors—the creation factor, the human factor, and the "other-worldly" factor.

The Creation Factor

Nature, being the result of creative activity rather than the product of impersonal forces, is an open system, capable of being stewarded—

now and in the future—to meet the needs of an expanding human family.

Development Principle # 1: Creation Is an Open System

God has created a universe composed of material and non-material reality. His creation is populated by angels and people (and who knows what other beings). Though governed by natural law, the system is open to the intervention of the Creator, angels, and people.

In this open system, nature is dynamic rather than static. New resources can be created by human conceptual activity. New ideas open whole new worlds of opportunity. Oil—that dark gooey ooze—was a nuisance until the need for light and power established its usefulness and purpose. Suddenly, that which lay ignored under people's feet for generations became a resource. Likewise, two bicycle mechanics in an emerging nation dreamed of flying. As their dream became reality, it opened a new world for the human family. Michael Novak, Roman Catholic author and scholar, captured this spirit when he wrote:

> Countless parts of God's creation lay fallow for millennia until human intelligence saw value in it. Many of the things we today describe as resources were not known to be resources a hundred years ago . . . The cause of wealth lies more in the human spirit than in matter (1982:103).

This open-system principle establishes limitless opportunity for discovering new worlds and creating expanding resources, thus making *positive sum societies*. It stands in sharp contrast to a closed-system view of the universe. The closed system states: "Nature is all there is." There is no creator, and nature is without design, order, or purpose. Humankind is part of nature, not an intervener in it.

Based on the assumptions of the closed system, wealth and resources are static: "What you see is what there is, and there isn't any more." Thomas Malthus, English economist, articulated this position in the west. Malthusian theory states that as the world's population increases, the amount of resources available for each person decreases.

The size of the pie is fixed, thus creating what Lester Thurow calls the "zero sum society" (1980:24). Using an external critique, the closed-system model looks to statistics for answers and concludes that some people are poor because others are rich. Therefore, to resolve the problem of hunger and poverty, scarce resources must be equally distributed.

This same concept is called "limited good" in materially less-developed societies. Good things such as wealth, health, time, power, and security are fixed. If any man's family or community seeks more than what it already has, that deprives someone else of those same resources (Stockwell, 1981:121). There is no way to increase what is available, no way to develop more wealth. This "limited good" perspective generates strategies for the maintenance of the status quo.

Whether explained as a zero-sum or a limited-good society, the closed-system model breeds underdevelopment. The open-system model creates a framework for development and opens new worlds of opportunity.

Development Principle # 2: People Are to Have Dominion over Nature

God has created the universe, placed people on earth, and established them as his stewards or vice-regents. People are to have dominion over nature, rather than be dominated by it. This dominion provides impetus for people to harness nature and fight against such ravages as drought, disease, and famine. Abraham Kuyper, the great Dutch prime minister and educator, founder of the Free University in Amsterdam, wrote eloquently on the subject:

> We with our own human nature are placed in nature around us, not to leave that nature as it is but with an urge and calling within us to work on nature through human art, to enable and perfect it . . . Human art acts on every area of nature, not to destroy the life of nature, much less mechanically to juxtapose another structure, but rather to unlock the power which lies concealed in nature; or again to regulate the will power that springs from it (p. 19).

It has been said that God used mathematics—systematic, predictable order—as the language of creation. *Natural law*, therefore, stands behind creation. By sheer rational ability, a person can discover the design behind nature (science) and then use those laws to intervene and harness nature for his or her own benefit (applied technology). But a person is also a created part of the universe; a person is on the same level as nature; a person is nature's "brother" or "sister." Creation is to be honored, tended, nurtured, and stewarded by people.

An illustration of man's intervention to create a hospitable environment from an uninhabitable one is the modern city of Phoenix, Arizona. Like many other arid regions, the "Valley of the Sun" is marked by high summer temperatures (over 115 degrees Fahrenheit), little rainfall (seven inches per year), and massive flooding when it does rain. By harvesting the water which falls, the people of Phoenix stopped the destructiveness of floods and created the sixth largest agricultural county in the United States. By utilizing insulation and cooling systems, the people were able to create a comfortable environment which attracts tens of thousands of residents and visitors.

In the open-system view of the world, disease, death, and natural calamities are aberrations. They are the consequences of humankind's rebellion against the Creator. Therefore, a person must stand against the destructive forces of nature and fight disease, suffering, hunger, poverty, and death.

The open-system view of life stands in contrast to naturalism, which perceives people as merely a part of nature, living in harmony with whatever fate it delivers. Animistic cultures are strong examples of naturalism. All of nature is inhabited by spirits and is controlled only by appeasing those spirits. The people of such cultures have no concept of the laws behind nature—for example, the reality of microscopic germs. Disease, death, and hostile environments are normal. The goal is to live in harmony with nature and thus attempt to survive. Such a survival mode usually engenders a sense of resignation or fatalism.

Food for the Hungry, an international relief and development agency, was responsible for the nutrition program at the camp hospital in the Hmong refugee camp located in Ban Vinai, Thailand. One day, in a small back room of the hospital, three young mothers stoically watched their newborn children slowly die from tetanus. What had happened? Someone had cut each of these precious children's umbilical cords with a rusty knife. The knowledge of disease and germ theory which is so common in the west and painfully missing in many Third-World cultures would have saved the lives of those children.

Underdevelopment is spawned by the mind-set that nature has dominion over people. A person's goal is merely to survive. But to live in harmony with nature is to live in harmony with death. The development ethic, on the other hand, begins with the assumption that humankind is to have dominion over nature and that hunger, disease, and death are abnormalities that are to be conquered.

Development Principle # 3: History Is Directional

History is purposeful because the "Lord of History" has a purpose. The development ethic, as spawned by Judeo-Christian theism, introduces a radical new perspective on the concept of time—that is, that time is lineal. It has a *past,* a *present,* and a *future.* Time had a beginning, and it will continue into the future. This viewpoint creates an expectancy and introduces the concept of progress in the material world. It provides a place for human activism, ambition, discovery, and hope. Things may not only be *different* in the future— they may be *better.*

In the development ethic, life is purposeful, progressive, and hopeful. A person is the creator of history, not its slave. Just human relations are possible. Similarly, a person is not to be mastered by the environment, but rather, is to master it. One is not a cog in the machinery of the universe; instead, a person is the developer, the secondary creator, and the dramatist. Michael Novak relates the spirit of adventure and excitement that prevailed in North America during its growth years:

> Making history is an appropriate vocation, DeTocqueville commented on the spirit of the future that seemed to sweep through every family in the new world. Individuals break out of the ancient sense of imprisonment with eternal cycles and began to work towards, save for, and invest in the future. Migrants poured from the countryside, immigrants crossed frontiers and set sail upon forbidden oceans (1982:99).

The development ethic also recognizes the spiritual dimension of development. Development is more than the growth in material resources or control over the environment.

In contrast, the ethic that spawns underdevelopment assumes that time is one endless cycle, with history going nowhere. In this view, time is defined by nature's cycles. The two most prominent are the *seasons*—spring, summer, autumn, and winter (or dry and rainy)— and lifecycles—birth, life, and death.

John Mbiti, a Kenyan theologian and educator, studied two hundred and seventy of the thousand-plus language groups on the continent of Africa. Not a single one of those language groups has a clear view of the future. Instead, the long-term past and the present are the key realities. The past is filled with tradition and ancestral values. The present is "now," almost as if there is no other time—and tomorrow is vague at best. Mbiti wrote:

> It [time] moves "backward" rather than "forward"; and people set their minds not on future things, but chiefly on what has taken place.
>
> This time orientation, governed as it is by the two main dimensions of the present and the past, dominate African understanding of the individual, the community and universe (1970:23).[2]

Where, in this scheme, is there room for development? Development is, by its very nature, an activity of the future, an expression of faith and hope. If there is no future, how does one proceed with development?

This cyclical view of time has a profound impact on people's concepts of history. Life is often viewed as "on the wheel" in which history simply repeats itself again and again. The Pakkred Children's Home in Bangkok, Thailand, is a poignant example of life "on the wheel" without hope. The home is filled with children who are physically or mentally handicapped. For the most part, they have been abandoned by their families and their culture. After all, as Buddhism teaches, handicapped persons are simply being punished for sins in their previous lives—the bad *karma* from previous existences. Being handicapped is something they deserve and must suffer through in order to have hope for the next life. There is to be no improvement in this life.

In contrast, the development ethic assumes a world in which there is a past, a present, and a future with hope. History is going somewhere, and progress can be made in this material world, in relations with others and with God. In the ethic of underdevelopment, however, history is going nowhere. Hope is missing. Time has no future. Progress in the material world does not exist and the time frame of the past does not provide a sufficient framework for development.

Development Principle # 4: Bounty Is to Be Created and Stewarded

Development is practically impacted by ideas and values. This truth was illustrated by a professor at a school in Israel. As his class sat on a hill overlooking the Judean hills, he stated that the land of Palestine has historically been fought over by two opposite sets of ideals. The Arabs have believed that Allah had put a curse on the land; the Jews believed that Jehovah had promised that the land would flow with milk and honey (a contrast of fatalism and hope). The same geographic location, the same climate, the same land, the same natural resources—but conflicting worldviews and thus vastly different "realities." For centuries under the Arabs, Palestine had lain dormant, resulting in subsistence-level living for its inhabitants. Today, under the vision of the Jews, it is among the most bountiful arid regions in the world.

The development ethic postulates that bounty—abundance—is found in the cornucopia of personal creativity. The "Primary Creator" has fashioned a universe in which the rational mind and the creative intuition of a person—as a "secondary creator"—may operate. New bounty and new horizons wait only to be envisioned by an artist, a scholar, a writer, a poet, a discoverer, or an explorer. Novak writes:

> Creation left to itself is incomplete, and humans are called to be co-creators with God, bringing forth the potentialities the Creator has hidden. Creation is full of secrets waiting to be discovered, riddles which human intelligence is expected by the Creator to unleash. The world did not spring from the hand of God as wealthy as humans might make it (1982:39).

Likewise, Boorstin, writing in the introduction to *The Discoverers*, states,

> My hero is Man the Discoverer. The world we now view from the literate West—the vistas of time, the land and the seas, the heavenly bodies and our own bodies, the plants and animals, history and human societies past and present—had to be opened for us by countless Columbuses. In the deep recesses of the past, they remained anonymous. As we come closer to the present, they emerge into the light of . history, a cast of characters as varied as human nature. Discoveries become episodes of biography, unpredictable as the new worlds the discoverers opened to us (1983:XV).

Human beings are among the greatest of our resources. The next child born may be the Bach, Einstein, or Mother Teresa of our future.

In contrast, the ethic of underdevelopment believes that wealth is limited to the physical or natural resources currently observed. These, by definition, are limited. Humankind is seen as part of nature, and the increasing size of the world's population is viewed as part of the problem. Rather than developing an environment that would stimulate the discoverer, artist, or poet in each human being, the ethic of underdevelopment creates structures that stifle the human spirit and arbitrarily limit population growth.

The development ethic affirms that bounty is to be created by human discovery and innovation and that development goes beyond a simple increase in goods and services to include the compassionate use of those goods and services to just relations among people in their environments with God. The ethic of underdevelopment, by contrast, defines resources strictly in material terms and believes that those resources are limited.

The Human Factor

A person bearing the image of God is the greatest resource for development, and as a rebel against God is also the prime hindrance of development.

The next four principles may be summarized into two thoughts: humankind's significance and corruption, and the unity and diversity of the human family.

Development Principle # 5: Human Life Is Sacred

What is a human? What is one's purpose in life? In a sophomore sociology class, a professor posed the question, "What is the purpose of the life of a Third-World baby that dies in infancy?" After a pregnant pause which gave his students time to think, the professor responded, "The purpose of the life of a child that dies in infancy is to be fertilizer for a tree." Students were shocked by such callousness. The professor was absolutely correct, if one employs naturalistic premises. In the ethic of underdevelopment, life is cheap. A person comes from dust, and to dust returns.

The clash of the ethic of development and the ethic of poverty can be clearly illustrated by a 1985 trip to Ethiopia by Tetsunao Yamamori, the president of Food for the Hungry. Yamamori found a child who had been left alone and was having difficulty breathing. He picked the child up and carried it to the mother. The mother's response? "Put the child back; it is *meant to die.*" Yamamori replied, "The child is *not* meant to die." He took the baby to a clinic for medical care. Death was thwarted for yet another day. The two opposite ethics have very dramatic consequence in terms of life and death.

The development ethic affirms the sanctity of human life. A person, made in the image of God, has a primary identity—pointing upward towards the Creator, not downward towards nature. Being thus made, each individual has intrinsic worth and personal dignity. Life is sacred and therefore is to be preserved even in the weakest, most broken, vulnerable, or wretched human being. The measure of the development potential in any society is found not in the way its members treat the greatest in that society, but in the way they treat the least.

The development ethic advances the significance of human life. In the ethic of poverty, life is of much less value.

Development Principle # 6: Humankind Is in Rebellion

While a person is a wonder—the highest of all creatures—he or she is also in rebellion. Every person stands autonomously against the Creator. Every person's soul has been corrupted. A person is prone to evil and not to be trusted. The development ethic remembers that rebelliousness and acknowledges that evil is real, personal, and abnormal. Alienation from the other person, from God, and one's environment all result from this rebelliousness. Redemption and reconciliation for all three sets of relationships provide the good news of the Christian development ethic.

This point of view contrasts with the values of underdevelopment expressed in both modern and traditional cultures. Modern underdeveloped society categorically denies evil. Humankind is basically good, it says. If there is a problem, it is due to a lack of good manifesting itself in ignorance or to an environmental or social condition. Utopian models of society are based upon this thinking. In many underdeveloped cultures, however, there is no denying the power and personification of evil. Evil spirits inhabit the world and bring flood, famine, disease, and death. Evil is normal. It is not to be fought against, but merely appeased through ritualistic practices and sacrifices.

The development ethic acknowledges that evil is abnormal, and thus has grounds to oppose it. Knowing that evil is real and personal, the development ethic takes precautions not to give too much authority to one individual because of the human "thirst for power." Novak in The Spirit of Democratic Capitalism, articulated a classic historic critique of the development experiments in North and South America. At the time North and South America were settled by Europe, each continent had nearly identical ratios of native populace and European settlers. The wealth in natural resources favored the south. Five centuries later, the north is economically and politically more developed. Why?

Different ideals drove each experiment. The governments of South America were structured similarly to those of Southern European countries and Roman Catholicism. The Catholic church was governed by one man, the pope, through a hierarchical political structure. Likewise, the governments of the south were oligarchies headed by a single man or family with highly centralized dictatorships. In contrast, the North American experiment was based on the Northern European and Protestant models which recognized that every person is sinful and not to be trusted. These governments did not want power to reside in one individual and therefore created democratic government. The checks, balances, and political pluralism produced very different results.

Development Principle # 7: All People and Nations Are Equal

Recognizing that the image-bearers of God are both male and female produces one of the foundation stones of the development ethic: All people, as they stand before God, are equal in value and worth. This equality may sometimes be acknowledged, as in the Declaration of Independence:

> We hold these truths to be self-evident, that all men are created equal, that they are endowed by their Creator with certain inalienable rights, that among these are Life, Liberty, and the pursuit of Happiness.

This profound truth counters bigotry, which says, "Because we are different, I am better than you!"

The ethic of underdevelopment establishes inequality as a virtue. It endorses one person as better than another. Autocratic caste systems are the result. Examples abound. In Hinduism, the Brahman priestly class rules all others while those in the untouchable lowest classes are deemed subhuman. Similarly, the apartheid system of South Africa institutionalizes one race of people as superior over another.

While the ethic of development sets people and nations free before the law, the culture of poverty imprisons people and ethnic groups into rigid caste systems.

Development Principle # 8: Each Person and Nation Is Unique

The ethic of development, recognizing diversity of person, function and role within the Godhead, appreciates God's creative diversity and expects individuals, and culture, to be unique in character. The development ethic says diversity is real. It marvels at the variety of creation, and it sets people free to be all they can be. The individual is wonderful!

The ethic of underdevelopment, however, establishes conformity and numerical equality as virtues. Its social order is one of utopian egalitarianism: People are equal and should be insured of equal outcome or equal results. Coercive structures and raw power are used to implement this uniformity.

The development ethic recognizes human, cultural, and national uniqueness; it celebrates diversity. The ethic of underdevelopment spawns uniformity.

The last two development principles—that all people are equal and yet unique—may be seen as a "unity among diversity" couplet. Patterned after the Trinity, unity among diversity is the foundation for human community. Diversity without unity is the libertarian ideal, but unity with diversity is the communal ideal. Understood together, unity and diversity uphold both the social rights and the individual responsibilities of each member of a society.

Development Principle # 9: Work Is Sacred

The "Protestant Work Ethic" is probably the most familiar of the development ethics. It stems from the representation of God as "the Divine Worker, the Creator, and the Great Developer." Humans, standing as God's vice-regents over creation, were designed to work. Work is a sacred task. To deny a person's work is to attack his or her dignity. Our life work is a calling which affirms our dignity and glorifies the Divine Worker. Abraham Kuyper framed this eloquently:

> Wherever man may stand, whatever he may do, to whatever he may apply his hand, in agriculture, in commerce, and in industry, or his mind, in the world of art, and science, he is, in whatsoever it may be, constantly standing before the face of God, he is employed in the service of his God, he has strictly to obey his God and above all, he has to aim at the glory of his God (1983:16).

The "religious worker" is not the only person called to the sacred task. So, too, is the farmer, painter, maintenance worker, scientist, educator, homemaker, plumber, writer, or carpenter.

This work ethic is defined in an "other-centered" context. It differs from the self-centered escape mechanism of a workaholic or the hedonistic lust for things. The work ethic is tempered by an internal asceticism and, thus, must also be termed a savings ethic and a giving ethic. In the "Protestant Work Ethic," work is service-oriented, serving God, the future, and one's fellow man. The cry of this ethic is "work as hard as you can (capital development), save as much as you can (capital accumulation), and give as much as you can (capital sharing)."

Within the ethic of poverty, only certain types of work are sacred; for example, services performed by a priest, pastor, religious leader, medicine man, or "politician." These positions are considered high callings. For all others, work is a curse to be endured. Work is not sacred in modern consumer-oriented cultures, either, where it is merely a means to an end, the price to pay in order to obtain personal pleasure and "toys."

In less-affluent societies, people work to put daily food on the table. A peasant may work hard when work is available and resources are needed. However, the spirit of fatalism fosters dependency—first on nature, then on the government, and finally on the larger community—for survival. Well-intentioned outsiders can reinforce this dependency by acting paternalistically.

In cultures of poverty, work is conceived merely as a means to an end. In the development ethic, work is a sacred task. Its fruits, while privately owned, are aesthetically stewarded.

The Other-Worldly Factor

Perhaps, nothing provides a greater contrast between the ethics of underdevelopment and development than the factor known as "other-worldly." The development ethic assumes that a person exists in a personal universe where spiritual, moral, rational forces, and absolutes are present. This assumption starkly contrasts with the ethic of poverty which posits a uni-dimensional, "flat-earth," pantheistic, or monistic model of the universe. If one denies the existence of a personal, infinite God, then one must cease being worshipful and must also deny everything that has its existence in him. Ultimately, love, morals, and rationality disappear as underdevelopment of the spirit, the heart, and the mind reigns. What does the ethic of development teach about man's spirit, ethics, and intellect?

Development Principle # 10: The Spirit—The Universe Is Ultimately Personal

The development ethic assumes that we live in a personal universe. A person's aspirations of personality, love, communion, creativity, and volition are encouraged, not denied. A person's primary identity is found in his or her relationship with the Creator. This relationship defines the context and the ultimate purpose for both of the major areas discussed previously—the creation and the human factors.

Because ultimate reality is personal, the system is open to opportunities for liberality and an optimistic future. Love, self-giving love, reigns. A person is called to love God and to "love his neighbor as himself." It was said of the early Christians that they were a new breed of humankind: They not only cared for one another, but they cared for those outside their ranks. Emperor Julian (332–363) wrote:

Atheism [Christian faith] has been specially advanced through the loving service rendered to strangers, and through their care for the burial of the dead. It is a scandal that there is not a single Jew who is a beggar, and that the godless Galilaeans care not only for their own poor but for ours as well; while those who belong to us look in vain for help that we should render them (Neill, 1964:42).

In contrast, the ethic of underdevelopment leaves a person adrift in an impersonal universe, one without love and charity. Human aspirations of significance are denied, creating a climate of insufficiency and a pessimistic future. An English poet, Steve Turner, describes this stark scene in *The Conclusion:*

> My love
>   she said
>   that when all's
>   considered
>   we're only
>   machines.

> I chained
>   her to my
>   bedroom wall
>   for future use
>   and she cried (1983:18).

A classic distinction between the ethic of development and underdevelopment is in their demonstration of charity. As Ethiopia faced massive famine during 1984 and 1985, who was there to help? Those who responded were agencies from the West, where the great reserves of compassion and charity run deep in the culture. The majority of agencies had their beginnings in Judeo-Christian institutions. Conversely, charity from Buddhist, Hindu, Marxist, Animistic, or Muslim cultures was almost completely absent.

The ethic of development is personal, extending compassion and creating a mind for liberality and hope for the future. The ethic of underdevelopment, stemming from impersonal roots, creates a climate of indifference, insufficiency, and despair for the future.

One must look beyond creation and the human factor to understand the kind of developmental perspective intended for Christians.

*Development Principle # 11: The Ethical —The Universe Is
Ultimately Moral*

God's character provides the standard for moral absolutes. These
are values of right and wrong, good and evil. A culture supports
either development or underdevelopment, depending upon which of
these value it chooses.

Not only are there moral absolutes, but there is also moral freedom in the development ethic, allowing for a person to make significant choices in life and also to be tolerant of the values of others.

A companion to the concept of moral absolutes and moral freedom is the recognition of personal evil in the universe. Both people
and angels have rebelled. The ethic of development understands this
rebellion and a person's resulting need for both a rule of law to
govern corporate life and self-discipline to govern personal life.

In contrast, the culture of poverty recognizes no moral absolutes.
Cultural or historic determinism replaces personal freedom. Survival
of the fittest is the ultimate personal and societal value.

The culture of poverty either denies evil or assumes that evil is
normal. The result is usually the same. In modern "value neutral"
societies, as in more fatalistic societies, evil imprisons people with
poverty and underdevelopment. A classic example of life without
morals is the genocide that took place in Cambodia following the rise
to power of Pol Pot and the Khmer Rouge. It is estimated that three
million of Cambodia's seven million people died during Pol Pot's brief
reign. David Aikman, then *Time Magazine*'s Eastern European bu-
reau chief wrote:

> In the West today, there is a pervasive consent to the notion of moral
> relativism, a reluctance to admit that absolute evil can and does exist.
> This makes it especially difficult for some to accept the fact that the
> Cambodian experience is something far worse than a revolutionary
> aberration. Rather, it is the deadly logical consequence of an atheistic,
> man-centered system of values, enforced by fallible human beings with
> total power. . . . By no coincidence the most human Marxist societies
> in Europe today are those that, like Poland or Hungary, permit the
> dilution of their doctrine by what Solzhenitsyn has called "the great
> reserves of mercy and sacrifice" from a Christian tradition (1978:39–40).

The culture of development acknowledges moral absolutes and
moral freedom, thus providing the foundation for government by
law and self-discipline. The culture of poverty denies both moral

absolutes and moral freedom, thereby contributing to a cultural death-wish.

Development Principle # 12: The Intellectual — The Universe Is Ultimately Rational

The development ethic believes that the universe is rational. It is orderly, purposeful, and governed by natural law. Objective truth exists because there is an *objective standard* for it which is revealed in the created order. It can be known objectively and is open to all who will pursue it.

Frances Bacon, writing in *The Advancement of Learning*, artfully stated it:

> Nay, this same Solomon the king, although he excelled in the glory of treasure and magnificent buildings, of shipping of navigation, of service and attendance, of fame and renowned, and the like, yet he maketh no claim to any of those glories, but only to the glory of inquisition of truth; for so he sayeth expressly, "The glory of God is to conceal a thing, but the glory of the king is to find it out"; as if, according to the innocent play of children, the Divine Majesty took delight to hide his works, to the end to have them found out; And is as if kings could not obtain a greater honour than to be God's play-fellows in that game (Boorstin, 1983:ix).

We are the play-fellows of God, included in the grand discovery of the universe.

The principle of the rationality of the universe establishes a foundation for science, discovery, and education. Accumulative knowledge may be passed on from generation to generation and from one culture to another. Education prepares people for life and provides tools for solving present and future problems.

This perspective stands in stark contrast to the ethic of underdevelopment, in which the universe is ultimately irrational and unknowable. Objective truth does not exist. The universe and all of life is mystery; it is unfathomable. There is no foundation for science and, consequently, for exploration of the universe. The ethic of poverty stifles humans the discoverers, the explorers. It robs them of the tools needed for solving present and future problems. An example of life without rational knowledge is the Zen practice of conceiving the impossible: "Talk without tongue; play your stringless lute; clap with a single hand" (Chang, 1969).

The ethic of development establishes and affirms the rationality and purpose of the universe and man's ability to explore and learn from it. The culture of poverty stifles the spirit of discovery and problem-solving.

Why are people poor? Why are people hungry? Some argue that poverty is primarily a state, a condition, a set of circumstances. People are poor, they say, because there are not enough resources in the external world. On first glance this may have some merit; in some parts of the world, this is indeed true.

However, there is a much more profound factor: Underdevelopment, and its corresponding hunger and poverty, has its root in the minds and hearts of individuals and in the moral and ethical ideals of cultures. Value-neutral critics imprison people in poverty, as do cultures which embrace values that produce underdevelopment.

Two opposing sets of values exist. One set of values supports development, creating a "life wish" for its people; the other hinders development, producing a cultural "death wish."

The development ethic acknowledges the God of the universe. His supernatural existence provides the ultimate framework for development. Humankind, bearing the image of God, is both the greatest resource and the greatest obstacle to development. Nature—being the result of God's creative activity rather than the product of impersonal forces—is an open system, capable of being stewarded both now and into the future to meet the needs of an expanded human family.

While elements of the development ethic may be found in many cultures around the world, the ethic has been most clearly articulated and strongly manifested in the Judeo-Christian culture of the West. May we of this culture, at the close of the twentieth century, have the courage to acknowledge the development ethic. And, may we have the vision to take its principles to those who hope for freedom from cycles of poverty. We will not create development by paternalistic intervention or mere formal instruction. Rather, true development will occur when its ethic is conveyed through the process of discipleship—as the members of the human family work, live, and play alongside one another.

---

[1]"Ethic" is used here to depict what is described elsewhere as worldview.

[2](Editor's Note: Mbiti's description of the African's view of the future presents a bleak view of the development which can be done. However, while African

worldviews and languages may not view time in a linear sense, opportunities for change do exist within them. They provide strong bases for building relationships within their environments with other people and with God in an event, oral-oriented world—a worldview perspective demonstrated in the scriptures, but generally foreign to western development workers. To work effectively in development with the African whose sense of the future is limited, one must begin with the aspects of his or her worldview which are not time-bound, such as relationships and events, to build faith and hope and reduce constraints. In these developmental interactions their worldview will be enlarged, as will be the worldview of the ethnocentric westerner.)

7

A Missiological View of Christian Relief and Development

C. Peter Wagner

WHEN SEEKING TO UNDERSTAND the rationale for relief and development from a missiological point of view, it is essential at the outset to
know which of several possible missiological paradigms is assumed.
As a matter of fact, the issue of just how Christian social ministries in
general relate to missiology is one of the chief current points of
discussion among professionals in the field. It must be frankly admitted that my own personal views on the subject would not be shared
by all of my fellow members of the American Society of Missiology.

Let me explain.

Missiology, in its bare-bones definition, is simply the cross-cultural
communication of the Christian faith. Those who specialize in the field
can deal with historical trends in missiology, with comparative religions,
with leading personalities and their contributions, with dialogue with
non-Christian religions, with social ethics, with evangelism as defined
in many different ways, with relief and development, with theology of
mission, with interface with the social sciences, with Bible translation,
or with any number of other facets of the discipline. Because missiology
includes such a wide spectrum of option, it is necessary for the author
of an essay on missiology to define his or her point of view by the use of
several qualifying adjectives.

C. PETER WAGNER is professor of church growth at the Fuller Theological
Seminary School of World Mission and the author of over thirty books on missions
and church growth. He joined the Fuller faculty in 1971 after sixteen years as a
missionary to Bolivia.

THREE QUALIFIERS

My perspective, first of all, is that of an evangelical missiologist. Those who do not follow the evangelical point of view frequently criticize us for being "conversionist." Rather than seeing all religions as different pathways leading to the same higher power, as do some missiologists, evangelicals are much more exclusivistic. They hold that the one true God is the Father of Jesus Christ and that only through Jesus can men and women be reconciled to God. Evangelicals believe that decisions made in this life concerning Jesus Christ irrevocably determine whether the individual will spend eternity in heaven or in hell. Because of this, the chief goal of missions is conversion to Jesus Christ. The best favor an evangelical missionary can do for a Muslim or a Buddhist or a Jew or a Hindu is persuade them to believe in Jesus as only Lord and Savior.

Secondly, my perspective is in conformity with the Lausanne Covenant. The Lausanne Committee for World Evangelization, formed in 1974, is the chief networking agency for evangelicals worldwide. Article 4 of the Lausanne Covenant makes a strong statement for the ministry of evangelism and article 5 addresses Christian social responsibility. Article 6 relates the two and affirms that "in the church's mission of sacrificial service evangelism is primary." This, quite obviously, has a direct bearing on Christian relief and development. It is not my purpose here to argue the legitimacy of this statement—I have done that in some depth in *Strategies for Church Growth* (Regal Books). It is only necessary at this point to affirm my personal agreement with it.

Finally, my missiological perspective is strongly influenced by the Church Growth Movement. Not only does the Church Growth Movement agree with the Lausanne Covenant that evangelism is the primary task of the mission of the church, but it goes beyond that to insist that evangelism is not just proclaiming the gospel of Jesus Christ but it is also making disciples. Evangelism's goal is to see men and women commit themselves to Jesus Christ as Savior and Lord and become responsible members of Christian churches.

None of this stress on the conversion of non-Christians, on the primacy of evangelism in the mission of the church, or on centering the missiological task on making disciples of Jesus Christ is to be construed to imply that Christian social ministries are unimportant in mission. Quite the contrary. Having clearly set forth my assumptions, I intend to devote the remainder of this section to arguing that

Christian social ministries are indeed a vital aspect of mission. I believe in what many today are calling "wholistic mission."

It wasn't always like that.

THE "GREAT REVERSAL"

I become a Christian in 1950, during what is now being called the "Great Reversal." When I was converted in university and joined Inter-Varsity Christian Fellowship, I became identified with the evangelical wing of Protestantism, and I have been an evangelical ever since. I soon learned that our group was engaged in serious theological warfare and that we were mostly on the losing side. We were battling against liberalism, against postmillennialism, against evolution, against Freudian psychology, against naturalism, against humanism—all of which could be more or less summed up in the term "the social gospel." What did this imply?

The origins of the social gospel have been traced back to the latter part of the 1800s.[1] Its principal advocate in America was Walter Rauschenbusch, who used the kingdom-of-God motif as a major integrating element in his theological development. "The social gospel," Rauschenbusch says, "tries to see the progress of the kingdom of God in the flow of history . . . Its chief interest is the kingdom of God" (Rauschenbusch, 1917:146). By association, then, the kingdom of God became an enemy of evangelicals. Feelings were so strong that some went to the extreme of opposing any sort of Christian activity designed to heal the hurts of society.

In reaction against the social gospel, evangelicals during most of the twentieth century chose to concentrate largely on soul saving. Wes Michaelson is correct in his observation that the evangelical heritage has been "dominant individualism," with its great emphasis on "converting" while assigning a peripheral status to "questions of discipleship, justice and the shape of the church" (Michaelson, 1979:66). A gradual change began shortly after World War II.

Most observers list Carl F. H. Henry's *The Uneasy Conscience of Modern Fundamentalism*, published in 1947, as the first stirring. Fuller Theological Seminary, which was founded that same year and where Henry himself taught, was given a mandate by its president, Harold John Ockenga, to spearhead a neo-evangelical movement in which concern for justice, peace, oppression, racial equality, and other major social issues would be restored to the evangelical agenda. Through the 1950s it was a lonely road, but during the 1960s the group Richard

Quebedeaux calls the "young evangelicals" joined the movement and energetically proclaimed, with considerable success, the need to restore evangelical social concern. They may have swung the pendulum back a little too far, but that could be expected. When the decade of the 1960s had concluded, David Moberg could observe that, overall, evangelicals were "awakening to their inconsistencies" and "returning to the totality of the Christian Gospel" (Moberg, 1972:177).

Two important emphases helped swing evangelical missiologists back toward recognizing that mission included more than winning souls to Christ. One was the recognition of the biblical emphasis on the kingdom of God in the here and now. The other was taking seriously the Cultural Mandate. The two are closely related, but they need to be examined one at a time.

THE KINGDOM OF GOD

John the Baptist, Jesus, and the apostles all preached the kingdom of God. It was an important theme both before and after the resurrection. Since God's kingdom is not a territorial rule, it is understood as a reigning of the King of kings and Lord of lords over all who will submit to his lordship. The kingdom came to earth when Jesus was incarnated and entered directly into conflict with the kingdom of Satan, which had enjoyed relatively free dominance of the human race up to that time. The New Testament teaches that Satan was defeated by Jesus Christ on the cross, but that he continues to exercise tremendous power and will do so until Jesus returns the second time. At that point the eschatological kingdom will be inaugurated. God will reign supreme, swords will be beat into plowshares, justice will roll down like a river, poverty, discrimination, oppression, sickness, and all other social ills will disappear like mist in the morning sun. Some Old Testament prophets caught glimpses of the eschatological kingdom. John describes it in the Book of Revelation as a holy place where there will be no more tears or death or sorrow or crying or pain (see Revelation 21:4).

When all this will happen, no one knows. Meanwhile, as the kingdom of God is preached and more and more people submit themselves to the reign of the King, the wider blessings of the kingdom of God will be more evident here and now. God's people are people who are committed to the promotion of justice and peace. They oppose those in the kingdom of Satan. Since the kingdom of Satan, as the late Orlando Costas said, "stands for what oppresses, dehumanizes, and enslaves man, the kingdom of God must stand for what humanizes, liberates, and enriches man" (Costas, 1974:66). Churches full of people who serve Satan rather than God are not the kind of churches that the Church Growth Movement has ever recommended. Church growth teaching advocates people living the kingdom lifestyle. I like the way Ronald J. Sider puts it: "In the power of Christ, Christians can begin now to live in Christ's new kingdom even though it will come in its fullness only at the eschaton" (Sider, 1980:156).

THE CULTURAL MANDATE

As with any significant kingdom concept, the Cultural Mandate has its origin in God. It was first given before the fall, when only Adam and Eve comprised the human race. As the creation narrative unfolds, God says, "And now we will make human beings; they will be like us and resemble us. They will have power over the fish, the birds, and all animals, domestic and wild, large and small" (Genesis 1:26,TEV). It was done, and Adam and Eve were ready to receive their first recorded divine commandment: "Have many children, so that your descendants will live all over the earth and bring it under their control. I am putting you in charge of the fish, the birds, and all the wild animals . . . " (Genesis 1:28, TEV). These first human beings were given what Robert Webber calls "delegated sovereignty" over God's earthly creation (Webber, 1979:37). They were to treat creation as God himself would treat it. That was the Cultural Mandate.

In New Testament times, Jesus not only exemplified the Cultural Mandate in his own life and ministry; he summed up the entire teaching of the law and the prophets by saying, "Love the Lord your God with all your heart, with all your soul, and with all your mind. This is the greatest and most important commandment. The second most important commandment is like it: Love your neighbor as you love yourself" (Matthew 22:37-39, TEV). No one can be a kingdom person without loving one's neighbor. No Christian can please God without fulfilling the Cultural Mandate.

The specific content of the Cultural Mandate is awesome. God expects a great deal of those to whom he has entrusted the earth and all of its goodness. Distribution of wealth, the balance of nature, marriage and the family, human government, keeping the peace, cultural integrity, liberation of the oppressed—these and other global responsibilities rightly fall within the Cultural Mandate. Since it is

God's will that the human race live in shalom, those among them who have been born again into the kingdom and who purpose to live under the lordship of Jesus Christ are required to live lives that will promote shalom to the greatest extent possible. Psalm 144 lists some of the blessings of God on his people: They have victory over their enemies, their sons grow up like strong plants, their daughters are like stately columns, their barns are filled with crops of every kind, sheep bear young by the tens of thousands, cattle reproduce plentifully, no cries of distress are heard in the streets, and their God is the Lord. While it must be kept in mind that such an ideal situation will not occur until the age to come, it is God's desire that the people he has called out in this present age reflect and promote such blessings to the best of their potential.

Some specific demands of the Cultural Mandate were set forth by John the Baptist when he said that those who had affluence should share with the less fortunate, that tax collectors should not over-charge, that soldiers should not be brutal or accuse falsely, and they should be content with their wages (Luke 3:11–14). This is only a sampling of the requirements of the Cultural Mandate; the Sermon on the Mount and numerous other biblical passages add significantly to the list of God's expectations.

The Cultural Mandate has never been rescinded. It was given at creation and will be in effect until Jesus returns. Christian people are God's chosen agents for doing what they can to make it happen. Every Christian and every church should be contributing in some way to the effective fulfillment of the Cultural Mandate. It is not enough to think and theologize about it. It takes doing. It is not enough to even pray about it. It takes energy and involvement. Changed persons do not automatically move out to change society. They need to be taught, they need to be encouraged, they need to see exemplary models that they will desire to imitate.

For most Christians who have committed their lives to Jesus as Lord, this is not new information. One of the most influential books among American Christians in recent years has been Billy Graham's *Peace with God*. In it, Graham acknowledges evangelical criticisms of the social gospel. "But," he argues, "Jesus taught that we are to take regeneration in one hand and a cup of cold water in the other. Christians, above all others, should be concerned with social prob-lems and social injustices . . . The Christian is to take his place in society with moral courage and stand up for that which is right, just and honorable" (Johnson, 1978:138). Few evangelical Christians would take exception to Graham's statement.

Perhaps the most representative evangelical statement in our generation, the Lausanne Covenant, puts it this way: "The message of salvation implies also a message of judgment upon every form of alienation, oppression, and discrimination, and we should not be afraid to denounce evil and injustice wherever they exist. When people receive Christ they are born again into his kingdom and must seek not only to exhibit but also to spread its righteousness in the midst of an unrighteous world" (Article 5).

Orlando Costas saw four major areas in which church growth takes place: numerical growth, organic growth, conceptual growth, and incarnational growth. The latter, incarnational growth, has directly to do with the Cultural Mandate. Incarnational growth, Costas says, means "the degree of involvement of a community of faith in the life and problems of her social environment" (Costas, 1974:89–90). Most Christians would agree that incarnational growth is an important part of service to God. Most, I think, would also admit that neither they nor their churches are satisfactorily involved in it.

Measuring instruments have yet to be developed that can help us monitor our progress toward incarnational growth. As an ideal, Costas argues that "the church is faithful to her witnessing vocation when she becomes a catalyst for God's liberating action in the world of poverty, exploitation, hunger, guilt and despair . . . " (Costas, 1974:33). He suggests that Christians do three specific things: they "stand in solidarity with the people," they "show with concrete actions that God cares" and "they help them understand" their situation. If these ideas are to become practical, and I hope they soon will, measurable guidelines will have to be drawn up so that a given local congregation will be able to know whether it has grown incarnationally from year to year or how it compares with similar churches in similar cultural settings. Perhaps one could begin by measuring the percentage of total church income given to causes outside the local parish. This is a challenge for future research.

SOCIAL SERVICE AND SOCIAL ACTION

As the church moves into the world to fulfill the Cultural Mandate, two general avenues of potential ministry open up. Students of the social concerns of the church have called them by different names. I have chosen to follow the lead provided by the International Consultation on the Relationship between Evangelism and Social Responsibility convened jointly by the Lausanne Committee for World Evangelization and the World Evangelical Fellowship in Grand Rapids, Michigan, in 1982. There "social service" was carefully distinguished from "social action."[2]

Social service is the kind of social ministry geared to meet the needs of individuals and groups of persons in a direct and immediate way. If a famine comes, social service will provide food for starving people. If an earthquake or tidal wave devastates an area, social service will provide food, clothing, blankets, and medical supplies; also resources to rebuild homes, schools, and churches. If agricultural production is low, social service will introduce new crops, livestock, and farming methods so that food production will increase.

Within social service there is a further technical distinction of terms that has been fairly well accepted: *relief* and *development*.[3] Relief treats the symptoms. It comes after the fact. Development treats the causes. Development would include establishing medical and dental clinics and training local people how to staff them, digging wells where the water supply is inadequate, setting up cottage industries, or providing short-handled hoes in Niger. Both relief and development are social service; there area not social action.

Social action is the kind of social ministry geared toward changing social structures. Like development, it treats causes, but the scope is much broader and the effects more far-reaching. Social action, by definition, involves socio-political changes. If a government is mistreating a minority group, for example, it involves whatever is necessary to correct the injustice. It might mean picketing the legislature; it might mean organizing an electoral campaign to unseat a senator or even a president; it might mean supporting guerrilla bands that will overthrow the whole government and rewrite the constitution. Social action might or might not involve revolution, violence, or civil disobedience in some degree. The end goal of social action is to substitute just (or more just) for unjust (or less just) political structures.

PLANNING FOR CHRISTIAN SOCIAL MINISTRY

In fulfilling the Cultural Mandate, especially in ministries involving social service, churches need to see clearly what should be done and why. Most Christians agree that their churches should help the poor, for example, but, in fact, less than 1 percent of American churches have what they themselves consider "especially successful" programs to help the poor.[4] Most American churches are far from perfect, of course, and need improvement in many areas of their life. But do they need to be *that* far from perfect? If so, they may find it embarrassingly difficult, if not impossible, to respond to the biblical question: "But if anyone has the world's goods and sees his brother in need, yet closes his heart against him, how does God's love abide in him?" (1 John 3:17–18, RSV).

In planning for greater social involvement, it is helpful to consider three questions that are frequently raised when churches begin to develop programs for social ministry: Why? What? and Who?

Why do we engage in social ministry? Basic to the answer to this question, of course, is all we have been saying about the Cultural Mandate. Social ministry glorifies God because it is done in obedience to God. Beyond that, however, many Christians wonder whether engaging in social ministry can be considered a legitimate end in itself, or if we should do it only as a means to the end of winning souls.

As I see it, social service can be both. One church in America, which is growing rapidly by attracting a large number of unchurched people to Christ, has as its motto for ministry: "Find a need and fill it; find a hurt and heal it." By discovering the felt needs of unchurched people and designing church programs of service that will meet those needs, the church uses social service as an evangelistic means. Hundreds of examples could be drawn from world missions which establish schools, hospitals, or orphanages in order to help open people's hearts to the gospel message. In the New Testament accounts of the spread of the faith, as we see with the lame man at the temple in Acts 3, social service in the form of miracles and wonders seems to have functioned as a means of preparing people for the message of salvation.

But, having said this, I do not believe it necessary to justify all Christian social ministry on the basis of its help in saving souls. The Good Samaritan bound up the wounds of the person who was robbed and beaten with no conditions attached. When Jesus healed the ten lepers, his healing was 100 percent successful, though only 10 percent came to faith through it. Jesus healed the man at the pool of Bethseda despite the fact that a) he didn't even know who Jesus was, b) he didn't thank Jesus for his healing, and c) when Jesus later told him to stop sinning he betrayed Jesus to the Jewish authorities, who plotted to kill him (John 5:1–8). But the event is recorded as a significant part of Jesus' ministry. Carl F. H. Henry argues that "the primary reason for social involvement ought not to be an indirect evangelistic ploy"

(Henry, 1971:112) but rather a straightforward demonstration of God's justice in the world. There is biblical justification for doing good whether or not men and women are brought to faith in Christ as a result of it.

WHAT ARE WE AIMING FOR
IN CHRISTIAN SOCIAL MINISTRY?

If we leave aside for the moment the use of social ministry as a means toward evangelism and concentrate on the service itself, what would we like to see happen? An appealing answer might be "to make all poor people rich." However, I doubt that this is an adequate answer, for more than one reason. But before I give the reasons, let me say up front that our goals for people in crisis situations are not that ambiguous. For example, if a village in Ethiopia has been out of food for a month, the goal of social service is to deliver them the food they need to restore and maintain their physical strength. Situations of emergency relief form a category of their own.

But suppose people are making it. Barely. They never have enough to eat, they have no access to modern medicine or to schools, they have no sanitary facilities or sewers, they live in cockroach-infested shacks, they seldom bathe, and if they are fortunate they have one change of clothes. Should our goal be to help these people get rich? I think most of us would say, well, perhaps not rich, but at least middle class. We would like them to be more like us.

After saying this, however, it is well to pause and ask ourselves how much of our own cultural ethnocentrism we have injected into our ideals for the rest of the world, whether within our own nation, or the Indian reservations or in the Appalachian hills, or in the Third World, where a billion or so people are living much as I have described. Our Anglo-American tendency is to equate material prosperity with happiness and well-being. One negative effect of multinational corporations is their penchant to project Anglo-American material values as "the good life." Edward Stewart points out in his analysis of American culture: "Americans consider it almost a right to be materially well off" and they "tend to project this complex of values, centering around comfort and material well-being, to other peoples. They assume that given the opportunity, everyone else would be just like themselves. Hence they are disturbed by the sight of the rich churches of Latin America standing in the midst of poverty" (Steward, 1972:64–65).

My own sixteen years of experience living in Bolivia, one of the poorest countries of the Third World, has helped me to see Stewart's point. We need much more cross-cultural research on what exactly constitutes "quality of life" to each of the world's thirty thousand or so distinct groups of people, and that quality of life needs to be defined from *within* rather than from *without*. This may require more cultural humility than some Americans—Christian or not—could muster, but I believe it is the approach which best respects human dignity and cultural integrity. What right do we have, for example, to tell mothers in Kenya or India how many children they should have? Some American blacks who have "made it" economically are now wondering out loud how satisfying Anglo-American values really are. One says, "The keys to the executive suite did not turn out to be the keys to the kingdom after all." He goes on:

> This brings us to the heart of the black dilemma today: success in America does not mean the possession of such inward qualities as family affection, courage, pity, patience, hope, faith, self-sacrifice—qualities not unknown in the black community during its most appalling trials. Success means the ownership of things (DeLamotte, 1980:277).

I do not profess to know what constitutes true quality of life. But I do have ringing in my ears one of the most common statements that Latin Americans make contrasting their lifestyle with North Americans: "North Americans live to work: we work to live." When I think back on those easy-going ulcer-free days of long siestas in the hammock, guitar music on the dirt streets in the evenings, friendliness and hospitality, I wonder how important indoor plumbing is anyway. Who is it that has their values straight? I don't know, but I am quite sure that simply handing out material goods, except for emergency relief, may not always be the best goal of Christian social service. In this light, perhaps we need to reread Paul's words to Timothy: "So then, if we have food and clothes, that should be enough for us. But those who want to get rich fall into temptation and are caught in the trap of many foolish and harmful desires, which pull them down to ruin and destruction" (1 Timothy 6:8–9, TEV).

WHO SHOULD BE THE RECIPIENTS OF OUR SOCIAL MINISTRY?

It is helpful to think of Christian social responsibility as moving outward in three concentric circles from each Christian individual.

The first people I must reach out to in Jesus' name are the members of my own family. In our American culture this generally means the nuclear family; in many other cultures it means the extended family, which may be a circle of one hundred or so people. "But if anyone does not take care of his relatives," says Paul, "especially the members of his own family, he has denied the faith and is worse than an unbeliever" (1 Timothy 5:8, TEV).

The second priority for Christian service is our brothers and sisters in Christ. This is emphasized in Galatians 6:10: "So then, as often as we have the chance, we should do good to everyone, and *especially* to those who belong to our family in the faith." The believers in Jerusalem might have shared with the unchurched poor, but it is not recorded that they did. Their sharing was among *themselves* (Acts 2:44–45). They did not help widows in general, but Christian widows (Acts 6:1). Paul's collections in the Gentile churches were for the poor Christians in Jerusalem. It is not always recognized that the much-quoted "cup of cold water in Jesus' name" refers to helping Christian messengers of the gospel, not to humanity in general (see Mark 9:38–41; Matthew 10:40–42). In all probability, this also is the best interpretation of the passage about giving food to the hungry, drink to the thirsty, hospitality to the stranger, clothes to the naked, and visits to the prisoner, as recorded in Matthew 25:31–46 (Ryrie, 1977:223–224).

The third priority for Christian social service is the needy of the human race in general. Galatians 6:10 clearly says that we should "do good to everyone." Because it is a third priority it does not mean that this is optional. The poor and hungry and needy and oppressed of the whole world need to be helped by people who live in a kingdom lifestyle and who take seriously the Cultural Mandate. Christians who use these biblical priorities to deny global responsibility, as some unfortunately have done, are disobedient to God and should repent and mend their ways.

The subject of this essay is greatly expanded in *Church Growth and the Whole Gospel* which was in print under the Harper & Row label from 1981 to 1987.

[1]For a contemporary analysis of the Great Reversal and its origins in the social gospel, see David O. Moberg, *The Great Reversal: Evangelism Versus Social Concern* (Philadelphia: Lippincott, 1972); and John D. Woodbridge, Mark A. Noll, and Nathan O. Hatch, *The Gospel in America: Themes in the Story of America's Evangelicals* (Grand Rapids: Zondervan, 1979), pp. 240– 247. An earlier history of Christian attitudes toward the Kingdom of God is found in David J. Bosch, *Witness to the*

World: *The Christian Mission in Theological Perspective* (Atlanta: John Knox Press, 1980), pp. 140–158.

[2]Lausanne Committee for World Evangelization and World Evangelical Fellowship, "Evangelism and Social Responsibility: An Evangelical Commitment," Lausanne Occasional Papers No. 21, Grand Rapids Report, 1982, pp. 43–48.

[3]For extended treatment of the differences between, and complexities of, relief and development, see Mooneyham's chapter "Development: People-Building vs. Nation-Building, in *What Do You Say to a Hungry World?* pp. 197–219.

[4]See *Christianity Today* 24, no. 14 (August 8, 1980), p. 18.

8

Spiritual Formation for Relief and Development Workers

Lynn E. Samaan

LEADERS OF CHRISTIAN RELIEF and development agencies and leaders of Christian institutions of higher education are becoming increasingly concerned about spiritual formation of their students and workers so that they will be better prepared as true Christian witnesses. Why emphasize on spiritual formation? Is not the central issue better training for community development, not spirituality? Is it really a necessary component for professionals who are called specifically to deal with community and individual needs? Can we not assume it is occurring as development workers attend Christian schools or their local churches? And after all, is it not ultimately the work of the Holy Spirit and not a matter of training.

Christian character development is a growing concern in mission circles. Many mission leaders are now voicing a discontent with the present level of spirituality of missionaries. Phil Parshall, a veteran missionary to the Muslims, reported a survey he conducted among eight hundred missionaries in the *Evangelical Missions Quarterly*. He identified depression, frustration, emotional tension, anger, pride, sexual temptation, a need for better times of prayer and Bible study and intellectual stagnation as a few of the spiritual difficulties missionaries were having. "Are missionaries spiritual?" Parshall asked, "The question should cause not a small amount of probing and introspection" (Parshall, 1987:16).

LYNN E. SAMAAN is co-director of Servants Among the Poor, a ministry devoted to the equipping of Christians to serve among the urban poor.

Doug Stewart, a missionary to Mexico, voiced his concerns on this issue:

> I think the area you're proposing is much more vital than many would realize. I think it is taken for granted that a person who's been accepted to be a missionary will automatically keep growing spiritually. As a matter of fact missionaries are exposed to an unusual number of distinct pressures, which can snuff out or seriously damage their emotional and spiritual life, if they do not know how to respond (1986).

Clearly, the concerns about spirituality relate to Christian relief and development workers. Therein lies the significance of this study. Over half of the world's five billion people are unreached with the gospel. We have a commission to equip faithful men and women to be Christ's witnesses to all peoples.

DEFINING SPIRITUAL FORMATION

The term "spiritual formation" is not found in scriptures. Neither is the substantive word, "spirituality." However, the adjective, "spiritual" is frequently used in scripture to describe the character of people in the kingdom of God. It is very closely linked to the work of the Holy Spirit in a person's life and the holy character of life which develops as people live their life "in Christ" (Hastings, 1959:808).

Definitions of spiritual formation vary from the process by which God reshapes persons into newness and fullness of his intention for them and towards Christlikeness to deification and union with Christ, (a hellenistic and more Roman Catholic concept).

Dunnam provides one of the better theological definitions:

> The dynamic process of receiving through faith and appropriating through commitment, discipline and action, the living Christ into our own life to the end that our life will conform to and manifest the reality of Christ's presence in the world" (Dunnam, 1982:43).

The Spiritual Formation Task Force for the Association of Theological Schools has an educational definition (ATS, 1972:168), breaking the concept into three aspects:
1. Holistic development
2. Experience with God
3. Becoming holy; like God

I define spiritual formation as:

1. Knowing and experiencing God in an intimate relationship
2. Holistic development towards holiness and Christlikeness
3. Obeying God and doing the work of his kingdom

I prefer this definition because it clearly divides spiritual formation into the knowing-being-doing components which are so vitally important to any learning or growing process.

It is also important to note the crucial factors for this process to take place, namely: the triune God, the submitted believer, and the Christian community as he or she learns to live by the principles and values of the kingdom of God.

The word "sanctification" is more familiar to evangelical Christians than "spiritual formation"—a term adopted from the Roman Catholic Church. Sanctification is derived from the Latin words *sanctus* meaning "holy" and *facere* meaning "to make." In the New Testament, the term usually connotes a condition, state, or process of inner transformation resulting in purity, moral integrity, and holy, spiritual thoughts expressing themselves in an outward life of goodness and godliness (Douglas, 1974:1139).

A third word, "holiness," is also very related to spiritual formation. Scripture clearly indicates that holiness means consecration, being set apart and cleansed for the service of God. It means, in essence, taking on the very character and nature of God. Holiness is not just keeping rules or observances (Leech, 1980:33). It is therefore important that in striving for holiness, one not fall into the snares of legalism. Holiness flows from a relationship with God which demands a corresponding holiness in men and women (Leviticus 19:1-2, Psalm 15; Leech, 1980:34,36).

It helps to group the goal into knowing, being, doing categories while recognizing they are cyclical, intertwined, and interdependent. Only as we develop a close relationship with God and come to truly know him will we become like him (1 John 3:2). As we are transformed and become like him, we begin to more naturally act in godly ways. As we do what he desires, we are also transformed more into his likeness. Transformation leads to becoming like him, acting like him, and knowing him. Our goal must include all three aspects.

An element of mystery remains in these concepts of spiritual formation, sanctification, and holiness. This mystery forms a creative tension which is a part of all of Christianity. It must be seen to be an avenue for faith and not a stumbling block. Understanding the goal of spiritual formation is essential to helping people grow in this process.

The means to the goal differs widely according to the individual church tradition, culture, times, and individual personalities, experiences and theology.

METHODS OF FACILITATING
SPIRITUAL FORMATION

The search for methods of facilitating spiritual growth begins with an exploration of the scriptures regarding holiness. Some Christians believe spiritual formation is strictly the work of the Holy Spirit, while others place the responsibility on the believer. The scriptures clearly indicate spiritual formation is a cooperative effort between the person and God (2 Corinthians 7:1, James 4:8, 1 Peter 1:22, 1 John 3:3) and not a matter solely dependent upon just God or just ourselves. Throughout scripture is the principle and pattern of God working together with man. It is the pattern for salvation of human kind, for spreading the kingdom of God in the world, for cultivating the earth and harvesting its fruits, to name only a few examples.

This cooperative effort is also evident in the sanctification process. It is work, wrought in our hearts by the Holy Spirit (Romans 15:16, 1 Corinthians 12:11) in conjunction with our faith (Acts 15:9, 26:18; Galatians 3:14). The two are inseparable and complimentary (Ephesians 1:13-14, Philippians 2:12-13, 2 Thessalonians 2:13). To the extent we consecrate, the Spirit sanctifies (Hastings, 745). Furthermore, it is very difficult to mature spiritually in isolation from Christian community, (1 Corinthians 12:12-27, Ephesians 1:23, Colossians 2:19), or from growth in the knowledge of the Lord, obedience, doing his work, and truly desiring to change and grow. Tilden Edwards once said:

> Anything can contribute to our spiritual formation, but intentional spiritual formation is a conscious means of cultivating our attentiveness to grace; Christ's nature and our life assisting us in not missing, distorting nor fleeing from grace as it appears (Edwards, 1980:10).

In other words, our attentiveness can influence just how long it takes us to mature as Christians and just how far we can actually progress.

J. Robert Clinton developed an insightful formula in understanding the relation between our response, processing which God does in our lives, and the length of time it takes to grow in our spiritual formation. "Spiritual Formation = Processing × Time × Response" (1986).

He defines processing as "any providential event, person, lesson, or thing which God uses to develop, confirm, or move a person along towards their God-given potential" (1986). Time is the changeable variable according to the response to the processing. If the response is positive, the time is shorter than if the response is delayed, absent, or inappropriate.

Some of the foundational disciplines of spiritual formation include: worship, corporate and personal prayer, learning and applying scripture, and serving through love in action. However, the classic disciplines such as meditation, fasting, journaling, spiritual reading, self-denial, obedience, poverty, and contemplation have all been effective disciplines throughout Church history (Edwards, 1980:9).

Another ancient aid to developing Christian character or a mature spirituality is the use of spiritual directors. They provide spiritual counseling, edifying and encouraging the spiritual development of another person. Whereas people in Catholic and Orthodox traditions have used spiritual directors for years, Protestants have only recently begun to use them, a trend which appears to be increasing in popularity. Protestants have more often used parallel master-apprentice modeling, imitation modeling, or discipleship modeling.

Charles H. Kraft related a conversation which Jacob Loewen once had with some of the nationals in Panama regarding values the missionaries had taught them. Sadly, without hesitation they responded, "money." When pressed as to whether they had actually been told these were the most important values they replied, "No, but this is what the missionaries' actions clearly taught" and what they themselves now wanted (Kraft, 1987).

Christians have been called out of this world in order to live by the values and principles of the kingdom of God. These principles are vastly different and often the opposite of the values of this world. Why, then, do they not live this way? Possibly because they do not have a clear understanding of the kingdom of God, or possibly because they have not taken seriously their spiritual and value development as Christians. Possibly because it is difficult. As the following chart shows, every Christian is subject to many different subtle value systems, most of which exert a greater influence upon the person than the value system of the kingdom. For example, the average

Western Educational System Values	Kingdom-of-God Values
• Competition	Others should increase and I should decrease
• Hierarchical relationships	Identify with others and serve them
• Passivity	Responsible active learning and doing
• Status earned by knowing	Credibility earned by relationships and doing
• Dependence upon self and science	Dependence upon God
• Pride	Humility
• Manipulation	Human dignity and freedom
• Task-oriented	Relationship-oriented

Figure 5: Contrasts Between Western Education and Kingdom-of-God Values

young development worker who has recently graduated from technical school has had roughly twenty years of value training in the western educational system built on the pre-Christian Greek model of education.

Spiritual formation resembles growing a garden which requires a partnership between the farmer and God. The farmer sows the seed, cultivates the soil, weeds, guards from predators, and harvests the fruit of the plants. God provides the seed, the sun, the rain, the soil, and life to the plant. Both must faithfully do their part or the garden will produce little.

One may depict the components of spiritual formation graphically. Figure 6 lays out the knowing-doing-being components along with the other aspects of spiritual formation. Figure 6 may be a useful tool for evaluating and diagnosing spiritual development and problems.

Reflection helps facilitate the growth process. It can happen alone or with others using various methods such as journaling, meditation, or reflecting with others.

The categories are "Knowing," "Being," and "Doing." The listed items come into focus during each phase. Note how the focus progresses over a lifetime from knowing to doing to being.

Pre-Christian Foundation	Security	Commitment and Inner-Life Growth
K **N** **O** **W** **I** **N** **G**	• Nature of God as it relates to security • Christian basics • Fundamentals of prayer and Bible reading	• Nature of God and his demands on us • Nature of Christ • Overview of the Word of God • Discipleship • Evangelism • Nature of the body of Christ
D **O** **I** **N** **G**	• Celebration • Small group meetings • Family • Fun	• Obedience checks • Integrity checks • Word checks • Ministry tasks • Spiritual disciplines • Ministry assignments and skills • Exploration of calling
B **E** **I** **N** **G**	• Security with God • Security with body • Inner healing • Zeal	• Deeper commitment to Christian life and values • Growth in discipline • Tempered zeal

Reflection—Alone or with Others

S **T** **R** **U** **C** **T** **U** **R** **E**	• Small group • Church/parachurch • Togetherness	• Small group fellowships • Church/parachurch • Ministry in small teams • Mentoring • Training seminars • Accountability groups • School/formal training

Barriers

	• Wounded past • Broken family • Fear of getting close	• Fear of commitment • Rebellion to discipline • Rebellion to authority • Poor relational skills

Figure 6: Phases, Categories, Patterns and Process Items of the Christian[1]

Gifts, Calling and Ministry	Quality and Ministry Maturity	Convergence
• Gifts • Calling • Self (strengths/ weaknesses) • Patterns and Principles in Scripture	• Growth into union life • Cultures and people • Deeper biblical insights	• Intimacy with God and with people
• Gifted power • Prayer power • Power encounters • Networking power • Ministry insights • Influence challenge	• Spiritual authority • Influence-mix discovery • Isolation • Life crisis/breaking • Destiny revelation	• Spiritual authority • Ideal role • Teaching through life and words • Destiny fulfilled
• Character and moral development	• Maturing in Christlikeness (patience, humility, love)	• Christlikeness • Fruits of the Spirit • Wisdom
• Spiritual Director/ Mentoring • Individual and team ministry • Personal life involvement • Leadership experience	• Leadership in ministry • Personal life involvement • Spiritual director	
• Personal ambition • Pride • Preoccupation with power gifts	• Too busy for spiritual disciplines • Discouragement and depression	

Figure 6: Phases, Categories, Patterns and Process Items of the Christian (*Continued*)

METHODS WITHIN THE CHURCH TRADITIONS

Methods of fostering spiritual development within the major church traditions tend to be similar. Often the major difference is semantic. However, some differences do exist.

Western churches tend to put more emphasis on the mind or reason, while the Eastern churches focus on the heart (Spidik, 1986:17). The Western church has developed religious orders and programs of discipleship, each developing its own methodology of spiritual formation, while the Eastern church is without these schools (Spidlik, 1986:17).

The Roman Catholic and Orthodox churches have both similarities and striking differences from the Protestants. The Roman Catholic Church has developed a greater use of the sacraments, liturgy, orders, and spiritual directors as important means of spiritual formation. Orthodox churches, on the other hand, have depended more upon mass methods such as preaching, teaching, individual and corporate prayer and Bible study, and the use of informal small groups as principle means of formation.

One may simplistically compare the strengths of each of these three major church traditions by these categories noted above: Protestants have majored in *knowing* God (through his Word and relational experience with him), while the Eastern church has emphasized the *being* part of formation, focusing on the imitation of Christ, the mysteries, and the living liturgy as they travel down the road of self-denial and other-worldliness towards God, and the Roman Catholics have emphasized the *doing*. All of the categories are present in every church tradition, but by focusing on their strengths it helps to clarify their distinctions and identifies areas where we can learn and grow from the strengths of other traditions. It is helpful to recognize the weaknesses of one's traditional background and seek ways to grow in areas which are not stressed by one's own church.

SPIRITUAL FORMATION AND PARACHURCH ORGANIZATIONS

Parachurch structures have played a special role in spiritual formation since their inception. Some of the earliest structures were the Roman Catholic and Orthodox religious orders which established contexts of poverty, community living, rules and fraternity to provide spiritual reflection, direction, prayer and nurture. The orders maximized the advantages of community and discipline to foster spiritual formation. Each can teach some valuable lessons. They have worked hard to develop their spirituality and continue to rank among the world experts and thinkers in the subject. The dangers of monasticism and clericalism, however, must be understood, for much of Roman Catholic (and Orthodox) monastic spirituality presupposes a differentiation between the ordinary masses and the spiritually elite, a distinction which is contrary to the biblical idea of the priesthood of all believers (see Hestenes, 1982:85). Unfortunately, a monastic approach often so removes Christians from society that they can no longer relate to the problems and trials of the common people, and the average person often excuses them as too "other worldly."

The Protestants, in contrast, have focused on the masses rather than an elite few, utilizing mass communication methods such as preaching, small-group Bible studies, seminars, and Sunday schools. Often among these churches the results have been too "this worldly."

The Protestant tradition has its own parachurch structures focusing on spiritual formation (discipleship). Places such as Herrnhut and more recent groups such as Youth With A Mission, Campus Crusade for Christ and the Navigators have been developing their own unique forms of developing spirituality. Most of these groups, however, have developed a "method" rather than flexible comprehensive approach. Most Protestants do not have a clear concept of spiritual formation and feel it is rightfully the responsibility of the church or something God does as long as individuals are obedient and maintain regular times of prayer and Bible study. Unfortunately, relatively few churches clearly and intentionally help their people grow spirituality, either.

SPIRITUAL FORMATION IN INSTITUTIONS OF HIGHER EDUCATION

The Association of Theological Schools surveyed what was being done about spiritual formation in seminaries in 1980. A key question was, "Has your school developed an intentional mutually explored set of assumptions and practices in spiritual formation?" Sadly, but not surprisingly, most schools answered, "No." The exceptions, for the most part, were Roman Catholic.

The ATS made some interesting observations about the divergent church traditions.

Roman Catholic

Although many seminaries had a full-time spiritual-formation team, spiritual development still could not be guaranteed. In fact, many students developed a passive dependence upon others and the system for their spiritual formation instead of taking their own active initiative in it. A strength, however, was their appreciation of the rhythms of contemplation/action, solitude/community, critical analysis/devotional life.

Evangelical

No general consensus regarding spiritual formation existed among the evangelical schools. Many saw this issue as the responsibility of the church and denomination and not something in which educational institutions should be engaged.

Ecumenical

For the most part, the ecumenical churches have an ambivalence and tension on the subject and preferred a strong psychological interpretation for such things (Edwards, 1980:23).

In conclusion, the ATS Task Force stated:

> Spiritual formation cannot be left to chance but includes: intelligence, instruction and discipline of practice. Holiness is an art which needs guidance, challenge and support. Faculty, staff and students all have reciprocal roles in it (Edwards, 1980:37).

From my 1986 study about spiritual formation I found twenty-one different methods of spiritual formation in use. The major methods are similar to those used in the local churches. Schools' commitment to spiritual formation had significantly grown in intentional spiritual formation since the 1980 study. Almost half of the schools responding to the survey now offer at least one course in spiritual formation, ranking them number one of all the methods used. It is interesting to note that, unlike the Roman Catholic institutions, very few of these schools have a department in spiritual formation or major in this field.

The first Protestant Theological Seminary to have a department of Spiritual Formation was Asbury Theological Seminary (1964). This institution and Fuller Theological Seminary are among the most progressive Protestant schools with offerings in this area. Other seminaries such as Dallas Theological Seminary require all of their students to take spiritual-formation courses.

SPIRITUAL FORMATION AND SPIRITUAL IDENTIFICATION

An often overlooked dimension of spiritual formation is spiritual identification—that is, the adapting of one's spirituality to that of another culture, where appropriate and biblically acceptable.

Protestant Christian missionaries have often failed to identify spiritually with the various peoples and cultures, and as a result failed to incarnate the gospel for them in a manner the local people understand. Instead of representing holiness, they often represent materialism, immorality, pride, arrogance, insensitivity, and secularism.

Holiness to a Muslim, for example, may mean:

- humility
- regular prayer life
- fasting
- alms giving and concern for the poor
- a life of sacrifice and suffering
- a power to heal, deliver from demons (jinns) and miracles
- memorization and meditation on the Word of God

Certainly, this list is biblical, but it is different from characteristics of the average western Protestant as it maintains many of the ancient Semitic forms of holiness practiced in the days of Jesus. A Christian called to work among an Islamic people has a responsibility to carefully learn the forms of spirituality and then diligently adjust to these forms as daily habits of life and worship.

INTENTIONAL SPIRITUAL FORMATION FOR DEVELOPMENT WORKERS

Christian relief and development agencies are looking for truly spiritual people who would make a significant impact for the kingdom of God and in the lives of the people to whom they were sent, rather than just doing good for humanitarian reasons. Their development should be no different than other Christian workers.

Christians regularly ask two questions regarding any situation: "What is Jesus doing in this?" and "What does he want me to be doing?" This questioning may help a development worker seek to join in with what God is doing in a particular culture and people, rather than to ask God to bless what he thinks is best.

To map out a path of intentional spiritual formation training, the entire structure needs to be a constant mix and balance between knowing-being-doing and reflection. Some areas to learn for the *knowing* component may include:

- The utilization of spiritual resources in overcoming and growing in the midst of culture shock, loneliness, disappointment and spiritual warfare.
- Creative ways for having his or her needs met for nurture, spiritual direction and community in areas where there is no Christian community.
- The history of the church and its spiritual disciplines for that country as well as a thorough understanding of the religions of that country and their spiritual disciplines.
- Techniques for effective journaling for spiritual growth and reflection.
- The scriptural perspective of the spirit world, and cultural biases against them in order to more effectively minister in the power and gifts of the Spirit and do spiritual warfare.
- The ways by which the incarnational model can increase the effectiveness of the relief and development worker.
- The ways how one's theology and worldview affects one's approach to spiritual formation.
- A comparison of the host and home culture's values with kingdom values.

The following activities may help develop the *doing* component for development workers:

- Meet regularly with a spiritual director and write a brief reaction/evaluation of the experiences.
- Meet regularly with an accountability group on a regular basis for reflection, personal evaluation, feedback and discussions based on topics related to spiritual formation.
- Interview several people from different church traditions/ religions on how they do spiritual formation.
- Take regular spiritual retreats, preferably away from normal relaxation destinations.
- Spend time with people who are spiritual role models and reflect on what was learned.
- Practice spiritual disciplines for a period of time, and then reflect afterwards on the experiences, difficulties and victories.

While the most difficult to directly address, the following suggestions are offered for the *being* component:

- Spend some time reflecting upon ones' spiritual journey and character using the chart of Phases, Categories, Patterns, and Process Items.
- Identify one's character type and explore how spiritual formation can differ for each type using the *Enneagrams*, Myers- Briggs, or other standard tests.

Paul recommended Christian workers take time for serious training as soldiers or athletes, through self-discipline (see 1 Timothy 4:7). Peter also exhorts his readers to work at spiritual formation in 2 Peter 1:3–11:

> His divine power has given us everything we need for life and godliness through our knowledge of him who called us by his own glory and goodness. Through these he has given us his very great and precious promises, so that through them you may participate in the divine nature and escape the corruption of the world caused by evil desires.
>
> For this very reason, make every effort to add to your faith, goodness; and to goodness, knowledge; and to knowledge, self- control; and to self-control, perseverance; and to perseverance, godliness; and to godliness, brotherly kindness; and to brotherly kindness, love. For if you possess these qualities in increasing measure, they will keep you from being ineffective and unproductive in your knowledge of our Lord Jesus Christ. But if anyone does not have them, he is nearsighted and blind, and has forgotten that he has been cleansed from his past sins.
>
> Therefore, my brothers, be all the more eager to make your calling and election sure. For if you do these things you will never fall, and you will receive a rich welcome into the eternal kingdom of our Lord and Savior Jesus Christ.

---

[1]The terms used in Figure 6 are defined as follows:

Security—the time when a new Christian comes to grips with the fact that he or she is loved by God and the body of Christ and finds true belonging, security, love and closeness in these new relationships. Some Christians never mature beyond this phase.

Commitment and Inner Life Growth—the period when the Christian begins to understand the fundamentals of the Christian faith and its demands. It is the time when the inner life begins to grow, deeper commitments are made and discipline and obedience to God begin to be understood. Many Christians never grow beyond this point.

Gifts, Calling and Ministry—is the time when a Christian discovers what his or her gifts, calling and ministry are, as well as patterns and principles in Scripture. This phase can pass quickly in the early years of ministry or last for most of one's life.

Ministry Maturity—is the phase when Christians truly begin to show the fruits and qualities of a mature Christian character and significant ministry.

Convergence—is the final phase which only a small handful of Christians reach, where they enjoy a special intimacy with God and Christlike qualities in their life.

9

Defining Development
in Social Terms

Samuel Wilson

SOCIAL RELATIONSHIPS AND associations impact on everyone's life and behavior. As westerners, we pay little attention to the social origins of behavior, and usually concentrate on individual choice. Individual action and behavior are important, but social continuity and transformation cannot be understood without considering the patterned behavior of many individuals and groups in society. Even an individual's rebellious behaviors are largely "steered" by social forces. Activists in the 1960s invariably grew long hair (although a few females shaved their heads for a short time), went barefoot, and supported the same slate of sometimes unrelated causes.

Social forces are our prime interests if we wish to understand development. We may speak meaningfully of "developed," "developing," and "less-developed" countries or societies; to do so points us to explore such social explanations.

CHRISTIANITY AS A SOCIAL FORCE

Christianity is not only a supernatural, spiritual force, it is a social force for change. By its very nature, vital Christianity is an active social change agent. A secular, agnostic graduate professor, forced by what he saw in the data he was analyzing, commented: "Ah,

SAMUEL WILSON is the director of research for the Zwemer Institute and formerly directed the MARC division of World Vision International. His Ph.D. in the sociology of development was granted by Columbia University.

yes, the d--- Pentecostals. They keep messing up everything!" Christianity was acting with evident social impact.

Christians and Social Influence

Religion in general and Christianity in particular is one of the strongest, most powerful social forces affecting social transformation.

In spite of this obvious social influence of religion, most western Christians are ambivalent about social influences and openly resist recognizing them. We are quite willing to make general statements about cities or regions, but would probably attempt to deny that social structure is at the root of what we are observing. For instance, even those Christians who think only of direct, personal evangelism will classify persons by ethnic or religious background as open or closed to the gospel. In this practice is an unrecognized acceptance of the merit in sociological approaches and structural views of the world. And when we are acting realistically, we Christians accept the fact. A sociologist says these social facts are what we should study, the lens through which we need to flesh out our interpretation of life—the "real" world. These social facts are the basis for making a difference in bringing about change and development.

Development can only be understood through such analysis.

Frustration in Ambivalence

When as western Christians we try to think about development or system transformation, we are hamstrung on at least two counts. We have a built-in bias against thinking about systems and their organizational forms, their structures. Second, we interpret the scripture in an ambivalent way that leaves us uneasy with the whole question of becoming active to improve the quality of life. As a result of this curious mixture, we either get the "guilts" about productivity that lifts some set of people above subsistence (Christians should suffer and be deprived) or we go overboard with a theology that enshrines material goods as automatically a sign of God's blessings. Worse, this way of thinking gets attached to individuals, and justifies cutthroat competitive actions. Christian business people are apt to take as great delight in a "shrewd" deal as any "bottom-line" manager!

This ambivalence may be especially true of missionaries. It may induce a polarization on the field between the missionaries and development workers. After World War II, when western Christianity deployed its maximum work force in the mission field, it was sending people as missionaries who were predisposed against seeing social systems' developmental influence. Western (northern) Christianity was acutely individualistic. It sought individual conversion. Mission theology and practice imbibed the essence of the western humanistic individualism. Missionaries were (and maybe still are) not capable of thinking about the world or interpreting their own scriptures from a collective point of view. Consequently, thinking in terms of societies and their differences was anathema.

This individualistic bias existed at the time that anthropology was enriching and disciplining mission to grow in regard and respect for other cultures. Ironically, true children of western cultures could, as by-products of their societies, also be emissaries and apologists for institutions they were constitutionally incapable of critiquing.

Meanwhile, lay Christians filled a disproportionately high percentage of government and corporate overseas slots. Part of their motivation was a disguised attempt to discharge Christian charitable impulses. These two sincere factions found themselves residing in the same locations with very different views of Christian duty. In the 1960s, a missionary pastor approached two members of an English-speaking congregation who were engaged in animated conversation about national development. One was the AID program officer in Peru, and the other a Ph.D. candidate in economics who was acting in an advisory capacity to the national government. As the pastor approached, the animation switched to an embarrassed silence, and an awkward change of subject. The laypersons "knew" that evangelicals shouldn't be involved in transforming society.

Any societal or group-level focus for scripture interpretation can still raise a howl of protest that "everyone knows that if you want to transform society, you must transform individuals."

Missionaries went, and are still going, with an attempted apolitical agenda. This agenda is a direct consequence of their social environment, not of the emphasis of the Bible. Northern conservative Christians defend individualism with all the fire of a struggle for substitutionary atonement. However, without realizing it, they are defending a social value taught them by a secular system that claims its base in individualism. The power of such a society is demonstrated in that it convinces virtually all its members that this is the only way to think.

DEVELOPMENT: A SOCIAL
HISTORICAL PERSPECTIVE

What is "development"? Does anyone know? Something occurred once and only once in human history. It happened in the west. We may call it renaissance, modernization, or the industrial revolution. We may fixate on a single aspect of the transformation. According to taste, we may prefer to define what happened by emphasizing either the political, scientific, economic, or social dimensions. But the whole bundle is the epochal social transformation which westerners prefer to call "development."

For the first and only time in history, people started aggressively and freely to save and to seek personal advantage. Newly developed values not only justified this effort, but encouraged it in all its "true" members. At no time in history had production raised the quality of life while political dogma embraced egalitarian standards, and social value was placed, at least in ideal, on fair participation for all.

The West was transformed. And through its colonialism began to export, some of the institutions of transformation and the values of exploitation.

Exported Self-Determination and Reforms

Then, much later, in a burst of typical enthusiasm, Americans tried to export whole their particular brand of economy and political system, thinking of it as capitalist democracy. Late in World War II, the two most powerful western leaders had met on a destroyer in the North Atlantic and issued a declaration framed by the European context. It forthrightly and staunchly affirmed the right of every nation to self-determination. Concepts of western democracy undoubtedly boxed in this declaration and their expectations of where it might apply. Brashly, most of the colonial world took advantage of this commitment by Roosevelt and Churchill to dare to build independent nations. The general political principle prevailed, if only after significant violence.

Transformation—More Than Economics

In the period immediately after World War II, although the general egalitarian political principle was accepted, development was thought of almost exclusively in economic terms. And these economic terms were chauvinistic. Productivity was a function of capital, labor, and technology in the "right" mix. The task of an economist working as an advisor in a Third-World situation was to discover a way to bring these three into balance, at least in the urban, industrializing sectors. However, profits could stay in the hands of military or oligarchic elites. Drug mafia in more current times can organize whole regions to great productivity, but this does not represent, by any stretch of the imagination, "good" development. Military dictatorships can rape the countryside, indulge their inner circles, and still produce growth in the GNP. In fact, they may be able to make an economic system out-perform one that allows participation and reasonable vocational and social mobility. This way, however, is not desirable.

How well did our Two-Thirds World brothers diagnose these situations, and force a political perspective that includes oppression and liberation into our vocabulary as definitional dimensions of true development!

The 1960s and the Alliance for Progress finally tied economic aid in practice to the notion of democratic reforms. Now the number of strongmen toppled during a particular administration provides the base by which to judge the foreign policy performance of the "developed" nations.

Values Recognized

In the disillusionment of the late sixties, development theorists added "values" to the development equations and attempted to take more complete and comprehensive views by adding other social sciences to the dialogue.

DEVELOPMENT: A COMPLEX DYNAMIC

Development as a dynamic relates to the total social system. Its elements involve at the very least, technological innovation, economic structures, and political system. These combine in their effects to launch growth in productivity. They modify the "feel" of life in a society by broadening distribution. In most instances, some informal upstart sector of society forces the change. Henri Pirenne described the transformation of law and commerce forced by the development of the middle class outside the ramparts of the medieval city. The informal economies are doing the same thing in current settings.

Historically, development had introduced sweeping technological change fostered by a unique curiosity and notion of causality, coupled with the belief that a person can change things. This we have glorified as the "scientific" view of life. Economically, it involved the creation of a set of values and institutions that threw monetary investment, the production of capital, and savings into a whole new importance. Politically, the plains of Runnymede and the heritage of the Bastille contribute major egalitarian strains to our western idea of democracy. From them, the West believes that self-determination and equal rights ought to be a part of appropriate transformation and democratization of politics. The "masses" ought to be enfranchised and the common people ought to have a right to speak for themselves in determining their present and the future.

Development and Political Change

Historical development involved political change. Political change is a peculiar problem for western Christian theologians, whose interpretation of the scriptures relating to the "powers that be" predispose them to arch conservatism. Should a thoroughgoing Christian have participated in a Boston Tea Party? Activism in the political arena is not comfortable to western Christians.

To favor transformation, political structures can be neither greatly centralized nor absolute, nor so weak as to be unable to sustain order. Though most writers and theorists in the West shy from comment on it, military force subject to political control was historically a powerful aspect. Technology for defense was a key to survival. In modern times, research and development in technological areas have used the smokescreen of national self-preservation and military preparedness to carry out "pure" research and fund materials research which has tremendous impact on day-to-day life. Thus, even current technological advance depends to a degree on weapons development.

Alongside the notion of stability and preservation of order, our notions of development were and are full of ideological strains of individualism and personal rights. We seem unwilling to admit the need for authority in a system by providing a rationale and structures for implementation. This is, perhaps, one of the roots of our anti-institutional posturing.

In the ancient kingdoms of the East, commerce and production had undeniably produced fabulous riches, but had also left them in the hands of hereditary or military elites. Skill and innovation were not directed to producing surplus (saving) and distributing a modicum of benefits to a majority of society as the products of the effort. Workers could not and did not expect to participate fully in the bounty that resulted from their labors. Nor was sufficient mobility permitted to lead the masses to believe that they might participate in such bounty.

Development in the Judeo-Christian Tradition

Curiously, while most of the above processes involved a desacrilizing of life and behaviors, the combination of Christian and Jewish religious principles played a strong part in producing most of these changes. The same mindset that rebelled against religious authority in expressing its right to think was nurtured at the breast of the motifs of the Hebrew Christian scriptures which strongly invite an investigative spirit. Max Weber intuitively recognized this in his most famous work, *The Protestant Ethic and the Spirit of Capitalism*, and in his work on the great religious systems.

Our egalitarianism surely owes its strength to the prolific Old Testament foundational statements on equal justice before the law. The same law was to be applied evenhandedly to rich and poor, orphan and widow, and strangers dwelling in the midst.

Part of what produced the changes was the capability to organize in new, legal ways. What this means, quite simply, is that development involves reorganizing relations. These relations then become legally and socially legitimate. When sociologists analyze the period of western development, they are apt to call great attention to the evolution of financial structures such as banks and lending houses. They may also generically call attention to the changes in legal structure that made an entity like the modern corporation possible. Evolution of credit and other economic institutions, and the development of the burgher class outside the old medieval city, forced sweeping legal change. Indeed, these changes led to a totally new jurisprudence and set of laws.

Consider so simple yet so profound a device as the thing we call the modern corporation. Bureaucracy comes to a peak with the evolution of the modern corporate structure. A crazy idea this, that persons should be able to formally associate to accomplish set goals (make money?) and not be personally responsible for debts incurred by this legally fictitious entity. This kind of entity was an unheard of innovation. Yet, it is a crucial institutional form for the economic systems of the more developed nations. People can agree to treat an association, formalized before the law, as if it has real existence. It can act independently of those who direct it. At the same time, this fiction makes it possible for participants to risk as much of their possessions in a venture as they wish, and also defends them from personal fault and loss of any unrisked capital.

It has, incidentally, migrated everywhere as the predominant form of local and national church structure.

SURPLUS AND DEVELOPMENT

Before "modern" times, the great religious, military, and government bureaucracies had evolved systems of authority and accountability which made enormous projects possible. Involved in all these ventures were the development of many of the bases of modern business and economic life. Statistics probably originated in the need of Pharaohs to know how large the pool of personnel and food and weaponry was and to be able to direct campaigns with reasonable logistics.

In modern, developed states, the application of these methods geometrically increase the amount of surplus produced.

Development Broadens Distribution

The many strands came together for one and only one time in history. A large region of the world was producing surplus through manufacturing. At the same time it was restructuring the relationships of production and finding ways to manage and administer. Yet it was also both freeing and motivating segments of its populace to work under new conditions. Still, at the same time it was incorporating them in the processes so that the quality of life for a majority was upgraded.

We attempted to export and impose these aspects of life. Fortunately, we have begun to refine our understanding of the historic social settings of the shifts. We have also begun to recognize that no one-to-one comparison exists by which, in the words of one past author,"the West shows to the non-West the mirror image of its own future." Social transformation in the South (non-West) should not and cannot be made slave to any single model of economic or political system.

Social Relations, Power, and Productivity

Even if exact generalizations are not possible, we do know that an intimate relation exists between the elements of organization for social relations, governance, and production/distribution. One cannot modify the values which drive and determine economic structures solely by investment tactics. Nor can one directly intervene by teaching or instruction alone with assured results in education or political enfranchisement. These changes depend, rather, on the vital dynamic of real social groups. They emerge from interaction and social process, including collective interest which may not be explicitly conscious.

For example, it appears that no group is ever included in the political system without posing a threat to the currently powerful actors. The threat may be tacit, but there must be evidence of power to force one's way into consideration. The basis may be raw force and its threat of violence or sophisticated politically subtle suggestion—but a threat is necessary to cause systemic change. Cases where groups who posed no threat were politically enfranchised might not produce a wordless book, but certainly do not require a library holding shelf. The political dimensions of development, like all the others, involve competition and potential conflict. And conflict can be salutary.

DEVELOPMENT: A DEFINITION

Generally, development is the struggle of a given social segment to transform itself toward improved life quality and participation for an enlarging percentage of its members. Almost inevitably, any such segment will encounter the need to integrate, at some point, into an environing and usually threatening larger system. This larger system will usually be composed at least in part of competing elements which attempt to limit participation in its available rewards.

It becomes evident, then, that development is based on both production and distribution.

No system exists where distribution is perfectly equal, and where authority is absent. Even where every person sits "under his vine and under his fig tree" a rod of iron rules over all, delegating legitimate power to intermediate levels of office holders.

Development involves powerful social forces rooted for strength in cohesive groups. These groups mold their members' perceptions, values, and motivations, and thus transform society.

Group Identity and Development

Someone has to feel much reassurance and support from a group in order to risk acting in their behalf. Groups confer an identity that is larger than individual life. When groups are newly emerging, their spokespersons will appear to be overreaching, and to be arrogating to themselves the privilege of speaking for segments they have no clearly visible legitimate basis to represent.

How often the cry is heard on the lips of politicians or labor organizers, "The people demand . . . " "The man in the street will not tolerate . . . " when they are voicing their own opinions and not those of the man in the street. One might wonder where they derive the right to speak for the "people" or the "worker." Indeed, individual actors can draw from a group identity which personifies the aspirations or needs of given groups. This is true regardless of the scale on which it occurs. We can talk about a single social class, a defined region within a country, a single city, or a total nation. People, however, are molded socially. While mavericks may lead for a time, only whole groups provide the basis for the set of transformations that we call development.

An aspiring social transformationist would do well, then, to seek and work with local leaders. Through these leaders, the development worker will be able to sense and express the inarticulate longings of social sectors which do not participate fully in the goods and rewards available in a social and economic system. Rarely will it be possible for someone from outside the group to achieve enough identification with and recognition by a group to be trusted by and speak for them.

THE CHURCH AND DEVELOPMENT

The church, ideally, has the tools to overcome all social barriers, and this is, surely, the church's call and ministry. Therefore, Christians who rightly understand the possibilities inherent in church unity as a social force are way ahead of the game in working for social transformation. Planting and edifying a church relates to the whole spectrum of social transformation. However, development workers who recognize the church's role in social transformation will be well-advised to work with social processes generated by the impact of an invasive power of the Spirit of God.

Transformation and Urban Ministry

The world is becoming increasingly urban, and urban forms are profligate in their creativity. Those who do not agree should try to find a single western social theory or philosophy which has been applied with good fit and without being modified in any overseas urban situation, or vice versa.

Urban factors deserve such extensive treatment that mere mention here cannot do them adequate justice. Among all the social forms important to social transformation, none epitomizes the possibilities and problems better than the city. Development transformed social relations and focused them in urban areas.

Cities are intensifiers of all that is good and evil and neutral.

Here again, the Christian is more apt to denounce the intensification of evil, rather than celebrate the power for good inherent in urban life. Of all the elements that might be looked at up and down the social scale, none is more important than the set of relations and institutions that we know as the modern, world-class city. Only transformation of technology makes cities habitable, political forms make them tractable to any government, and modern economic organization puts an infrastructure under them to make productivity possible. Cities alone provide the range of choices that make liberty significant.

Yet when we look at the literature or tap popular opinion, we are more likely to find unalloyed animosity than celebration, fear, rather than joy in the idea of transforming the city for good.

People involved in urban social transformation face two temptations: 1) they may focus on the macro-structural problems and fall into despair because the infusion of resources and personnel required for change is so massive that they despair, or 2) they may look for an isolated sector of the disenfranchised and impoverished and apply temporary poultices.

Just as city forms were intimately associated with historical western development, so they will be with any effective transformation in other situations. We cannot and must not avoid the city. We must learn what development means in urban context.

The church must be seen for its potential to mobilize Christians from all walks of life, who, working in coordination, can effect real transformation at both levels.

RULES OF THUMB FOR TRANSFORMATION

1. *Become comfortable with looking at the world in terms of meaningful groups, and with the need to organize to produce change.* To favor social transformation, facilitators must become concerned for groups and develop acute consciousness of their dependence on group processes for success. The change agent's role and agenda must grow out of some group's real and felt needs. He or she must live out the Christian virtue of humility.

Missionaries and development workers from the West need to overcome the deficit of their inbred predisposition against social institutions. Formal and informal associations and organizations are the only basis of transformation on a meaningful scale. While we may be highly impatient of the knee-jerk response of forming a committee to address any need, a good deal of realistic wisdom resides in working with already structured forms to reach goals.

Most westerners will need to cease looking for outstanding leadership, and learn to sense and develop community and communal spirit and cohesiveness. Massive research shows that leadership will evolve and be recognized by acting groups. This is especially sensitive and difficult in urban settings.

2. *Recognize that values are not taught, but caught from social systems to which they are essential.* Groups evolve views of life and perspectives for dealing with perceived reality. And local congregations, regional fellowships, and national associations of Christians and Christian organizations, under the discipline of the Word, move toward a "Christianized" definition of reality. They offer the only real hope of worthwhile transformation here, and in the hereafter.

3. *Serve local processes and needs, rather than slavishly importing foreign models.* Any Christian worker who approaches traditional or other social systems with a view to helping transformation from a Christian perspective must not, under any circumstances, come with a mind closed by a single model. Christian workers must give up the notion that eventually the social scene in which they are working must transform to conform to the systems which molded their own ways of thinking. Development is most certainly not the attempt to recapitulate the home social transformation in a host social setting.

Most Two-Thirds World peoples accept some communal notion of life which runs counter to northern, First-World, or western individualism. This perspective may begin with the extended family as the basic economic unit, or the notion of communal control of agricultural products. This collective view of life was inherent in the Inca socialist state, or in the communal backgrounds which predispose many of the African states to some form, automatically (and most often mistakenly) categorized in the West as socialism. Instead of resisting this sort of organization of life, the Christian interested in social transformation should welcome it and seek to work with it as the only adequate basis for achieving gospel goals. They should proceed with the kind of respect for the integrity of the peoples they can only learn from scriptures and the Spirit who inspired them.

4. *Be alert to the social systems in which the groups of interest are nested, and be prepared to react positively to almost inevitable conflict.* An awareness of society's inequalities and of the groups and social mechanisms surrounding a transforming group are essential. Sooner or later, improved integration into larger systems will come only after some degree of conflict. Will the transforming social segment be prepared to handle this conflict? We need theology that will make Christian entities comfortable in moving toward resolution of such conflicts. All too many make the automatic conservative assumption that in all instances of potential conflict, the only truly Christian response is stoic forbearance. Positive anticipation and loving Christian activism can preclude damaging conflict, improve social conditions, and include more people in enhanced life quality. Some conflict is healthful. But, preparedness in heart and mindset are essential. These can be affirmed from a biblical base.

5. *Create new formal forms of organizations as necessary to maintain momentum in transformation, with an eye to minimizing social disruption.* The most important resources lie in the social cohesion and shared gifts of the group active for its own transformation.

In major urban settings, the prime hope of constituting a powerful group active in its own interest is the existence of a large pool of individuals whose powerlessness and disenfranchised, oppressed state makes them aware of their need to relate to others and act in concert along lines of shared interest. They know they currently have no power. Their entire experience of life is of being mere objects which are acted upon. Find the hopeless, and inject hope by promoting concerted action. Any project around which a set of diverse individuals may make common cause may become an affirming experience of strength. Such pools of individuals become groups only when they are organized and successful in rebuffing real or imagined enemies. They thus manage to gain a sense of power over against the powerlessness in which they had previously been steeped. Only projects with a high likelihood of immediate success are worth such risk, however.

6. *Make the church comfortable with exercising organized influence for positive change.* Some scriptural motifs are missing in our modern Christian schizophrenia toward development. The Bible includes strong goals of overcoming, of triumph over evil. Historical missions have completely transformed traditional cultures. John Paton's efforts, for example, eradicated head hunting and violence from the New Hebrides, modern Vanuatu. We rightly caricature puritanical missionaries who felt a compulsion to clothe naked "natives" in Victorian garments from temperate zones, but selectively exclude a positive rationale for eliminating suttee or cannibalism. These we attack as "obviously" demonic practices. They were part of social systems, systems that needed the radical judgment of Word and church. Without being triumphalistic, Christians ought to be able to champion biblical principles of social transformation. They should undergird and ennoble being salt and yeast not only without apology, but with a developed apology for positive action.

7. *Recognize and welcome the urban institutions as allies.* We can trace our fears to false historical attitudes and see the biblical focus on the city for redemption, benign authority, and markedly enhanced and enriching social life. The arena in which the struggle of good and evil is played out will finally be an urban arena. Any attempt to bypass the centers of power will limit and marginalize all social transformation.

Probably no greater challenge exists than Christian transformation in an urban context. Just as the city concentrates, magnifies, and intensifies all other features of life, it puts immense obstacles in the way of identification—but it also heightens the satisfactions associated with significantly important ministry.

We must learn what Christian social transformation means in the pluriform city.

10

Economic Perspectives Undergirding Christian Relief and Development

Stephen Weber

THE PURPOSE OF THIS CHAPTER is to make the reader aware of some basic economic issues related to Christian relief and development. Experience has shown that significant economic knowledge gaps exist in the preparation of many Christians engaged in relief and development activities. In some situations this lack of economic perspective has been the primary reason for the failure of relief and development projects.

We have learned over the years that the acquisition of "church-growth eyes" allows the Christian to view the potential of any given opportunity somewhat differently than people who have not yet been sensitized in this very important area of missiology. A somewhat similar analogy applies to the Christian relief and development worker approaching the less-developed countries (LDC's) without "economic eyes."

"ECONOMIC EYES" AND MARKET STRUCTURES

What are the primary economic perspectives which are needed in order to begin the development of "economic eyes?" Foremost on the list is the question of markets. It is quite amazing when one

STEPHEN WEBER has served as the coordinator of Nazarene Compassionate Ministries for the International Church of the Nazarene since 1984. He has been responsible for approving funding for various relief and development projects in over seventy countries. Formerly, he served for ten years as a missionary in Haiti.

examines the number of Christian relief and development projects undertaken in LDC's without proper knowledge of the market structures.

Basically, two major systems of social coordination must be taken into consideration. These two systems are defined as the arrangements which people have designed for trading and interacting economically with each other. These are macroeconomic descriptions which Peter J. Hill calls

> . . . the private property, market system which relies primarily upon prices to convey information and to structure incentives; and the centrally planned system which depends much more heavily upon non-market means of securing social coordination (1987:41).

In traditional LDC societies, these systems for establishing social coordination are complex arrangements of material capital and human capital which find equilibrium based on such things as investment incentives, income streams, technological change, and consumption patterns.

One example will clarify what is meant by markets. Many times the Christian relief and development worker will see the need for some type of technological innovation, such as the inclusion of solar ovens into a society. The idea of solar ovens sounds reasonable. If solar ovens were utilized they would eliminate the need for charcoal or wood-burning fuel. The elimination of wood consumption for fuel would greatly decrease the need for cutting trees. This reversal of the deforestation pattern would ultimately positively effect the weather and drought cycles which have plagued the economies of LDC's for decades. Sound familiar? No matter how well this particular solar oven development project is planned, it will not be successful because local market systems have not been properly considered. Think for a moment of all the market aspects related to the charcoal fuel business: First, people cut and prepare the trees; other people transport both the wood itself and the finished charcoal fuel. In addition, other people make their living via the selling of the fuel in the wholesale and retail marketplace.

In this example, any solution dealing with the problem of wood or charcoal fuel that does not take into account the complex levels of market structures from the forest to the traditional long-run equilibrium of an economy built around localized use of charcoal fuel is doomed to failure. Most Christian relief and development efforts take place within the context of a market structure where prices are determined by the relationship of complex factors relating to supply and demand.

This chapter is not the proper place to debate the relative merits of the various markets which peoples have developed. However, it is the proper place to begin to deal with the reality that these markets do exist.

THE MULTIPLIER EFFECT

Once we have been made aware of the importance of markets and their integrated structures, we can move on to a more narrow subject of designing limited or closed markets. This move will require a basic understanding of what the Keynesians call "the multiplier effect" (Baumol and Blindes, 1979:163).

The multiplier effect is one of the central pillars of Keynesian macroeconomic theory. It is not necessary for this discussion to know the mathematical formulas behind the theory, nor is it necessary to be in agreement with the Keynesian models. What is important are at least these four terms:

- *Marginal propensity to consume* (MPC) (Baumol and Blindes, 1979:166)
- *Marginal propensity to save* (MPS) (Baumol and Blindes, 1979:133)
- *Aggregate demand* (Baumol and Blindes, 1979:113)
- *Nominal income* (Dolan, 1980:92)

The basis of the theory is simply that one person's spending is another person's income. If a circular flow of income and expenditure can be created, then everyone connected to that particular market structure will benefit economically. Without using any mathematical formulas or much economic vocabulary, I will attempt to illustrate how the multiplier effect works in a closed or limited market.

Assume for the moment that we are exposed to a traditional economy at long-run equilibrium. This equilibrium means no technological change is currently taking place; and stable preferences exist with respect to consumption, saving, and investment. It also means that there is efficient allocation of resources and settled interpersonal relations (Curley and Gift, 1985:50).

Into this situation we introduce a development grant (or loan, or expenditure relating to relief activities—the issue is new nominal income from outside the system). If the recipients of this hypothetical grant are assisted in their development of a proper structure of consumption incentives and saving opportunities, the original amount of the grant will be multiplied several times over through the circular flow of income and expenditures.

Let us assume that the grant is for the purpose of manufacturing concrete construction blocks. The original cash grant which is infused into the closed-market system (such as the Christian community) is used to purchase sand, cement, water, as well as to pay salaries on a per block basis to those responsible for the fabrication of the blocks, the transportation of the raw materials needed to make the blocks, and the actual wholesale and retail sales of the finished product.

Several members of the closed-market system benefiting immediately in the form of salaries and wages (nominal income). These primary benefactors will create what we will call "an aggregate demand for goods and services" (Dolan, 1980:248). They will all have "a marginal propensity to consume" (MPC) and also "a marginal propensity to save" (MPS). Their consumption patterns will be centered around our assumption of an economy in long-run equilibrium. These primary benefactors will spend a certain portion of this income on what is called permanent income streams. This would be various consumables such as food, clothing, and related construction materials. It would also include service sector expenditures such as education, transportation, and health-related felt needs.

After the primary benefactors exercise their MPC, we see the multiplier effect take place. Their expenditures for consumables and service sector needs become income for the providers of these goods and service. These secondary benefactors also will spend a portion of the realized profits based on a similar MPC. The multiplier effect increases the actual benefit of the original grant by a factor of several times the original amount. The actual benefit depends upon such things as the amount of "leakage" outside the system (goods and services not provided by members of the closed or limited market), and the amount of each benefactor's marginal propensity to save (MPS).

At this point, the need for a saving system becomes apparent to the adherent of the multiplier-effect closed-market system. If members of the market also have access to a safe and reputable savings structure, the multiplier effect has additional impact on the community in question. If this closed-market system is a Christian community such as a local congregation, it is not difficult to see the increased multiplier benefits of such a grant which includes a savings function.

This example of the multiplier effect opens the forum for the discussion of the next phase of necessity economic perspectives for the Christian relief and development worker. Our assumption called for long-run equilibrium. It assumed the absence of technological change, something which is no longer true in the world of LDC's. It also assumed stable consumption, saving and investment, one of which is stable in most LDC situations. Last on our long list of assumptions is the efficient allocation of resources which resulted from settled interpersonal relations—which would mean that our market system is just. We know of many ways to describe the actual market system situations in LDC's, and none of the descriptions would be close to using words such as "just" or "fair" or any other similar words. The poor simply do not take part in any type of just economic market system. At this point we leave much of the traditional economic thought, and open our thinking to such revolutionary ideas such as Schumacker's "economics as if people mattered" (Schumacker, 1973).

The Christian relief and development worker needs to make several adaptations of economic models.

APPROPRIATE TECHNOLOGY

First, we begin with technological change. Traditional economics call for the most cost-effective methods possible. The theory calls for the marketplace to determine the utility of the product and how it is to be produced. In technological change, normally, this means something other than labor-intensive technology. However, this approach is not the case in LDC's. Theirs is a world of labor-intensive systems. For example, never in the history of North American interstate construction have our eight-lane super highways been built using thousands of men and women without the benefit of dozens of labor-saving machines and heavy equipment. However, in mainland China, on the super highways being built to accommodate the needs of the economic free zones (the windows to the west for the twenty-first century), one will see thousands and thousands of laborers building the super highways—which rival any modern U.S. interstate—without one piece of heavy equipment or labor saving machine in sight. The reason: labor-intensive technology. The western relief and development worker must learn to understand and deal with this perspective. The objective is to build meaningful and cost-effective economic systems which take into consideration both the dignity of those involved as well as the reality of the actual lower labor costs found in LDC's.

Secondly, we look at the assumption of stable consumption, saving, and investment climates. Economic models explain that as the aggregate demand increases, if the supply can be increased, the cost will decrease proportionately. However, LDC's do not benefit from stable patterns of consumption due to the lack of available raw materials. To the contrary, in most LDC situations, the price will increase as demand increases due to the lack of raw materials. Therefore, before any development project is undertaken, the availability of raw materials must be considered. A successful project will normally be tied directly to the ability to develop and maintain a stable supply of raw materials used in the manufacturing of both the desired consumables and non-consumables produced. In the case of our earlier block-making example, extreme care would be needed in order to ensure the availability of adequate sand, cement, and water. The ultimate decision concerning the infusion of electricity into the project would be decided upon after the costs associated with an electric block-making machine were calculated against a non-electrical machine using more labor-intensive methods.

Stable consumption is dependent upon the availability of various raw materials. Equally related to this availability is a stable saving and investment system. Very few issues are more germane to the understanding of Christian relief and development than credit.

Imagine for a moment a world of triple-digit annual inflation, a constant devaluation of the national currency, plus 20 percent per-month interest rates. Few of the traditional economic models were designed to cope with these types of realities found throughout the LDC's. How does one adapt the economic principles to this type of LDC world?

If credit is one of the keys, then some type of organized credit system is a large part of the answer. What if low-interest or non-interest loans were introduced into our closed or limited market system? If qualified members could borrow at rates far below the typical "loan shark" schedules, it is natural to assume a large demand for such revolutionary credit. The problem is not lack of demand for credit. No, the problem is collateral, organized methods of repayment plans, and foreclosure procedures on assets of the members. All of these very real questions require viable answers before stable credit (saving and investment) structures can be developed. Few of those living in the developed nations can properly visualize what a cadre of highly trained and skilled "credit brokers" could do to bring about lasting development opportunities in the world of LDC's. Yet, here is one of many areas that most Christian relief and development workers defer to secular or less-than-ethical credit structures.

Our last assumption concerned the effective allocation of resources resulting from settled interpersonal relationships. We would like to assume that settled interpersonal relationships have resulted from the elimination of sin from the social/economic equation. Unfortunately, sin is still very much a part of every LDC development situation. Therefore, we many times stabilize interpersonal relations by recognizing economic realities, markets, and such things as vested interests and competition for limited raw materials. Some Christians have been known to resort to "contextualizing" and falling into the pattern of paying "service fees" and other dignified sounding names for bribery. Fortunately, most Christian relief and development workers are looking for other, more biblical solutions.

One solution to effecting a more just allocation of resources and stabilizing interpersonal relations is accepting reality: It is possible to create wealth. Most Christians (and non-Christians) assume the size of the economic pie is fixed. Which is to say that if "those Christians" or "those poor people"—or whatever closed-market system we would choose to see as the primary benefactors of the relief and development infusions of resources—if those people increase their share of the pie, then the rest of the community is placed in a position of losing their current share of that pie. The objective here is simple: Convince the interested observers that they too stand to benefit economically from the positive results of a continually increasing pie (the creation of wealth, from which all benefit economically).

This approach works quite well for all types of macroeconomic markets. For example, in a centrally planned economy such as Cuba, where the state controls the market structures, a Christian community can use the state system as a partner, a purchaser of items required by the state. What is needed in these types of situations are visionary Christians, relief and development specialists who can understand both the objectives and the complexities of a centrally planned economy. In non-centrally planned economies, one must deal with various types of free-market systems. These systems are described by Paul Samuelson as "systems of coercion by dollar votes" (Dolan, 1980:156). In a true free-market economy, when it is properly understood, it is possible through barter or other structured agreements to conclusively prove that a bigger pie *is* possible, and thereby allow the just allocation of resources to help guarantee the success of the relief and development project being undertaken.

Return once again to the block-machine illustration: The supplies of cement become the key to success. In many LDC situations, the supply of cement will be a state, or some similar monopoly. Therefore, it becomes imperative that those in control of the cement are made aware of the reciprocal benefits of the steady supply of cement to the proposed block-machine project. In many small projects, this awareness will not be much of a problem. However, as the size of the project increases (and thus the need for cement also increases), it becomes critical that the supply of cement is kept constant. Perhaps in this illustration the supplier of cement is either the state or is controlled by the state. The reciprocal benefits must be spelled out. The blocks will build schools, low-cost housing, clinics, all of which will benefit all the people in the particular sector of the economy in question.

If proper needs-assessment research has been completed, the state (the controller of cement or whatever raw materials are needed to make the project a success) will actually assist the project by giving tax advantages or discounts or other forms of cooperation. The flip side could be some type of anti-Christian bias which may mean various forms of economic persecution. In these situations, alternative structures must be developed in order to accomplish the objective. This development of alternate structures will make the task of a more just allocation of resources more difficult to accomplish, but not impossible. Our point at this juncture is to briefly introduce the worst case scenario: the Christian relief and development worker ignoring these very necessary ingredients for long-run economic equilibrium, and not dealing with these factors in advance of beginning the project. To ignore them would mean failure or frustration in most LDC relief and development activities.

As our world moves from its recent "east versus west" political stalemate to a more tense "north versus south" economic debate concerning the misdistribution of God's abundant resources, the Christian relief and development worker must understand the issues involved. Recently, as evangelical relief and development workers, we were invited to Cuba, Nicaragua, Mozambique, Napal, and Pakistan. How do we effectively respond to these requests for assistance? We respond with highly skilled Christians, looking through "economic eyes" at a world suffering from the effect of sin. Until we finally regain a proper understanding of how economics is critical to missiological concerns for church growth, we will continue to miss golden opportunities of involvement in bringing a lost world face to face with the ultimate hope found only in the person of Jesus Christ.

11

Christian Social Transformation Distinctives

Edgar J. Elliston

CHRISTIAN SOCIAL TRANSFORMATION differs from the relief and development work of such agencies as USAID, World Bank, CIDA, SIDA, NORAD, or other government related agencies. The differences in Christian social transformation appear principally in its goals, motives, and methods as they relate to spiritual, social, and/or physical or environmental issues.

Robert Moffitt defines Christian social transformation or development in terms of the Christians' three key relationships. Development according to Moffitt is "every biblically based activity of the body of Christ, his church, that assists in bringing human beings toward the place of complete reconciliation with God and complete reconciliation with their fellows and their environment" (1987:236). Moffitt's definition suggests an active intervention of the people of God into the three key relational domains with God, others and the environment. Ed Dayton defines Christian social transformation as "a process of external intervention intended to enable a people to become better than they were before" (1987:55). Dayton's definition of intentional social transformation, while lacking Moffitt's broad relational directionality, certainly underscores the issues of the process, enablement, external intervention, and the social issues involved. Tito Paredes defines development as a "movement toward that freedom and wholeness in a

EDGAR J. ELLISTON serves as assistant professor of leadership selection and training in the School of World Mission at Fuller Theological Seminary. In that role he coordinates the Development Concentration.

just community which persons will enjoy when our Lord returns to bring the Kingdom in its fullness" (1987:82). His definition, written from a Latin American point of view, emphasizes freedom, wholeness and justice as linked with the kingdom of God.

God took the initiative to redeem. Now Christians are called to actively engage or intervene in redemptive activities. The activities have spiritual, social, and physical dimensions (see Revelation 21:1-4, 22-24; 11:15). While occasionally a secular person will take the initiative to work for others solely for their benefit, Christians are commanded to do so continuously with a scope as wide as "all peoples" and "all creation."

Costas addresses the scope of Christian social transformation by writing,

> The fundamental missiological question before the Christian Church is not whether mission should be conceived of as vertical, horizontal, or both; not whether it should be thought of either as spiritual and personal, or material and social; nor whether we should emphasize in our practice one aspect or another. It is rather whether we can recover its wholeness and efficacy, whether we can see it as a whole and live up to its global objectives (1979 xii-xiii).

Christians approaching social transformation or development, however, reflect the worldview perspectives from which they come and often struggle with these prevailing cultural views. These worldview perspectives affect their motives, methods and goals. Hiebert (1987:104-105) notes three of these issues which have profoundly influenced Christian social ministries in the past and which continue to inhibit the effective contextualization of developmental efforts in the present. These issues include colonialism, social evolution and positivism.

Churches have been closely tied with the classical colonizing processes of the past and more recently with both neo-colonialism and even "internal" colonialism (Altback and Kelley, 1978). In each of these forms of colonialism the local culture was/is considered as inferior. The traditional "inferior" ways of religion, social organization, and economics required replacement or modification toward the position of the "colonizer."

Many Christians embrace a second inhibiting perspective based on the theory of cultural evolution (see Hiebert, 1987:105). People holding this perspective assume that culture change is not only directional, but is moving toward their own form of culture. For them the issue of contextualization is irrelevant if the people with whom they work are already inexorably moving toward their own cultural forms.

Many Christians struggle with the perspective in which science and technology provide both the means for knowing and the ultimate answers. Christians working in development have often fallen into the trap believing that western technology provides the best answers to all kinds of situations and that development just requires the transfer of technology. People holding this perspective have often failed to recognize existing technologies which have served well to bring an integration of the existing worldview and ecology. The simple transfer of technology, even modern "appropriate technology," has seldom, if ever, fully served the developmental needs.

Christian social transformation, however, emerges from three distinctive concerns: 1) the motivation, 2) the process values, and 3) the intended goal.

CHRISTIAN MOTIVATION FOR SOCIAL TRANSFORMATION

Christians, because of their commitment to Christ, are by their "new nature" concerned about the well-being of their neighbors, both in the present and in eternity. Two concerns focus the Christians' attention on their neighbors. First, is their need to be reconciled to God through Jesus Christ, and secondly, is their need for food, clothing, shelter, dignity, and a realization of the potential for a full and meaningful life.

Government officials often promote development with a great deal of rhetoric, announcing their altruistic goals to help the poor and underdeveloped nations. However, at the governmental level, development generally serves either to provide raw materials or to open new markets for the providing government. Often, it serves both objectives, as well as providing a means to propagate the donor's ideology. In any case, the primary benefit is for the donor. President Richard Nixon made the purpose all too clear when he said, "Let us remember that the main purpose of American aid is not to help other nations, but to help ourselves." There will nearly always be an economic benefit to the donor, as well as a potential military strategic advantage. The ethnocentric assumption that the donor's way is best, especially for the donor, appears clearly in the policies and practices of governmental agencies.

The believer's motive for helping others arises from a personal obedience to Jesus Christ and the desire that others similarly know and follow Him. Christians working in compassionate ministries differ from the typical secular development workers in their driving motivation. Their motivation comes from significant differences in terms of *whose* they are, *who* they are, and their *view of the future*. Each of these distinctives serves to motivate Christians to work toward a clear goal and to work with the people where they are.

Whose Disciples Are They?

Jesus said that anyone who gives a cup of water in his name because he belongs to Christ will certainly not lose his reward (Mark 9:41; cf. Matthew 10:40–42). Jesus' focus is on the primary controlling allegiance of the person and how that allegiance motivates the person. The focus in this text is not on the authority of Jesus, but the identity of the disciple and master. Whose follower is the Christian? Under whose discipline is he? Here the question of lordship arises. Who is one's master—Jesus Christ or the state? The question of lordship determines the ultimate allegiance of the disciples and the direction they will go. One's allegiance profoundly influences his motivation.

Who Are They?

The Christian is a different person because of what Jesus Christ has done. The apostle Paul wrote that the believer is a "new creation." Jesus described the change in terms of a "new birth." A Christian is different from within and has a different set of motives driving toward ministry.

Christians have experienced and continue to experience several developmental initiatives of the Holy Spirit which not only change them, but which drive them to ministry with others. Some of these freeing and developmental events and processes include: forgiveness of sin, reconciliation with God, adoption as heirs of God, being "called," receiving "spiritual gifts" for ministry with others, and the bearing of "spiritual fruit" which deeply affects relationships with other people.

The personal transformation through the renewing work of the Holy Spirit motivates a person to look outward and to participate in the converting, redeeming, reconciling transformation of what surrounds him. This motivation in a social ministry may be seen in interpersonal relationships before it appears in institutionalized forms. The motive comes from the good news of a changed life which now has hope and peace and a life which has experienced an undeserved justice and any oppression lifted. The motive again is kingdom-based and focused on others for their good.

View of the Future

Since the Christian's view of the future differs from the views of the secular community, the motivation for working for the future differs. Most westerners see the future in material, technological, and economic terms. Government-based development can be counted on to focus on technological or economic issues. The bright future is defined in terms of a successful technological transfer, an improved gross national product, high level employment, the absence of debt, and a surplus in the budget. While an active participant in the economic structures, the Christian sees both the immediate future and an eternity with hope in terms of the kingdom of God. With a different view of the future, the present motives for both personal growth and working with others take on a very different character. With a different view of the future the issues of economics, although important, take a somewhat different priority. What is of eternal significance also comes into focus.

Sinclair, describing the wisdom of God as it relates to development and eschatology, writes,

A biblically balanced wisdom . . . increases our anticipation of the good that God will do; it also gives us the strength to endure what Satan will do. Thus a balanced biblical wisdom encompasses both vision and realism. It guides a widespread transformation of society radiating from a revived and vigorous church. . . .

Wisdom provides the means to discern the true qualities of a developed society. Wisdom also helps define the goal of social transformation: what sort of society are we trying to create? A biblically based development or social transformation should reflect the characteristics of the messianic kingdom of wisdom and peace (1987:167).

The Christian's view of the future is described by the prophet Isaiah as he notes the work of the Spirit:

The Spirit is poured upon us from on high, and the wilderness becomes a fruitful field, and the fruitful field is deemed a forest. Then justice will dwell in the wilderness, and righteousness abide in the fruitful field. And the effect of righteousness will be peace, and the result of righteousness, quietness and trust for ever. My people will abide in a peaceful habitation, in secure dwellings, and in quiet resting places (Isaiah 32:15–18).

The Christian's view of the future is one of hope. Sharing this hope with others provides good news both for the present and for eternity. "We must celebrate its greatness. Hope from God bursts our circle of experience wide open and it promises us 'what eye has not seen' and what 'has not entered the heart of man'" (Sinclair, 1987:170). The Christian has hope because of the resurrection.

God's kingdom is characterized by love, justice, freedom, peace, and hope. It has entered into the present bringing hope for the future. David Bosch writes of the salvation offered in the kingdom,

> Our concept of salvation must include both the personal spiritual aspect and also the social concrete aspect, and it must emphasize neither to the detriment of the other. We must reject a gospel that is ultimately spiritualized to such an extent that it does not touch reality, but also one that has been secularized to the point that there is no call to repentance and no relationship with God above (1987:184).

The Christian's view of the future and the salvation in the kingdom provides a unique motive for involvement in social transformation. The motive for Christians reflects who they are as they have been changed by the Lord, called by Him and serve as His disciples with hope, both in the present and for the future. As believers experience conversion, every dimension of life is changed giving freedom for them to become all that God intended. The excitement of the good news of this conversion provides the motivation for the incarnational witness wherever they are. A characteristic of their incarnational witness and ministry is that it is always other centered, that is, for the benefit of the other with a kingdom perspective.

CHRISTIAN SOCIAL
TRANSFORMATION PROCESS VALUES

Evangelical leaders clarified the move back to an integrated view of evangelism and social transformation in the Grand Rapids Report. In that report, two great concerns of the church are inextricably related. Their social ministries were described as a "consequence of evangelism," a "bridge to evangelism," and a "partner to evangelism." The processes of carrying out the Great Commission and the Great

Commandment do intertwine and contribute symbiotically with each other. With the worldview change that comes with conversion resulting from evangelism comes an openness to the transformation of all of a person's primary relationships. With compassionate ministries of mercy, the good news is demonstrated in such a way that a person is attracted to accept Christ as Lord. In many activities, both love is demonstrated and the message of good news is communicated.

Christian social transformation differs from secular relief and development in that it serves in an integrated, symbiotic relationship with other ministries of the church, including evangelism and church planting. The same Lord who commanded and demonstrated love for his neighbor also commanded and demonstrated his concern for men and women who were estranged from God or their neighbor, whatever these values might cost.

Additionally, Christian social transformation processes view and value both the person and the community in a different way from secular approaches. The men and women who are to benefit from these activities are among those for whom Christ died. The relationships in the process are expected to be characterized by the fruits of the Spirit: love, joy, peace, patience, kindness, faith, gentleness, goodness, and self-control.

Christians recognize the importance of the ways social transformation work is done. The demonstration of ethical behavior is as important, from a Christian perspective, as the teaching about it. Christians also see that the social transformation process carries powerful developmental or counter-developmental messages.

While many "surface level" methods or processes parallel secular development, other "deeper level" methods or process issues differ. Needs assessment, planning, funding, staffing, training, managing, evaluating, making reports, relating to other agencies, social groups, and political structures, coping with cultural and communicational differences and many other similar complex issues face both the secular person, as well as the Christian, in development. However, in the midst of the treatment of these issues comes a set of distinctive Christian processes or methods.

The concept of the incarnation (living among, within, sharing, reciprocating) distinguishes Christian social transformational processes from secular development. With an incarnational—context sensitive approach—Christians act with a different set of relational attitudes. They build and encourage others regardless of their culture. These attitudes include *respect* (for the divine authority, calling, and commission under which they serve, for the individual, family, community, and culture whom they serve), and *meekness* (on the part of the development worker—restrained pride, ethnocentrism, and insistence on one's own way).

Respect begins with a recognition of the divine authority under which one serves. The God-given mandates are accepted and sought to be fulfilled in the context of one's giftedness and commission.

Respect for the other person and the other person's culture also characterizes the Christian's approach. Respect for the other person facilitates both learning from that person and the building of a relationship of trust. Trust facilitates communication and change. The behaviors which characterize this respect include patience, kindness, gentleness, and goodness.

On the other hand, meekness on the part of the Christian is that restrained self-control which enables one to control his pride and potential misuse of power. Paul said Jesus did not "grasp," but rather humbled himself. Meekness is not the weak groveling of a slave, but the voluntary disciplined submission under the lordship of Christ to serve others. Moses was meek, but he was not weak. Jesus was meek, but He had full authority in heaven and on earth.

The incarnational approach demonstrates the essence of a contextualized Christian approach in social ministries. The obvious lessons provide much fruit for meditation: 1) one lives with the people, 2) the focus is always on the people with whom one is working and their benefit, not one's own, 3) one addresses the people where they are in their frame of reference, 4) the message is delivered prophetically (i.e., God's will is faithfully interpreted for that time and place). It will always have redemptive implications for all of one's key relationships, with God, with others and with the environment, 5) the messenger is at unity with the people and so learns and participates with them in their life processes, and 6) common development issues such as "needs" are experienced from "inside"; therefore, they are not insensitively projected.

An incarnational approach moves the person away from both an egocentric and an ethnocentric approach to a receptor centered approach which is mutually beneficial. The level and quality of participation can be expected to improve as one moves in an incarnational mode. Both motive and process then change for the Christian. Ward suggests five successive levels of participation: giving, helping, teaching, leading, and sharing (1979). The motive for each is honorable, but only a reciprocal sharing engages both parties in a non-dominating truly enduring developmental relationship. Each of the other levels results in some kind of inequality and risks oppressive behavior.

The Christian takes the context seriously in the process of development. By approaching the context incarnationally, the Christian "brings together the spoken message of hope, the compassionate actions of hope, the selfless service of the needy, and the Christian nurturing of the reborn" (Sinclair, 1987:173).

CHRISTIAN SOCIAL TRANSFORMATION GOALS

The goal of Christian social transformation differs sharply from self-serving secular goals. A primary goal is the reconciliation of the people to the living God. Certainly the physical, psychological and social needs are crucial, but the goal always moves beyond the immediate economic, social or political sphere into the spiritual sphere. The ministries of the church touch every aspect of a person's life. Each ministry of the church seeks to bring women and men into the kingdom of God and under the lordship of Jesus Christ. Entry into the kingdom brings responsibilities of obedient discipleship, which in turn not only reproduces obedient disciples, but disciples who demonstrate love for their neighbors. Bosch writes,

> The central aim of the Great Commission is making disciples, which includes simultaneously practicing love and righteousness, that is, upholding justice. The tendency to narrow mission down to personal, inward, spiritual, and heavenly concerns makes a travesty of the gospel; yet this tendency is not far from much of modern evangelism. In the minds of some foreign mission administrators, "the church exists for the purpose of worship, communion, spiritual growth and evangelistic witness . . . Preach the gospel, win the lost, and social ills will gradually vanish as the number of believers in society increases." But as we have seen, such interpretations distort the gospel. Falsely, such evangelism teaches that pious individuals who have a personal experience of Christ automatically get involved in changing society. Christ teaches otherwise! When he talks about making disciples, especially in Matthew's Gospel, he means commitment to both the King and his kingdom, to both righteousness and justice (1987:188).

The goal of Christian social transformation differs from some other commonly held goals such as economic growth, modernization, justice or westernization. While economic growth, justice, modernization all may be desirable, the goal moves beyond to what is affirmed in the Lausanne Documents and commanded in scripture.

The full inter-locking implications of both the Great Commandment and the Great Commission are to be affirmed in Christian social transformation.

While Christians will see intermediate goals such as improved economics, roads, water systems, social structures, and justice as deserving of their very best efforts and support, they will also see the issue of reconciliation with God as having eternal significance. Three kinds of relational goals distinguish a Christian's perspective: 1) relations with God, 2) relations with others, and 3) relations with the environment. Christians seek each of these sets of relationships to be "right," recognizing that a failure in any one affects the other two. The right relations with God begin from where the people are. Right relations with other people require attention to where people are culturally, socially, economically, politically and spiritually. Right relations with the environment require attention to the broad ecological situation. In every case the goals can only be achieved through a "contextualizing" process which begins with the context and moves toward the "ideal" as authoritatively revealed by God and interpreted in that context.

A developmental goal for Christians which relates both to the individual and to the community is the establishment, the re-establishment and/or the maintenance of "right relations" with others. Right relations with others facilitates not only one's own growth, but the development of others as well. Much attention is given in the scriptures to the matter of relations with others. Good relationships are not to be maintained at any cost, that is, at the cost of integrity or one's faith. But good relationships are a key element in our own development, as well as the development of others.

This relational goal includes the pursuit and living out of justice, mercy, and peace. It includes the employment of one's spiritual gifts in the context of the fruit of the Spirit for the benefit and good of the the other person in that person's context.

In western cultures, many have not given much attention to the stewardship or trusteeship of the environment. Our attitude and approach is often one of exploitation rather than with an attitude of a trustee. People have been given the environment to master. But we are not to destroy it. The cultural mandate initiated in Genesis (1:28–30), where God commanded Adam and Eve to subdue the environment, did not carry the implication to exploit it to the point of destruction. As the Old Testament law was given, several principles emerged which relate to the environment. "The earth is the Lord's"

(Psalm 24:1-2). The land was to be used, but cared for as an enduring trust (Leviticus 25:18-24; Numbers 36:7). Every seventh year it was to remain fallow in order to preserve it.

Whatever one's ministry or vocation as a Christian, the goal ought to be focused on the reconciliation of others with God (2 Corinthians 5:17; Matthew 28:10-20). This goal does not exclude, but rather includes, right relations with others. Part of maintaining our own right relationship with the Lord is obediently pursuing this goal with others. The process is not specified in scripture, but the goal is. The interactive nature of these relationships further clarifies the goal of Christian wholistic development. The wholism must not only be for the individual, but with others, God and the environment as well.

The *motivation, process,* and *goal* of evangelical Christian social transformation work all differ from the secular humanistic, capitalistic, socialist, or Marxist approaches in all of the key relationships. If the Christian worker is trained in any of these perspectives and accepts it uncritically, all three of these basic concerns will likely drift from the range of acceptable Christian motives, processes and/or goals. Thus, there is a danger in pursuing all of one's training in secular colleges, universities or government agencies whose values and worldview systems do not reflect a Christian perspective. Christian relief and development agencies should then be warned of this danger. Likewise, the recruitment of faculty from the secular sector, who have not seriously considered the distinctive Christian differences in social transformation, can quickly subvert the Christian message and purpose in a Christian college's, university's or seminary's social transformation instruction.

12

Issues in Contextualizing Christian Leadership Development

Edgar J. Elliston

Stephen J. Hoke

Samuel J. Voorhies

NONGODIA LIVES WITH HIS EXTENDED FAMILY at Loringilup. His influence extends among all of the widely scattered nomadic Turkana in his area. In his area more than 99 percent of the people are Turkanas. He was a traditional diviner (*emeron*) before his conversion. Since his conversion, he has been a key leader both in evangelism and in other forms of "lift" or social ministries in his area.

Ron has just moved into his new home in a housing development in metropolitan Los Angeles. He serves as the senior pastor of a church whose members come from twenty communities which together number more than a million in population. The communities served have a wide range of ethnic diversity. White midwestern immigrants, white "native" Californians, white Europeans from many countries, Black Americans, Hispanics from more than twenty different

EDGAR J. ELLISTON serves as assistant professor leadership selection and training in the School of World Mission at Fuller Theological Seminary. STEPHEN J. HOKE is president of LIFE Ministries, an evangelistic and church-planting mission agency working in Japan. SAMUEL J. VOORHIES has been involved in rural community development in Africa with World Vision International for more than seven years.

Spanish-speaking countries, Portuguese-speaking Brazilians, "American born" and "overseas born" Chinese, Indonesians, Iranians, Vietnamese, Thais, and Filipinos are only a few of the many communities. As he seeks to equip people to serve in this boiling cauldron of change, the simple training answers of the past will not suffice.

Nongodia's family is facing the trauma of moving from a stock-based economy into a money-based economy. Ron's family faces the questions of gangs, drugs and leveraged credit. Nongodia has seen the building of a road bring profound change into his area with regular bus service and consumer goods available within walking distance from his home. Ron has moved three times in the past five years to different cities, each with different ethnic mixes, economic bases, and dominant cultural patterns. Five years ago the area where Ron's house is built was undeveloped rolling hills. Now it is a city.

CONTEXTUAL CONCERNS

Ministry contexts are changing. Technology is affecting change in leadership patterns. In 1980, two hundred cities numbered one million. However, before the year A.D. 2000, more than five hundred cities will number more than a million. Family structures and other social structures are experiencing new pressures and shifting patterns. New economic structures, political structures and communication patterns continue to stretch the imaginations of us all. Missions and relief and development agencies used to focus on the traditional populations. Social ministries and evangelism are now shifting into the cities where now half of the world's population lives and where there is great opportunity, as well as much suffering.

The context where women and men exercise their influence is crucial. It affects their own development, influence potential, and the development of others as leaders of social and worldview change.

Christian leaders always emerge as leaders in a context. A person cannot be a leader without followers in a situation in which they interact. Contextual variables shape a person's status, roles, power bases, goals, worldview and the myriad of cultural forms which both the leader and followers simply take for granted. As the context changes, the leader must also change to remain in leadership. Or, on the other side of the picture, if one wants to develop leaders for these changing contexts, the development patterns must also change. To develop leaders effectively requires a continuing adjustment to many simultaneous change processes. Too often leadership development falls into the trap of institutionalized irrelevance.

CONTEXT AND CURRICULUM

Leadership development planners must look at a variety of issues and how they interact to design appropriate and effective curriculum. All of these issues interact in the processes of design and the implementation. Each one, as well as the distinctive balance of the whole, affects the results of the training program. These issues also influence the evaluation and the recycling decisions that feed back into the curriculum process.[1]

Many different issues relate to designing an appropriate curriculum for developing leaders, but for this chapter only twelve of these issues will be identified. These twelve show enough of the complexity to suggest the importance of working through these questions in the process of either new curriculum design and implementation or the process of curriculum improvement. One could begin with any one of these issues. However, in the process, any initial issue will likely have to be readdressed as the others come into balance. One cannot take one of these issues, treat it separately and then just go on to the next issue, because each of these issues interacts with the others. If one does not recognize this interaction, then the curriculum will not hold together, the curriculum will not be functional, and the desired results will probably not be produced. A poor choice in any one of the twelve issues will likely lead to dysfunctions both within the program and with the program leaders as they seek to lead.

To consider these issues, at least five different perspectives ought to be brought to bear on each one. Each of these perspectives will affect the design of the curriculum with the introduction of values options and constraints. If they are not considered, it will remain incomplete and may be inappropriate or dysfunctional. The twelve curricular issues include: purposes, needs, control, costs, delivery systems, content, selection of learners, timing, evaluation, selection of resources, spiritual formation, and evaluation.

FORMATIVE PERSPECTIVES

Five key perspectives provide bases from which to judge whether the curriculum is appropriately designed. Each of these five perspectives provide both latitude and constraint. The latitudes and constraints of these perspectives will not likely exactly correspond as each of the curricular issues is considered. Hence, the wide range of options which may be available from one perspective may be constrained by another perspective. The basic rule, then, is the range of options allowed by the combined constraints to meet the curricular issues. This is the place to begin.

Where these perspectives are applied cross-culturally, the combined constraints may occasionally offer very little leeway for action. At times some of these constraints may be the focus of the curriculum to bring change.

Perspectives to consider in the design of curriculum include: a) perspectives from the community to be served by the learner; b) perspectives from the learners themselves; c) perspectives from subject matter specialists; d) perspectives related to the psychology of learning and learning styles; e) perspectives from theological or philosophical value bases (see Tyler, 1949).

Community to Be Served

The community to be served provides a dynamic set of perspectives from its worldview and cultural forms. A wise communicator will continually focus his leading on the followers to fit within their perspectives.

The community to be served defines the status and roles of the workers and of the leaders. The job descriptions come from the community being served. One must then look at the work to be done in the community to be served from the community's perspective.

Jobs and Leader Types

Following a typology suggested by Donald A. McGavran (1969) and then later more fully tested and developed by Elliston (1976 and 1986), McKinney (1982), and Clinton (1984), five kinds of leaders are suggested. The present development of the typology comes from several related variables: expertise, sphere of influence, and nature of the influence process.

A Type I leader influences a small local group in a face to face context. His level of expertise is non-professional and may be limited to a given job. In a food-for-work program, for example, he would lead with one of the work crews. This kind of work is generally done as a volunteer.

A Type II leader influences on a somewhat wider scale among several small groups in a local context. His expertise is generally limited to a specific area, but he serves as a para-professional in that area. His influence is limited in comprehensiveness and extensiveness, but may be very great in terms of intensity with a limited number of followers. The influence continues to be direct or face to face. An example of a Type II leader in a food for work program might be one of the community elders who not only leads a local work crew, but who has helped a local project manager in the planning and in local organization. The intensity of the influence may be great, but the extent of the influence and the comprehensiveness of the influence would be limited. This kind of work is often as a volunteer, but the worker may begin to receive some part-time financial remuneration.

A Type III leader influences on a somewhat wider scale and is aware of how the local situation fits into a broader picture. He is moving into a semi-professional status/role with more experience and expertise. Often this person moves into this leadership role as a vocation or at least in a bi-vocational way. He may have had some specialized (either nonformal or formal) training for this role. One example in a food-for-work project might be a local project manager. His influence would be both direct and indirect in a local community. The intensity of influence remains high and is accompanied by a corresponding rise in both comprehensiveness and extensiveness.

A Type IV leader's role differs from a Type III in several ways. The influence becomes largely indirect. The expected level of expertise and training increases. The sphere of influence widens in terms of extensiveness (the number of people involved) and may increase in comprehensiveness (the domains in which he has the potential for influence). However the intensity of influence may tend to decrease except for a few close associates. His expertise has moved him to be considered as a professional. In a food-for-work program a Type IV leader would be a regional administrator responsible for planning and coordination across several districts or perhaps a national level leader.

A Type V leader moves in a wider sphere of influence on a national or international level. This kind of leader influences indirectly or organizationally through multiple levels. The extensiveness dimensions of his influence reaches its fullest potential for the organizational structure or for the community. The comprehensiveness of the influence tends to decline, as does the intensity, except for the "inner circle" of followers. He is considered a professional who influences professionals. This kind of leader contributes through forming ideas and broad administrative policy making. This kind of leader may be a teacher whose influence directly influences these Types IV and V leaders. In a food-for-work program, a Type V leader might be the international director of food-for-work programs in a relief and development agency who coordinates the procurement of food from other international agencies.

When one looks at the jobs to be done and the distribution of the people to fill these jobs, the importance of Types I and II workers leaps into prominence. Undoubtedly, we should focus more of our concern on Types I and II leaders because of growing commitment to the indigenization of our relief and development work and because of the disproportionately larger numbers of these leaders who are needed. Types I and II leaders suffer most from the cultural, economic, and educational dislocation which occur when removed from their cultural contexts. They generally should be trained as leaders in their contexts. Technical skills and theoretical bases might be taught in some "extracted" settings on the field which do not cause dislocation of these workers.

Most formal educational programs focus on Types III and IV leaders. They are crucial to the whole context, but they cannot replace Types I and II.

Type V leaders seldom need new institutions for their development. While they are important, our focus is more toward the leader with the direct influence. The number of these leaders is limited, and it would not be economically feasible for training institutions to design many programs for this kind of leader. Secondly, most of these men and women are already employed full time, so any training program would have to be a combination of nonformal and informal modes. It is unlikely that educational institutions could spring enough of these men and women loose from their heavy schedules to participate in formal programs. The specialized nature of the training programs which are needed frequently require agency-specific training.

One can identify some ambiguities in classifying the relief and development workers' jobs in this way. However, the general picture provides an overview of the different kinds of expertise (technical, interpersonal, administrative and conceptual) which are expected for each kind of leader. In terms of priority, one can see a high priority for each kind of worker, although the numbers of workers in each category differ markedly.

Ministries to Be Done

The task or ministry to be done provides a certain community perspective from which to view any related training. While one can identify a variety of jobs to be done, the evangelical relief and development worker has been given the same mandates as other Christians for his Christian walk. Both the Great Commission and the Great Commandment apply to the Christian relief and development worker as well. One is not given a choice of which to obey. Both are mandated with an expectation of fruitful obedience. The legitimate question which occurs is *how* to do both effectively and to equip for both. To effectively obey both commands requires a flexible balance of emphasis which recognizes the "logical" priority of evangelism, but which also recognizes the occasional "pragmatic" or "logistical" priority of relief and development. Neither excludes the other, but rather contributes both to the other's acceptance and growth.

One may chart the balance in the following diagram (see figure 7). The issues of the receptivity to the gospel, stage of acceptance of the gospel (see Soggard-Engel Scale), political hospitality, and the needs for development must all be considered in determining the balance. The balance may vary widely from country to country and even within a single country. However, neither concern can be omitted. Both must remain in a dynamic tension with each contributing to

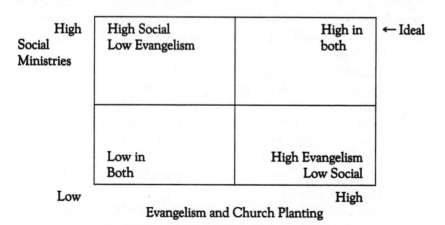

Figure 7: Projecting a Ministry Balance

the other. Ideally, one would seek to be high in both variables, but seldom can one begin that way or even end that way.

Both discipling and loving one's neighbor come under God's rule. Both domains are to be done in obedience to and controlled by our love for God. Our relationship with God is primary.

We often tend to dichotomize and polarize attitudes and actions when thinking about evangelism and social ministries. We emphasize either evangelism or social ministries. We may in a field situation be pressured to move more than is appropriate toward one or the other isolated extreme by the church, development agencies, the government, the community being served, and/or mission priorities and policies. In the past, local physical and economic needs and governmental pressures have frequently led to an ever larger emphasis/commitment to development because of the demands of growing institutions. On the other hand, some Christians, out of a deep concern for evangelism, have reacted against the older "social gospel" concerns and resisted any serious commitment to social or physical concerns.

We may see evangelism and social ministries as parallel and largely unrelated activities. Both may be valued, but attention and priority is given to only one or the other.

We may view one or the other as subservient to the other. For example, we may do development so that there will be "open doors." Or, we may do development while maintaining Christian values to establish a "Christian presence." Or, on the other side, we may do evangelism with the expectation that the new believers/churches will address physical and social issues at some later date without our leadership and/or participation. Non-Christian communities may see the "lift" that normally results from becoming a Christian and seek that lift before becoming a Christian.

Choices for budgeting (such as time, personnel, facilities, financial resources) may force less than an optimal balance.

A universal optimum balance cannot be described because of the wide range of local differences in terms of such issues as needs, political contexts, church contexts, economic, and social contexts.

Evangelism may be identified as social action (see Richardson, 1977:26–39) or social action may be identified as evangelism, as evidenced in many conciliar writings.

Evangelism and social ministries often appear in competitive, sequential, parallel, subversive, or even manipulative inter-relationships. All of these less than ideal relationships overlook or miss the potentials for positive interactions and relationships, which may result from a more wholistic approach to both evangelism and development.

Figure 7 can be used to *describe* the ratio of involvement between social ministries and evangelism. Some of the indicators of commitment in the balance include: time commitment, assignment of personnel, financial and material commitment. More conciliar churches who focus on social ministries only tend to cluster in the upper left sector of the chart. More fundamental churches who focus only on evangelism tend to cluster in the lower right sector of the chart. Churches which tend to focus only on their own needs, with little outward concern either in evangelism or social ministries, tend to cluster in the lower left sector of the chart. A single form or projected balance may be appropriate for one context, but it will not be appropriate for another.

Ideally, the balance would be moving toward the upper right sector of the chart where there would be a high involvement in social ministries and a high emphasis on evangelism. However, as the relevant contexts are considered—the immediate context of the projected development, the national context, and the context of the development agency/church—the ideal is seldom realized.

Figure 7 can be used to *project* an appropriate balance as the following factors are considered: a) values of the community to be served and of the agency, b) resources available, c) constraints such as political, economic, worldview, and religious, d) historical precedents, e) needs such as spiritual, physical, and social, f) receptivity to the gospel and to other change, and g) percentage of the people who are Christians.

One may chart the two emphases as in figure 7 with the two axes related to these two emphases. The ideal balance in any given situation would be the highest possible intersect of both variables. The reality of the immediate situation, however, conditions the balance. For example, if a person were working with an affluent middle class receptive population, the balance of effort should weigh heavily toward evangelism (at least initially) as seen in figure 8.

However, if one is working in a Muslim area with heavy restrictions, an appropriate balance may take quite a different form (see figure 9).

In both kinds of situations the context conditions the practical outworking of the mission. However, in both cases there ought to be efforts underway to raise the effectiveness of both evangelism and social ministries. In the affluent community, concerns for the poor

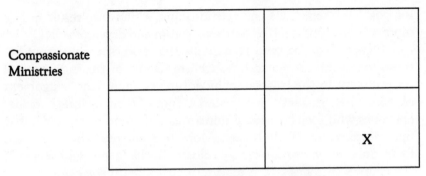

Compassionate
Ministries

Evangelistic Ministries

Figure 8: Balance in a Receptive Affluent Context

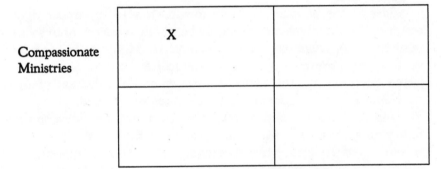

Compassionate
Ministries

Evangelistic Ministries

Figure 9: Balance in a Resistant Context

and issues of extending mercy for others, would certainly be a part of
the prophetic message. In the repressed context, the call to repentance and improved ways to persuasively proclaim the good news of
Jesus Christ would continue as a priority. In both contexts, some
activities would carry both kinds of messages, while other evangelistic
or development activities might not be appropriate either for a call to
repentance or a compassionate ministry.

Several variables should be included in the decision-making
process which aims at developing a dynamically appropriate balance.
The God-given mandates, both to disciple all the nations and to love
one's neighbor, require obedience. The contextual variables will include at least the following two sets of concerns: 1) "evangelistic"
variables—receptivity of the people to the gospel, the stage of

acceptance of the gospel, resources (people [including their gifted-ness and their use of spiritual power] and other resources), and the political and religious openness to conversion; and 2) social ministry variables—physical, social, psychological, spiritual, and economic conditions of the community being served, rate of social change, political restrictions and expectations, and resources available. While other issues will arise, these issues illustrate some of the issues which affect contextualizing decision-making.

The contextual balance among these variables is always in a state of change. Hence, the optimal balance between evangelism and so-cial ministries should remain in a state of dynamic support with the emphasis each of the factors capable of flexing to meet the changing situation. As people are converted, they will not only be able, but more willing to live out their good works to honor God and to demonstrate obedience. As these good works touch people, they may come to honor God by accepting Christ as Lord.

The Learners Themselves

Leadership developers must also be concerned about the learners themselves. Their skills, knowledge and attitudes, their hopes and aspirations, their levels of physical, social, and spiritual maturity, and their giftedness all provide bases on which to build or constraints for training and further development.

Several sets of variables emerge as one begins to think about who the workers are to be trained. Each set of variables may be used as a multiplying set for the other sets of variables. For example, we may have both insiders and outsiders who are Type III leaders.

Five sets of variables are described in this chapter. These five sets include the following: type of Leader, length of commitment, cul-tural/social proximity, "weekly" time commitment, and competency.

Types of Leaders

Five kinds of leaders were identified above. Each type of leader requires a different kind of training or equipping. The relative fre-quency distribution of these leaders ought to influence curricular decision-making.

One may begin to chart the distribution of these leaders on the basis of the number of people to which a person can effectively relate and influence. For the sake of simplicity and to suggest some guidelines for testing, the following table presents one such approach (see table 2). One basic assumption is that a given person has a limited potential for direct, frequent face-to-face influence at a worldwide level which may range between ten and twenty (see McGavran, 1969; Elliston, 1974; McKinney, 1982).

This distribution, while imperfect, does demonstrate the relative numbers of each kind of worker. The sheer numbers of people involved in Types I and II should capture our attention.

For the following table, the assumed size of the community to be served is one hundred thousand people.

The vast majority of relief and development workers needed are in Types I, II, and III. These people generally have the lowest entry level skills and knowledge, may be somewhat less motivated, are culturally within the context which are the focus of the development, and have the least accessibility to/from formal educational institutions (geographically, politically, economically, academically and/or socially). They are also the most unprepared for agencies to hire. They also lack the resources for training and are the least visible.

By "extracting" people from Types I and II to "change" or "develop" them toward Types III, IV, or V, several results emerge: 1) too many may be trained for those existing status/role positions, 2) the potential for local influence decreases, and a greater passivity often emerges locally along with a greater level of dependency, 3) the most able local leaders are "drained" from the local leadership, increasing the difficulty for the Types III, IV, and V leaders to influence locally,

Leaders who relate face to face with—	10 people	12 people	15 people	20 people
Number of leaders Required				
Type I	10,000	8333	6667	5000
Type II	1000	694	444	250
Type III	100	58	30	13
Type IV	10	5	2	1
Type V	1	0	0	0

TABLE 2: RELATIVE DISTRIBUTION OF
LEADER TYPES FOR A COMMUNITY OF 100,000
(Adapted from Elliston, 1987b:10)

4) the cost/benefit ratio investment of our training programs continues to be skewed in favor of the more highly trained people.

Matching the Trainee and the Training

What relationship exists between the "kind of development worker to be trained and the training program? Again and again designing of selecting training programs forces one to look at the learners. Their beginning and ending competencies and qualities provide the continuing focus in both the question of selecting among existing programs and developing a new training program. However, one cannot only look at the learner, but the program also comes under scrutiny.

Factors Affecting the Relief and Development Learners

Any educational context presents at least three variables which affect the learners. These variables may present consistent and complementary messages to the learners for his learning, or they may in both overt and covert ways present conflicting or contradictory messages. The covert messages are often the more persuasively powerful. These three variables include the content, the educational or training structure, and the learning process.

Naive training planners simplistically focus only on the information and skills the learner is expected to know and be able to do. The content and skill components of a given course certainly are important. They provide the bases on which the course will be developed and evaluated. They may also suggest some constraints for both the educational structure and the learning process which are used to communicate the content. While the content of a given course is an essential component, its impact on the effective functioning of the learner may well be less than the training structure and the process components. Think with me about the teacher who had the most impact in your life. My guess is that the reasons for the impact in your life went well beyond the content that the teacher taught. I would venture to suggest that the way the learning was structured, the process, and the personal interactions in the process also contributed significantly to what you learned. Yes, the information and skills are essential, but only one essential component is necessary.

The structure of the learning environment delivers powerful messages to the learner. A quick look at who really is in control, who makes the decisions, the ways the decisions are made, the expected formal and internal communicational patterns or procedures, the purpose or agenda of the people in control will either serve to confirm, contradict or confuse the instructional messages contained in the focus on the content and skills. For example, if in our curriculum content and skill development we teach relief and development workers the importance of participation in the community and teach small group skills to help develop participation, yet in our own training structure all of the decisions are made for them, they have no access to that structure and we do not engage them in participatory activities for their development, our structure belies what we are saying. We are saying one thing in our content and skill development, but denying its validity in our actions.

The truth of Jesus' statement may return to us as a blessing or a curse—"When a learner has been fully taught, he will be like his teacher" (Luke 6:40).

Some instructors in our training programs talk about the importance of the growth process. We lecture, test, read papers, and still remain inaccessible to our learners. We teach about the importance of a simple life style while we sleep and eat at the Premier Sheraton. We speak of spiritual formation and yet cannot testify of how the Lord specifically answered prayer for us today, yesterday, or even last year.

The process, procedures, or instructional method may contradict our stated goals. The method or process may carry as much or more information as the stated content. The impact of the method may neutralize the impact of the content or greatly enhance it.

When designing a curriculum, the designer must recognize that the structure, process and content all contribute to the learning messages and condition what is learned. The hidden curriculum in the structures and processes can either multiply the power of the teaching or subtly discredit and subvert it.

Matching Training and Leader Types

We have already identified various kinds of relief and development workers, a variety of educational modes, and their typical outcomes. What remains is the matching of the kinds of relief and development workers needed with these educational models. If the entry level knowledge, skills, attitudes, and spiritual maturity can be identified along with the exit competencies, then what remains is the design or selection of training models and their application.

For the sake of simplicity, let us look briefly at each of the five kinds of relief and development workers mentioned and project some values which may assist in both the selection and/or development of appropriate educational curricula. It should be noted that the planning of the training curricula relates only to the roles that the relief and development workers will be expected to fill in the communities they serve. A local school teacher, for example, may have a master's degree and years of experience in teaching and yet have little formal or nonformal training which would equip him for a relief and development role in a community resettlement program following a flood.

Type I

Skill needs—local, task-specific, and limited
Knowledge—recall and applicational
Spiritual Formation—Unquestioned commitment to Jesus Christ and personal growth, basic beginning ministry maturing
Competencies can be met by—a relatively high proportion of informal education; a moderate level of nonformal education; formal education may not be required or appropriate

Type II

Skill needs—multiple skills
Knowledge—limited ability to evaluate
Spiritual Formation—recognition and employment of spiritual gifts, recognition by others of spiritual authority
Competencies can be met by—continuing high level of informal education; increasing nonformal education on a paraprofessional level; introduction into some limited formal education

Type III

Skill needs—multiple skills at levels where he can teach these skills, able to administer, beginning to have some indirect ministry
Knowledge—local evaluation, wider awareness
Spiritual Formation—moving toward maturity
Competencies can be met by—consistent focus in informal education with an increase in reflection; a reduced focus in nonformal education; an increasing emphasis in formal education to provide the theoretical bases for explaining, predicting and local planning; often extracted from the work context geographically, socially and economically for training

Type IV

Skill needs—more administrative skills in indirect management, planning, organizing, problem solving, local organizational development

Knowledge—widely based, theoretical, able to evaluate from different perspectives

Spiritual Formation—experiencing the convergence of gifts, call, and the application of spiritual authority

Competencies can be met by—increasing informal education (personal growth contracting, imitation modeling, reading, personal research . . .); increasing nonformal education (conferences, workshops, seminars); decreasing formal education (degree programs will likely be completed)

Type V

Skill needs—definition of vision, motivation, administration at an indirect level

Knowledge—of the whole system, context, resources, processes at a level of analysis and evaluation

Spiritual Formation—experiencing the convergence of gifts, call, and the application of spiritual authority

Competencies can be met by—sharply increasing informal education (Apprenticeship and mentoring often become the key methods of instruction in which the emerging leader participates over what may be an extended period of time with his or her predecessor to "learn the ropes"); continuing nonformal education at a moderate level; almost no formal education

Each of the five basic kinds of relief and development workers requires a different mix of educational opportunities to develop in an optimally effective way. The balance varies for each kind of worker as one considers his career path and the context in which he will function.

Time Commitment

The time commitment of workers affects both the work to be done and the training design. Some workers may be expected to work part-time while doing other kinds of work, while others may commit themselves to full-time work.

Length of Commitment

The length of commitment workers make to the project makes a difference both in the training and in their attitudes on the field. The length of commitment also makes a significant difference as to the depth a relief and development worker can learn to function within the host culture with whom he has chosen to work. The time of training and/or orientation should be correlated with the length of commitment the relief and development worker makes.

Competency (Job Maturity)

Competency relating to the specific task at hand provides another perspective/variable for the development of curricula and instruction for relief and development workers. One may be highly competent in other areas, but when he is considered for the given job, the question of ability and motivation must again be raised.

Competency refers to the combination of skills, knowledge, personal traits, and motivation which enable a person to have the capacity to function in a particular situation.

A given type of leader may be highly competent for his present status and role, but would not necessarily be competent as a different type of leader. A Type IV leader, for example, would not necessarily be competent to carry out a Type II leader's functions or vice versa.

Subject Matter Specialists

The outside specialist not only knows the subject matter, but may, because of being an outsider, be able to bring fresh insight about relevant education in and for the context. The outsider generally has less entangling relationships which allow for more freedom of perspective. The outsider, however, may, because of a different cultural perspective, find it difficult to identify with the people of the local community or with the learners themselves.

Learning Styles

Learning styles like other cultural forms are learned/shared behaviors. Within a community, most people will share a similar set of learning styles. Ways of perception and learning styles differ as widely among cultures as do other cultural forms. Intercultural field training must be prepared to adjust accordingly.

Learning style differences between the learners and instructors or between the learners and communities to be served may create serious problems in terms of cultural distance in leadership.

The cultural or social distance of the learners or trainees from the host community significantly affects several key curricular issues such as purpose, content, perception of needs, timing, delivery system, teaching methods, control, and the like.

Hofstede (1980:42–63) suggests four ways to chart differences between cultures so that training programs for leaders and managers can be appropriate. These four scales could be described as *power distance, uncertainty avoidance, individualism-collectivism,* and *analytical-intuitive.*

Hofstede describes *power distance* as "the extent to which a society accepts that power in institutions and organizations is distributed unequally" (1980:45). In societies, for example, with a small power distance, inqualities are minimized; inter-dependence is recognized; subordinates and superiors in organizations tend to consider the others as "people like me." People in societies, however, with a large power distance tend to recognize inqualities in class relations; and people distributed in a hierarchy are seen as qualitatively unequal.

Hofstede describes *uncertainty avoidance* as

> the extent to which a society feels threatened by uncertain or ambiguous situations and tries to avoid these situations by providing greater career stability, establishing more formal rules, not tolerating deviant ideas and behaviors and believing in absolute truths and the attainment of expertise (1980:45).

People in cultures characterized as being weak in uncertainty avoidance would typically see life's uncertainties as normal and to be accepted; deviation is tolerated; aggressive or assertive behavior is frowned on; when rules cannot be kept, they should be changed; and, rules should be kept to a minimum. People in other societies, however, which have a strong uncertainty avoidance, tend to reduce ambiguities whenever possible; they are more assertive and aggressive; they develop more rules and ways to enforce the rules; and, they tend to work toward consensus.

Hofstede depicts the *individualism-collectivism* by writing, "Individualism implies a loosely knit social framework in which people are supposed to take care of themselves and their immediate families" (1980:42). People in collectivist societies base their identity in the group; extended families are valued and receive a person's loyalty. People in individualistic societies consider one's personal identity rather than one's family; family units tend to be nuclear only, and autonomy is valued.

The *analytical-intuitive* dimension is described by Hofstede as a "masculine-feminine" contrast. However, the issue is not really gender because it applies to a whole society. Rather, it takes a western gender stereotype to describe these cultural differences. In the intuitive (feminine) society, men tend to respond with more nurturing behaviors; there is less differentiation, but rather equality of gender roles; the quality of life is valued; and, interdependence is the ideal. People in analytical (masculine) cultures, on the other hand, see gender roles more clearly differentiated, with women being subservient. Independence, ambition, performance, and ostentatiousness are valued (see Hofstede, 1980:46, 49).

The cultural distance between the relief and development workers and the people with whom they are to serve will greatly affect their potential for effectiveness. Hofstede writes that for "managers who have to operate in an unfamiliar culture, training based on home-country theories is of very limited use and may do more harm than good" (1980:63). Contextualized developmental training which takes the local worldview and culture seriously provides the best hope for bridging the cultural differences for effective service.

Learning styles may also differ around the concept of *field independence vs. field dependence*. A recent study of African students showed 84 percent of those surveyed in both East and West Africa to be field dependent (Bowen, 1984). The following figures provide a quick reference to the differences in learner styles, appropriate teacher responses, and characteristics between field dependent and independent.

	Students who are Field Dependent	Students who are Field Independent
Techniques		
1. work alone	cannot do this well	prefer it
2. lecture only	not good	very good
3. film	good	OK, not needed
4. discussion	greatly needed	prefer not
5. small group task	greatly needed	really cannot stand it
6. use of story and outline	a must	only wants outline, but will sit for story
7. questioning/ discussion	do not expect them to do this well	can structure ideas quickly to answer questions

Figure 10: Learner Styles and Teacher Responses
(Adapted from Bowen, 1984:15)

Teacher Characteristics	Students who are Field Dependent	Students who are Field Independent
1. personal warmth	need	do not care
2. caring/friendly	need	do not care
3. supportive behavior	need	do not care
4. all business approach	scares them	prefer it
5. formal, organized/ logical/assertive	a must	prefer it
6. handouts/outlines	a must	prefer it

Figure 11: Examples of Instructional Practices

It is critical for the curriculum developers and instructors to understand what is being perceived. One may be understanding something very different from what is intended. Interpretation problems often exist. One might use words or phrases that are not directly translatable or have dual meanings.

Theological Perspectives

Christian workers serving in social ministries are no less accountable before God than other Christian workers such as pastors, teachers, or evangelists. Their overall mandates are the same. The biblical values by which pastors, evangelists, elders, or deacons are judged apply no less to Christian relief and development workers. They *ought* to, in fact, be "serving" in their vocations as part of the ministries of the church. Some key biblical values which apply to all Christian leaders apply equally to Christian relief and development workers.

1. Christian leaders should function as servants. They are to be evaluated primarily by the the criterion of the "servant" model of leadership as was lived and taught by Jesus and his apostles as the norm for Christian leaders.
2. Christian leaders should behave in ways which are beyond reproach in their communities.
3. Christian leaders should be distributed within the church with different persons "leading" according to the particular gift he may have, e.g., teaching, pastoring, showing hospitality, or one of the others.

Field Dependent	Field Independent
1. Display of physical and verbal expressions of approval and warmth	1. Formal student-teacher relationships
2. Use of personalized rewards	2. Instructional objectives; social atmosphere secondary
3. Teacher who gives guidance; makes purpose and main principles of lesson obvious	3. Teacher who encourages competition between students
4. Teacher who encourages learning through modeling	4. Teacher as consultant
5. Teacher who encourages cooperation and development of group feeling	5. Trial and error learning
6. Global aspects of concepts; clearly explained performance objectives	6. Details, facts and principles
7. Class discussion and interaction	7. Inductive learning and discovery approach
8. Intergroup interaction	8. Lecture and learning through discovery
9. Use of outline	9. Freedom to create own structure and/or outline; structure not necessary
10. Close supervision and direction	10. Distant supervision and less direction
11. Feedback to improve performance	11. Teacher as subject authority
12. Organization in order to aid performance; lack of organization hinders performance	12. Not dependent on feedback
13. Field experiences	13. Minimum amount of time in discussion; dislikes discussion

Figure 12: Preferences of Field-Dependent/Independent Students
(Adapted from Bowen, 1984:10)

4. Christian leaders should not base their leadership on their own rank, status, or power.
5. Christian leaders should contribute to the purpose, fulness, and functioning of the church.
6. Christian leaders should reproduce themselves through others, i.e., discipleship (Elliston, 1981:223–224).

When designing development curricula for relief and development workers, these criteria serve to guide in the selection of learners and curricula, the learning-serving stage of formal instruction, and the serving-learning stage following the formal learning. These six fundamental values only suggest much wider and deeper value bases in scripture. Biblical imperatives and clear instruction provide clear guidance for leadership values.

FUNDAMENTAL CURRICULAR ISSUES

Whenever an educational program is considered, some curricular value questions arise. These curricular issues are primarily *value* issues which are informed and constrained within the above perspectives. The journalistic questions of why, who, what, when, how, and where undergird the following expanded list of curricular issues. The addressing of these issues from the perspectives mentioned above is clearly for the purpose that the Christian worker may be fully equipped to serve appropriately and effectively in the context and ministries to which the Lord has led. The goal is to design and to implement a curriculum which is educationally, contextually, and theologically appropriate. The appropriateness is conditioned by the context which is to be served, by values which are brought to bear on the design and implementation both from scripture and from one's view of the people with whom he works.

Nongodia must be equipped to lead the nomadic Turkana Christians in ways which fit that community. Curricula which support Ron's further equipping, as well as the many "lay" leaders with whom he works, must similarly be adapted to the unique southern California context.

Contextualizing planners treat these issues from these major perspectives in each local context. They know that an educational model that fits in one context will not fit in another context. They recognize much of the dysfunctional leadership that is present in the church today can be traced back to inappropriate curriculum design, inappropriate curriculum implementation, or lack of evaluation and feedback into the whole curricula process.

None of these issues is difficult to understand. The complexity simply comes in the number of issues and the combination of the contributions or constraints of the perspectives that need to be brought to bear.

Purpose

The purpose issue answers the "why." Why is this curriculum being designed? What is the purpose that is to be served? A person who is designing curriculum should be able to finish the statement: "The purpose for this curriculum is . . . " The purpose may vary from one situation to the next. The purpose is the overall aim or the more generalized statement of *why* this curriculum is being designed. It is from the purpose that goals are derived and that more specific objectives which relate to behaviors may be derived.

Only when the purpose is clear can one determine whether or not it has been achieved. Without a clear purpose, clear goals cannot be established. Without clear goals, clear objectives cannot be established. Without clear objectives, the question of designing appropriate learning activities cannot be determined. The purpose gives the overall direction and guidance for the educational project.

Learner Needs

Effective training meets both the "felt needs" and "actual needs" of participants. It bridges from a point of contact with the learner related to their perceived need, to a future point of learning new knowledge, attitudes or skills. Given the diversity found in experience and community-relatedness, as well as the variance in education among new relief and development staff, accurate needs assessment will serve to pinpoint learners' questions and needs.

For example, many agencies hire young social workers in hopes of training them to be effective development assistance facilitators. They have a general understanding of a social approach to working with people, but may lack any practical experience in essential ethnological skills for working in communities, such as establishing relationships with leaders, identifying needs of the community, or planning development activities in a participatory manner. Rudimentary skill training must establish contact with what they do know and have experienced (the *known*), and help them develop additional skills in working with particular groups of people (the *unknown*).

Abraham Maslow's hierarchy of human needs is an example of a useful taxonomy for understanding human motivations in western culture, but may need serious revision before it can be used for analyzing the needs of learners in the Two Third's World. Self-directed learning has proven to be another useful educational approach for many adults in North America. However, regional and local cultural differences may dictate that "self-directed" means something very different in northeastern Brazil. For instruction to be effective in the Two-Thirds World, it must be rigorously adapted to the specific needs of the local learners.

Timing

Timing refers to several aspects related to the questions "when" and "how long." The educational program may be cyclical in terms of annual or multi-year cycles. It may have short cycles over a few days or weeks. It may not be cyclic at all. The timing needs to be looked at in terms of its relationship to the role of the learner. Is it preparatory? Is it recurrent? Or is it intermittent? Is it to be full-time, part-time or occasional? The question about "when" requires an answer. When should it be offered? When in the sequence of life's activities? When in the sequence of one's role development? When in terms of an annual cycle, a monthly cycle, the cycle of work, or a daily cycle? The timing simply requires attention.

Content

Content remains a critical component of the curriculum. What is the subject matter of the curriculum? Is it economics, appropriate technology, well drilling, or management? Content may be developed from several different perspectives. It may be *input* centered which is heavy in information. It may be *output* centered with a heavy emphasis in participation and function. It may be *context* centered. The content may be standardized, or it may be designed with the individual learner in mind. It may be academic or theoretical. It may be practical. Or, the content may not be in focus, but just serendipitous. This is what happens in the case of informal kinds of education where the content is not in focus as much as the relationship.

Delivery System

The delivery system responds to the "how" question. How will the instruction and related activities, planning, and evaluation be given to the learners? It is the system in which the student learns. Delivery systems exhibit wide variety. They may be based in an institution, in the local environment, or primarily around relationships. The delivery system may be isolated from the community, be very much involved in the community, or it may not focus on the community or its isolation, but rather upon a person. The delivery system may be unstructured or it may be rigid. It may be structured flexibly, or it may be structured in terms of life cycles or daily life experiences. The delivery system may be structured around teachers, around the learners, or around relationships. A person needs to describe what is important in the values that relate to the delivery system. A large part of the delivery system consists of the instructional or teaching methods.

Understanding and utilizing local knowledge systems in intercultural training is fundamental to contextualizing teaching methods. "Knowledge systems" include certain local culturally appropriate methods of retaining and transferring knowledge, such as storytelling. Storytelling is a primary characteristic in many African cultures. Instructors will be far more effective if they develop some storytelling as part of the presentation. A more effective method is to discover some local stories that illustrate a certain concept one wants to communicate. Researching literature about the culture, as well as books and stories written by local authors, is a way to discover these stories.

The understanding and use of a local knowledge system can also involve the way people communicate. In some sub-cultures in Kenya, verbosity is seen as a key characteristic to effective leadership. Whereas, in another sub-culture of the same country, the opposite is true. The effective leader is one who speaks little and listens much. Whenever possible, it is helpful to go to the location of the training event several days early to acclimate oneself to language accents, collect local stories, observe local communication patterns, and begin ascertaining appropriate group behavior.

In many Asian and African countries, communication is *indirect*, not *direct*. Westerners are known for their directness. We say what we mean and confront an issue, as well as confront the person. However, many Asians and Africans will avoid a confrontation at all costs, and will often approach an issue indirectly, perhaps alluding to it, but never mentioning it directly. It is critical to learn how to interpret their allusions as strong indicators, instead of expecting a direct outburst of their question or feelings about it.

This point cannot be over-emphasized. We may leave a training session thinking a person had no interest in the topic, when, in fact, he expressed a great deal of interest. This possible misperception can distort future encounters and contribute to both emotional and factual barriers to understanding.

Another area of local knowledge systems understanding is the emphasis often put on verbal, face-to-face communication, instead of written communication. In many African cultures, writing is not as important as face-to-face communication. In fact, some things, even in a training context, may be considered inappropriate to write. Feedback on the informal discussion that occurs over lunch may reveal how people are perceiving and understanding what the trainer is attempting to communicate.

Not only verbal teaching methods must be adapted to the context in which the training takes place; but, trainers must also be alert to possible needs in various settings for adapting media. Not all cultures are visually literate to the same degree, and not all training audiences understand the images in a given instructional video, for example. Using a local advisor is the best way to check for interfering meanings or images in instructional media.

One striking example of contextualizing media is Campus Crusade's creative use of a transportable voice encoder to assist in translation and accurate lip-sync dubbing of the *Jesus* film soundtrack into hundreds of different tribal dialects using local 'actors' who volunteered for the task.

Across Africa, AMREF (Africa Medical Relief and Emergency Foundation, known as the "Flying Doctors") has been highly successful in contextualizing the core of their "Community-Based Health Care Workshop" in many tribal cultures by using local stories and case studies, including proverbs, humor, and folk wisdom picked up in the villages in which they hold training sessions.

Control

The control of the curriculum in the design, in the implementation, in the evaluation, and in the implementation of decisions that are supported by the evaluation presents a set of crucial questions. One needs to ask, "Who is in control? Who should be in control? Is the control external as in a school? Is the control to come from within the community to be served or the community who is learning? Is the control to be hierarchical or more democratic or egalitarian? How is the issue of control to be addressed?"

Selection of Learners

The selection of the learners is a critical issue. The selection of the learners may well condition the outcomes of an educational program more than by what happens in the instructional process. One may approach the selection of students in several different ways to ensure appropriate selection for a given educational program. One may set entry requirements for students. They may be based on academic achievement, on age or experience, or they may be set on physical features such as height, or weight where the students are determined by entry requirements. Another way of looking at selection is to make the entry requirements determined by the clientele where those who are to be served will determine who is to learn. Another way to consider selection is not to base entry on certain predetermined requirements, but upon being in a context in relationship. The selection of learners is an important issue which is addressed in every training situation. Unless one knows who is going to be the learner, it is very difficult to design curriculum that will be appropriate for that person or for those people.

For formal educational programs to be successful, predetermined selection criteria is critical. Formal programs are highly structured and generally aimed at a particular goal. The educational processes and status and role relationships of instructors and learners are often highly structured. Students tend to face the same expectations in terms of content, assignments, and outcomes. Given this kind of structure, the selection processes should function to select a homogenous group of students who meet the pre-requisites.

For less homogenous goals or groups of learners, the process of selection will shift to the other curricular issues.

Costs

The issue of cost looks at another side of the "how" question. It must also be addressed when planning curriculum. A given educational program with an established delivery system, control structures, and content can be predicted to cost a certain amount. One may be constrained because of costs or resources to design a certain kind of curriculum. A curriculum may be resource intensive where the cost is less of an issue, such as a university. A university is resource intensive. There are laboratory facilities, library facilities, and a well-trained faculty. There may be a great deal of equipment, and many buildings. The resources that are brought to bear are many, and it must be considered as resource intensive. On the other hand, in another context, the curriculum may to be constrained because of values which say it should be resource saving. It should be labor intensive. It should not cost too much, but it should be appropriate for the context. If it costs too much, then the curriculum will have to be designed in another way.

Selection of Resources

The question about the selection of resources relates clearly to costs. This issue questions not only what resources are available, but what available resources ought to be used. One may think that is a strange question, but in the Two-Thirds World, resources are often available through funding agencies, through missions, or sometimes even through churches for educational programs, which in the long term perhaps should not be employed. Similarly, in many urban programs, the use of the "wrong" resources often seriously inhibits the long term development of the individuals, communities, and church. The same principle, however, applies in a local church. Some programs should be self-supporting. Resources can be applied to a situation which will be counter-productive for the development of that overall context. The resources may be brought to bear in ways that destroy resource development or could very much hamper resource development in that local context. So, not only the question of what resources are available, but which ones should be used needs to be addressed. This question would at least include facilities, personnel, money, and teaching materials, or all of the kinds of things that may be used in the structuring of the program.

Relevance

The question of relevance must be treated when curriculum is being designed. To whom is it to be relevant? Does it address children or adults, or is it to be non-age specific? Is it designed for the particular group of Christian relief and development workers who have clear distinguishing characteristics, status, or roles? Is it to be relevant to some specific situation designing particular skills and attitudes for that context, or is it to be more generalized and non-specific for the future? Is it relevant within the community to be served or to the educational planners? The question of relevance must be considered from early in the design.

Spiritual Formation

The internalization and development of basic Christian leadership values and other Christian values is not an automatic process, nor is it fully accomplished at baptism, at a recognition of one's "call" to ministry, at the time of one's entrance or even graduation from a theological training program. The formation of a Christian lifestyle and Christian leadership styles can not be assumed in a training program. Simply studying the content of the scriptures, theology, church history and/or other related subjects will not necessarily facilitate one's personal spiritual growth and formation.

Without a strongly formed spiritual base, spiritual authority will be missing. The overall influence for development may unfortunately be counter-productive to the purposes of the church.

Spiritual authority emerges as a person is formed or transformed to be the kind of person God desires! *Spiritual authority* is that God given right to exercise spiritual power to influence people toward God's purposes. A follower's allocation or attribution of spiritual authority to a leader and his recognition of this spiritual authority emerges from his recognition of God's working in and through the life of the leader.

Holland's model of learning goals (being, doing, and knowing, 1978:98) and his overall model of looking at theological education (input, reflection, experience and spiritual formation, 1978) both suggest that continual attention to spiritual formation is basic and essential to enabling Christian leaders to serve. His learning goals model suggests that the "being" domain is an essential part of the triad of goals.

All three modes (formal, nonformal and informal) of education should be brought to bear on this basic need of every Christian and, especially, every Christian leader. Since there are cognitive, affective, skill and spiritual domains to be addressed, integrated attention needs to be given to each. Formal or nonformal educational approaches may address the cognitive and skill aspects. However, nonformal and informal educational approaches which focus on relationships, those which incorporate supervision, observation and accountability over a period of time, and those which affect spiritual growth are also needed.

Spiritual formation and broader development in the community can be greatly enhanced by the developmental role of spiritual mentors or disciplers who are sensitive, not only to the spiritual needs of a person and community, but to the physical and social needs as well. It is interesting to note that the Greek word from which "equip" is translated in Ephesians 4:11-13 carries with it a sense of wholeness and "fitting into the context." One could readily point to Jesus or to the apostle Paul as examples of mentors who equipped people to fit into the context as part of an emphasis on character or spiritual formation.

While some spiritual formation issues are basic, especially for all Christian leaders in a given cultural context, some may require more attention than in another context.

Evaluation

Evaluation is that ongoing process which provides useful information for decision making. Evaluation is useful at every stage in the curriculum process: 1) in the design when objectives and goals are being set, 2) in the structuring when decisions about the delivery system, and, 3) in the implementation of resources. Evaluation is useful when looking at the process in terms of the way that the curriculum is being implemented in maintaining control and in observing what is happening. Evaluation is useful in the making of decisions for recycling and modification or continuance or termination. As the curriculum is planned, evaluation needs to be planned as a part of it. The results of evaluation feed in to the curriculum process at every point, and the curriculum process, on the other hand, should make allowance and plan for evaluation at each point.

One reason for initiating an evaluation is because of a discrepancy between the performance of the workers/leaders and the expectations others have for them. Often the goal of the evaluation is to inform the training decision makers.

Part of the problem of non-functioning leaders or dysfunctioning leaders may be traced to a training need. The training may have been inadequate or inappropriate. Or, the context may have changed so that additional training is needed.

The absence of the desired performance, however, may not be a training problem, but rather an administrative one. If the problem has administrative roots, additional training may not be helpful. In fact additional training may exacerbate the situation. Administrative changes may be required before the situation will improve. Performance discrepancies may also result from a motivational issue which discourages the workers and the community.

CONCLUSION

Designing appropriate and effective ways to intentionally develop leaders requires a continuing sensitivity to the context. The emerging leaders, the people they are expected to influence, and the situation in which they will work all bear on the design. If one were to consider the range of complexity that issues from this list of twelve issues and five perspectives, frustration and discouragement might occur. However, with an ongoing sensitivity to these issues, effective development programs can be designed. None will be perfect, yet the extent of the possibilities for effective equipping is beyond what most people imagine.

The beginning point is with the developer. This person must come to appreciate the insiders' point of view. The key theological term and pedagogical approach is "incarnational"; that is, to enter into the situation and work from within with and among the people being developed as a servant who does not grasp the "better ways" known in the past or in another place.

---

[1]*Curriculum* refers to the entire education process, not just written courses materials, books, or learning resources. Contextualizing the curricula does not refer simply to revising illustrations and translating the printed materials. It speaks to the necessity of rethinking and adapting the entire educational process.

13

Training Relief and Development Workers in the Two-Thirds World

Stephen J. Hoke

Samuel J. Voorhies

JACOB OKUWA WAS TWENTY-FIVE when he joined Vision of Mercy, a Christian agency focusing on small scale development projects in the Two-Thirds World. He had become a Christian in high school and majored in social work at the University of Nairobi. He decided in college to invest his life in Christian ministry among his own people. He had chosen an international agency only after lengthy discussion with his pastor about the limited options he would have working through his local church.

After one hurried week of orientation in the agency office in Nairobi, Jacob was thrust into the field, along with a co-worker, to "get a feel for the ministry." He visited eight communities in the first week, observed half a dozen projects, and began to see how the agency worked with people and carried out the ministry. He began to ask questions and to gain confidence in his ability to help the rural people. At the same time, Jacob was feeling some "culture shock" entering into the corporate culture of a Christian organization for the first time.

STEPHEN J. HOKE was associate director of field training for World Vision International 1985–1988. He is now president of LIFE Ministries, an evangelistic and church-planting mission agency working in Japan. SAMUEL J. VOORHIES has been involved in rural community development in Africa with World Vision International for more than seven years. During five of those years, he lived in Nairobi, Kenya, and traveled extensively across Africa.

Suddenly, Jacob was told by his supervisor that he would be given five communities the next week, and he should begin working with them. An emergency had arisen in the northern district, funding was held up on materials needed for a water scheme, and the staff were short-handed. Not only were staff unavailable to complete Jacob's training, but funds would not be available in this fiscal year to send Jacob for any practical training in how to enter a community, involve the community in planning, and project design or evaluation. Somewhat hesitantly, Jacob left the office on Thursday with butter-flies in his stomach and a sinking feeling of desperation.

"I thought I was going to get a three-month orientation," he told his wife that night, "and now I'm to administer five projects after only two weeks on the job. When will I get trained?"

Indeed! When will Jacob and his co-workers in Africa, Asia, and Latin America be trained adequately to engage in the highly sophisti-cated and complex task of Christian wholistic development? Increas-ingly, Christian workers from the Two-Thirds World are being hired to staff every level of personnel needs. To effectively equip these personnel, however, requires a sensitivity to learning styles and roles they are to have. They are being asked to function in organizations which are structured in "foreign" ways. As one is "trained" for roles whose sphere of influence is increasingly wider, cultural dislocation may occur along with other problems.

Too often, when the tyranny of the urgent, budget cutbacks, emergencies in other communities, and the everyday press of doing ministry descend simultaneously, energy and funds originally desig-nated for training are the first to be cut. The "tyranny of the emer-gency" often squeezes out the high priority of staff training. Training for the future is replaced by food supplies for poor communities today.

Nothing could be less developmental. Christian agencies en-gaged in relief and development must commit themselves to the strategic importance of staff training and development. A tremendous need exists for non-formal, practical training in human interaction with added managerial aspects. Community development staff must be growing and developing people themselves if they are to lead communities through the growth and change process.

PROCEDURES FOR TRAINING:
WHAT IS MOST IMPORTANT TO TALK ABOUT?

Certain essential dynamics of the training process cannot be omitted if effective training is to take place in a cross-cultural setting.

They are non-negotiable. Seven dynamics considered most crucial for effective training by Christian agencies should be considered briefly: based on needs not theory, experiential and action oriented, realistic and practical for the worker's tasks, biblically grounded, owned by and accountable to management, contextualized—compatible with the local context(s), and has a facilitative rather than an authoritarian teaching style.

Based on Needs, Not Theory

This principle is easily observable in the example of Jesus. He started with peoples' needs. He did not begin talking about issues he perceived to be the problem. He did not preach abstract theories to a generic audience. Rather, Jesus responded directly to people in terms of their self-disclosure about their own condition or situation. From the rich young man ("Why do you call me good?"), to Bartimaeus ("Go, your faith has healed you."), to the Samaritan woman at the well ("Go, call your husband and come back."), Jesus targeted his response of nurture, teaching, or healing to their point of need.

Development activity is often shaped by what the Christian agency is able to do or provide—rather than out of a specific analysis of the tasks that need to be done in participation with the community members. Too often, field training is the starting place for defining development work, rather than the other way around. The needs of the community and requirements for effective Christian development ministry should be the starting place for defining and planning development education. National development workers are the people most obviously caught in the crunch.

The first task is to determine the present circumstances and context in which the training strategy is to be planned. Although regional and international input are also important sources, this task will primarily include perspectives from the field about their particular situations answering the following questions:

1. What are both the *ideal* and *realistic* tasks of the development worker?
2. What are the strengths and weaknesses of staff as related to their tasks? How is performance measuring up against the job requirements? What "gaps" exist?
3. What training must be provided? Where? When? By whom?
4. What is the general academic and professional backgrounds of staff?
5. What are the particular country or cultural concerns?
6. What other training needs or problems are seen by the field?

Assessment of staff training needs should include both *quantitative* and *qualitative* measures. The quantitative will seek to answer such questions as: What gaps exist between task requirement and job performance? How many people evidence this/these needs? What different needs are there? How widespread is this need?

The qualitative concern will seek to describe the following questions: Where are the greatest needs? What are they? Can the staff meet the demands of the job? What training must be given?

Specific training needs can be assessed in a variety of ways including interviews of the worker or supervisor, direct observation of on-the-job performance, participatory group sessions, review of management plans for training, or survey questionnaires filled out by the workers themselves identifying those topics in which they most desire additional training. The list of ranked needs, however collected, should then be checked by management for accuracy and to affirm their commitment to training process. Integrating input on needs from several sources helps overcome the reaction or bias against gathered data by those who might otherwise disagree with it.

MAP International spends a lot of time talking with people at a place and time of their choosing. They listen for repetitive themes, and they listen for the people's sources of authority. What do they think they have control over, and what is controlled by an authority beyond themselves? An idea may sound good as a learning project, but if people believe they have no control over implementing the idea, then everyone is wasting time learning about it as a starting point. MAP has learned to start with something people, whether staff or community, believe they can control.

Richard Crespo, MAP's director of health training resources, illustrates the principle: "Find a common point of reference for talking about development" (Crespo, 1987:1). In one community, MAP staff started a conversation by using a story about another community's experience with a development project. Community members were then asked to compare their experience with that of the people in the story. People became so animated with the comparison that the MAP facilitators divided them up into small groups. The story about a similar community helped to establish a common point of reference. People began talking, and they wove into their conversation beliefs about what they could and could not change. This experience helped to define the learning and training tasks for the project (Crespo 1987:1).

Establishing learning objectives for training, in response to these identified needs, insures that instruction will be based on the needs of the participants. Need-based training thus avoids the trap of delivering inappropriate and theoretical content to expectant practitioners.

Experiential and Action-Oriented

How did Jesus teach? What approach to learning did he use? The answer is that he used a rich variety of styles. He lectured, told parables and stories, did miracles, and interpreted their meaning. He argued with those who could understand. He sent the disciples out in two's, and he told them how to begin. He employed many ways and many styles for many situations. Essentially, "Jesus taught by showing, and he asked them to learn by doing" (Meyers, 1987:16).

Effective field training uses active experience and learning activities. Action-oriented training gives everyone something to do all the time. Workshops focus on building skills which will make a difference on the job, not abstract discussions of theory removed from practice. Instructional exercises will cultivate attitudes, thinking and behaviors closely related to those required in their community tasks.

The Thai *khit-pen* (literally "to thing, to be") approach to functional literacy launched by the Thai Ministry of Education in 1970 and described by Srinivasan (1977:26–35), is a problem-centered curriculum focusing on problems of the learner's daily life. It includes critical thinking and problem-solving skills. The *khit-pen* man or woman is encouraged to be responsible for using human powers of analysis and reflection to get at the root causes of life's daily problems. "A man who has mastered the process of *khit-pen* will be able to approach problems in his daily life systematically" (1977:27).

A World Vision-sponsored one-week workshop on "Participatory Planning Processes" during 1983–1986 involved hands-on participation designing needs assessment techniques and planning strategies for use in communities. Typical activities included preparing one's own interview guides and using them to collect data during an actual project visit; constructing maps of project areas using locally available materials (grass, sticks, stones, and so forth); constructing nutrition charts with villagers using indigenous materials (corn kernels or beans to count children, animals, or amounts of food); using locally available materials to illustrate needs or teaching points (cutting up comic books to illustrate needs of youth). Varying the instructional time between individual reflection activities, as well as small and large group tasks, kept participants actively engaged in the learning process and modeled how they could involve community members in participatory planning activities.

Realistic and Practical for the Worker's Tasks

Students do not learn in the abstract or remote environment, but in the actual experiential context in which the knowledge must be applied. Samuel Rowan reminds us, "designing a sound professional training is broader than an institutional management question—extension or residence. The prior questions are: What constitutes a valid . . . education in Bogotá, Bombay, or rural Malawi? What does the student need to learn to know, to do, to be?" (Ward, 1972:3)

Good professional training requires a balance and blend among a variety of experiences. Achieving this balance makes effective training both an *art* and a *science*. Ted Ward's "Split-Rail-Fence Analogy" depicts the three major functions of a curriculum for training professionals (1972:6–11). The fence has three parts: the upper rail represents the cognitive input; the lower rail represents field experiences of the learner; and the fence posts represent the sharing experiences integrating knowledge with experience.

This analogy provides a helpful model for thinking about the field training of development professionals. *Cognitive input* includes the information that can be learned by reading, hearing, or looking and is provided through a wide variety of instructional modes: textbooks, assigned readings, lectures, recordings, films, videos, and programmed instruction. However, a curriculum that over-emphasizes cognitive input, Ward warns, "is likely to be characterized by high rates of drop-out and by frequent complaints about irrelevancy" (1972:8).

The Lower Rail: Field Experience provides the heart of the curriculum which books alone cannot provide. "Experiences of the practitioner's world thus become the sources of further knowledge, the motivation to learn, and the basis for evaluation, reconsideration, and planning" (1972:9). *The Fence Posts: Seminars* and other forms of

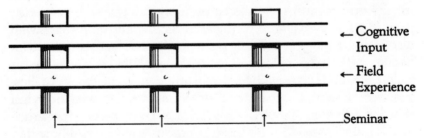

Figure 13: Split-Rail-Fence Analogy

sharing experiences provide the means for connecting the participant's cognitive input and his field experience. Ward observes:

> Something exciting happens when learners get together to put into *words* how new information relates to their doing an effective job . . . The seminar, as an opportunity for reflecting, evaluation and hypothesizing, can reduce the gaps and misapplications, resulting in more potent and responsible transfers from "theory" to "practice," and back again to better theory (1972:10).

Field experience spaced with interactive seminars help staff apply new principles and concepts to actual problems they are facing on the job. Participants in this kind of training immediately recognize the applicability of what they are learning relative to their local community, and they leave highly motivated to try it for themselves.

Educationally, we assume that the personal development of the individual development workers directly relates to their ability to facilitate change through their interaction with the community.

Development agencies have *task* purposes and *social* purposes. We must guard against the misconception that organizations exist purely to get things done. This purpose is only our work or *task* purpose. We also are responsible for helping meet human needs and achieve human goals.

Functional and consistent field training also facilitates the developmental needs of our staff to accomplish the *general* agency purposes. To be fully sensitive to the developmental needs of others in the communities, they must be growing persons themselves! Thus field training is not simply a problem of transmitting additional information nor informing the person of his particular responsibilities. The key is a change in values, attitudes, and ways of behaving so that individuals can creatively cope and make contributions in the varied situations in which they find themselves.

Two additional dynamics of Two-Thirds World nationals joining international organizations should be noted briefly. First, a natural clash can be expected between individual and corporate cultures when each operates from a different worldview. This clash also provides a potential "values shock" for which new staff should be prepared.

Western multi-national Christian organizations operating in the Two-Thirds World typically function and are organized in ways which are "foreign" to most locally-hired development workers. New staff orientation and subsequent training should explore ways in which western culture and worldviews influence the organization's structures, policies, and procedures. Biblical reflection could examine ways in which one's host culture either builds or inhibits the kingdom of God. We must continually examine ways that the organization's everyday procedures might inhibit effective development ministry in that host culture.

A second concern is to be sensitive to and to equip field workers for the different roles they will play within the organization and the surrounding communities. Careful attention must be given to helping national development workers function in multi-level international organizations. As a practical example, staff should be sensitized to and equipped for roles in which their sphere of influence is increasingly wider. When this occurs, cultural dislocation may occur. Almost all Christian agencies have, at one time or another, taken effective local facilitators and begun moving them forward and outward in ever-widening circles of international travel, speaking, and media exposure. In such instances, cultural issues of societal role and saving face must be considered when position changes might involve demotion, as well as promotion.

Effective field training will strive to make the content and process relevant to participants' back-home situation, whether that be in rural villages or in the central offices in urban centers. It will enable the worker to function more effectively in his practical everyday responsibilities. This is "appropriate education."

Biblically Grounded

Training for Christian development workers should be thoroughly grounded in Scripture. It is training that seeks to integrate new information and experience into a Christian worldview. Spiritual formation is an increasingly critical issue as described by Lynn Samaan's chapter in this volume.

First, "Christian" training means more than beginning each day's session with devotions and prayer. The Preacher of Proverbs expressed his worldview in this way: "The fear of the Lord is the beginning of knowledge . . . " (1:7a). Truly "Christian" training starts with God's Word, sees Scripture as the gateway to understanding, and is sourced or informed by God's Word.

Secondly, the revealed Word of God parallels and supports the general revelation of God available to us in creation. The same God is at once the Author of Scripture and the Creator of the universe. What is true about nature or mankind, as discovered through the sciences, will lend coherent support for whatever God's Word tells us about his creation and humanity. Scripture must inform our world-view.

Thus, when we begin development training with biblical reflection, we are attempting to discover new linkages and connection between God's story as revealed in Scripture, and God's story as it is being worked out in the communities of the poor. Our task is to interpret what God is doing around us and attempt to get involved with him. If Scripture reveals God's intentions for the poor, then biblical reflection becomes the laboratory in which to interpret what is happening and how to connect.

Third, training in basic Bible study, reflection, and interpretation must be part of any core curriculum in Christian development. Christian development workers should be people growing in their understanding and obedience to God's Word themselves if they are to be facilitators of change and transformation among the poor communities of the Two-Thirds World.

Modeling various approaches to Bible study along with providing time for biblical reflection also affirms the rich mosaic of diversity evident in our organizations and communities. One Christian agency in Brazil invited a young liberationist priest from the local Base Community to explain and teach how he lead Bible studies with his community. The young Protestant participants were at first amazed, and then thrilled to see the very same *dunamis* of the Spirit at work changing lives through exploration of the Word in Roman Catholic circles as they had experienced in their own evangelical circles.

Training *should* include devotional periods and individual or group Bible study. But more importantly, God's Word must be the referent for all we do, and the values of the kingdom of God must pervade all we think, say, and do as development workers. We recognize that even our instruction must be submitted to the authority of Scripture. In this way, training that begins with Scripture, seeks to discover the thread of what God is doing in the community and aims to equip staff to bring Jesus into the life of others in communities is field training that is biblically-grounded.

Owned by and Accountable to Management

Training is not a responsibility management can shift to outsiders or to a staff group without paying a price. Nor is it an operational area from which they can remain distant. While outside resources can be utilized, management must bear responsibility for the goals and outcome of training and support it intentionally and enthusiastically in order for it to be effective.

Management is also responsible in determining to what extent training will be linked to performance appraisals, staff evaluations, and supervision, and follow-up. Well-designed training workshops, dreamed up and delivered by well-meaning encourager-trainers, consistently fail to deliver the desired impact when supervisors do not follow up to evaluate the impact (if any) of training on actual job performance. Simply deciding before the training event that staff *will be evaluated* in certain skill areas at regular intervals following the event by their supervisors is a first step toward linking training to performance. The evaluations need not be formidable questionnaires, but could be done through on-the-job observation, informal interviews and discussions, self-reflection assignments, journaling, half-day reflection discussions with other training participants, or self-evaluations by the staff member.

From the perspective of project-level workers, two basic attitudes are present when evaluation takes place on a consistent basis. First, a mutual concern for effectiveness exists between management and staff and is nurtured by relationships of trust. If management only appears to be concerned with effectiveness and production, training will be perceived by staff as an enforcement tool. However, when management is able to communicate their commitment to the professional development of their staff as people worthy of continuing personal growth, then staff are more apt to respond favorably to training and be willing to submit their work to evaluation.

Also, managers must exhibit an openness to feedback and input from their own staff. When staff know their managers are willing to grow and change, and they see their supervisors attending training, then staff in turn will be more eager to grow and be willing to change as persons themselves.

Contextualized—Compatible with the Local Context(s)

Field training for relief and development sponsored by international organizations often, of necessity, takes place in contexts which are diverse geographically, culturally, religiously, economically, educationally, and socially. In such diverse contexts, serious questions exist as to what degree generalizations about teaching and learning can be made which apply across cultures. One thing is sure. This is the importance of understanding the local context(s) when planning and designing training which will be both effective and appropriate for field staff.

Contextualization will effect changes that will make training more relevant, meaningful, and understandable in other cultures. It attempts to make educational practice more appropriate to the receptor culture than exported western forms of instruction could ever be. Harvie Conn describes this kind of contextualization as "wrestling with the challenge of living as a Christian and sharing the gospel in different situations."[1]

Facilitative vs. Authoritarian Teaching Style

The final non-negotiable critical "given" to the nonformal training of relief and development workers is the person and attitude of the trainer as facilitator-encourager rather than authoritarian teacher. The "Jesus model" is again instructive for us at this point. Throughout the gospel accounts, Jesus appears as the master-discipler, totally committed to facilitating the growth and development of his disciples. He chose not to establish a school or to hold credit classes in an evening school. He chose a nonformal approach of instruction with those who possessed the change dynamic to bring about his "upside-down" kingdom.

The attitudes that the development facilitator takes into the community are essential. Two attitudes in particular are crucial: one's attitudes toward authority and toward control. Facilitators in the training environment must actually loosen control; they are not the only information givers. The learners should participate in every stage in the development process. The facilitators' task is to learn with them and from them. The learners are free to challenge, and the facilitators to challenge them.

A Christian leader does not operate from the same stance of authority as leaders in secular roles. Credibility and authority are gained by character and competence. The Christian's greatest authority, however, is the Word of God when applicable and presented with the Spirit of Christ.

One's self-perception and sense of security are also important emotional factors that must be considered. While it is necessary to establish credibility, promoting oneself in any way may become counter-productive. Personal security and self-confidence are also important in a cross-cultural training environment because accurate and understandable feedback is very difficult to obtain initially. The facilitator must be able to tolerate a high degree of ambiguity and operate in an environment of uncertainty. Reliable, accurate feedback is usually obtained only after much hard work in relationship-building, observation, and cultural understanding has taken place.

At the core, a facilitator is a co-learner . . . one who is willing to come alongside the learners and walk with them, talking, questioning, listening, reflecting, and encouraging. Spiritually empowered facilitators are a distinctive of Christian development training.

CHOICES

The trainer must consider a wide array of variables in the training process in instructional planning. These variables present themselves as *choices* or options that can be incorporated into the curriculum. Certain curricular options will prove to be more appropriate or effective in particular settings than others. They involve choices by those planning training. Six critical choices in curriculum development are outlined below.

Nonformal vs. Formal Approach

The training of relief and development workers falls somewhere in between *formal* education (a schooling process) and *informal* education (a socialization process). Such training includes a set of educational activities that are not a part of socialization, nor of schooling. That "other" sector of education has been called *nonformal education*.

Field training procedure must reflect this nonformal education concern for assisting people with change. Training people to fix motors or install light fixtures is one thing; it is quite another thing to train people to help others learn. Two keys to effective staff training help insure consistency between the training procedure used and the concept of nonformal education:

1. The spirit and focus of nonformal education is a concern for human development that must be clearly present in the process of staff training.

2. Consistency between the training procedure and field practice is required. Levine and Beeftu write: "If we learn a skill in a situation that is very similar to the way the skill will be used in the field, then there is a great likelihood that the skill will actually be put to uses in the field" (1987:11). Matching the training procedure with

the goal of nonformal education will strongly reinforce the very principles we are hoping to bring to the field. A synonym for nonformal education is "appropriate education," a kind of parallel to "appropriate technology."

Development training specialist Bryan Truman, formerly with World Vision, agrees:

> We're talking about an educational approach focused on adults, involving a new mode of operation called 'facilitation'—a non-directive process aimed at transforming values. This implies an attitude change within the facilitator (Ward and Truman, 1977:7).

> What we're talking about is a new approach to learning. Nonformal education as two aspects: first, a style of operation which we might call a facilitating approach to education. Second, it is an attitude about how adults learn. A far better term is 'development education' (Ward and Truman, 1977:8).

Ted Ward points out why choosing nonformal educational approaches for training development workers are important:

> The greater power for change is through the nonformal sector in a society. It inherently has a change dynamic to it. If you are concerned about processes of social change, and the potential of development in society, that is in the nonformal sector.
> You don't deliver development understandings by building schools. You do it by having workshops and training events, using church assemblies, and working with congregations, and you lift by helping people lift themselves. You use nonformal educational strategies. Second, you are concerned about the whole society. You are interested in what takes place in entire communities (1987:8).

Nonformal training events which are focused on the learners' needs will, of necessity, be highly participatory. However, participation in the learning process must start long before the event begins. Participation begins in the needs assessment phase as described above by feeding in participants' needs to planners. Participation continues as needs are clarified and ranked by participants to help focus training content on the most critical objectives. Active interaction during the learning event itself is the most visible form of learner participation, but not the only one.

Increasingly, in the Two-Thirds World, participants also want an opportunity to review and revise the objectives of planned learning events at the outset of the workshop. Early in any workshop schedule trainers must communicate to participants, "This is a collaborative event; there is still room for the agenda to be set participatively." Providing this kind of time provides an additional opportunity for all participants to insert and expand their values into the curriculum. Moving too quickly into the planned learning activities of a workshop may convey to participants the undesirable message that the content and process has been imposed from outside.

When dealing with adults, we must remember that they bring to the training situation existing knowledge, skills, and attitudes regarding the subject at hand, as well as ways of learning. This set of competencies requires us to consider, not only the goals we have for training, but also the goals and existing skills of the learner.

Learning is primarily active and involves the whole person— cognitive, affective, and behavioral. The adult learner can, and should, assume the more significant role in pursuing the educational process. The role and responsibility of the participants become more important in an intercultural learning context. If the training facilitators come from a different culture from participants, they must rely heavily upon them for basic indicators of effectiveness (culturally appropriate ways of asking questions, stimulating discussion, and ascertaining active participation and understanding, as well as styles of learning and group dynamics).

Three additional design considerations help keep field training more participative than passive, more functional than bookish. First, volunteering should be a continuous standard so the participants do not feel threatened or fearful.

A second guideline is used by MAP International: "Don't do for people what they can do for themselves—even if it means that the project (or training) will go slowly" (Crespo, 1987:2). In one community, people identified a need for training in veterinary care. The Mennonite Central Committee was recommended as a source for technical assistance. At first, MAP staff were expected to make the contact with MCC. Yet, when they reflected on the above guideline, MAP staff quickly realized that the community committee should write the request to MCC. In fact, the experience of writing the letter became a valuable learning task (Crespo, 1987:2).

Nonformal trainers continually need to turn over responsibilities in the training process to the learners themselves. This will insure that they are not creating a dependency in those staff they want most urgently to become self-directed and self-initiating actors in the development process.

Finally, nonformal field training must remain goal-directed at all times. The participatory and highly active nature of the learning activities should not detract from the goal of training for change. Nonformal training is intentional development education which, in its essence, is change-producing.

Flexible vs. School-Like

Nonformal education is "appropriate education" designed to be as flexible as the training situation requires. Unlike the traditional school where needs have been pre-determined, curriculum pre-set, and content pre-printed, the emphasis in field training may shift quickly, and it needs to adapt easily. Curriculum flexibility anticipates the need of planning to change the design content during the event itself as the needs of people change.

Extending field training into the community areas where staff are actually working, instead of extracting them from the communities in which they work, is wise. De-centralizing training efforts through mobile training workshops held onsite in local communities helps avoid the dangers of institutionalization.

The tendency toward institutionalization must be consciously resisted if field training efforts are to remain flexible and responsive to local needs. A promising nonformal development education curriculum was designed and implemented in Indonesia by a Christian agency in 1979. A two hectare site was leased for five years, and the underbrush was cleared for temporary bamboo structures to last only as long as the lease. But "what was good needed to be improved," and the intentional transience of the original designers was slowly replaced by permanent dwellings and structures in which to teach appropriate technology and development assistance theory and practice. Gradually, over a dozen resident faculty-facilitators moved in. The original flexibility and effectiveness was greatly reduced.

In Africa, on the other hand, Nairobi-based AMREF has been tremendously successful taking their "Community-Based Health Care" workshop to local churches, agencies and communities. They hold sessions in sanctuaries, offices, classrooms, and under the shade of village baobab trees. The training is shaped to fit the needs of the participants and may last from one hour to one week.

Developmentally Sequenced vs. Remedial Curriculum

Training may be viewed through two separate lenses, the remedial and the developmental. Through the *remedial lens*, we watch for a problem to surface which demands attention. As we focus attention on the problem and how it can best be remediated, we seek the best solution hoping the problem will disappear. If it dies, we turn our attention to another problem which may have arisen while we were focusing on the first one. Using health care as an example, the remedial approach is similar to putting a band-aid on a sore, with no thought as to how that sore might have been prevented or how we can avoid its happening again.

The *developmental lens* tends to focus more on people and how their lives can be enriched. Attention is directed more at enhancing the overall health of a person so that problems will not be as likely to arise. If problems do arise, however, they will be less serious. And, when problems surface, regardless of the seriousness, the person will be able to creatively discover means towards a resolution.

We have been doing an acceptable job at the remedial form of training (treating toothaches), but often little has been done of a developmental nature (total oral hygiene). As we become more developmental in our approach, the number of "toothaches" will be fewer and less severe.

Developmentally sequenced training will not only follow the natural progression of developmental tasks prescribed by the field worker's job, but it will also order learning activities in a manner which takes greatest advantage of the way in which adults learn. Ted Ward suggests a simple, three-mode model for structuring and sequencing development education activities (Ward, 1977):

1. *Reflect* activities: Reflection exercises are most helpful to begin adult learning because they help the learner pull together what they already know and have thought about a particular subject. This warms them up to the topic at hand with the often beneficial effect of surprising people with how much they already know about a subject. Essentially, reflection activities heighten the learner's sense of self-awareness.

2. *Detect* activities: During the second phase of a learning experience, learners are helped to discover or "detect" new information and meaning for themselves. A variety of different types of activities can be used which focus on learning new information and skills, or putting information together in new and more meaningful ways, such as lecture, discussion, games and simulations, forums, panels, question and answer, media starters, field trips, brainstorming, small groups problem-solving, and so on.

3. *Project* activities: Learners are helped to make specific applications to their lives from the general kinds of learnings gained. Learners

may be asked to think ahead of how the learning will apply, what changes they will need to make, what activities they will need to adjust or adapt, and to write synthetic guidelines or personal applications which project theoretical principles into future real-life situations.

One important caution in designing instruction is that every attempt be made to not plan more content or generate more information than can be talked through. The tendency is to over-structure and program with too much content. Developmentally sequenced training will be careful to block in open time in the schedule into which important issues can expand, and related issues which arise can be comfortably discussed without crowding an already jam-packed curriculum.

A related concern is to be sensitive to matters of pacing. Experience is the only guide for knowing when to keep things moving, yet being sensitive to the effect of fatigue on participants. Climatic conditions and environmental features of the training venue also influence pacing. Small, crowded rooms in tropical heat may make for animated discussions, but will tend to shorten the amount of time that participants can continue at that pace each day. More importantly, the educational and cultural backgrounds of participants may also heavily influence the speed at which they are accustomed to talking, discussing, dealing with matters of substance, and the level of abstraction in discussion.

To more clearly picture how to sequence staff training, the following three-phase model is proposed: *orientation* for new staff, *rudimentary* or basic *training* in development assistance, and graduate or *advanced professional courses*. A logical progression should exist in content and complexity as staff move through their field assignments.

The issue of credit or non-credit courses or workshops could be determined by each agency sponsoring such courses. An increasing number of North American-based institutions of Christian higher education have and are developing extension courses applicable to wholistic development, or have faculty members available to serve as faculty-facilitators for overseas workshops.[2]

Figure 14 depicts the aim of field training—to help staff progress through four levels of learning: from mere memory and understanding to personal application and transfer.

Simply put, developmentally sequenced field training offers the greatest promise of helping staff progress in developmentally appropriate ways parallel to their professional growth and experience. In addition, unless agencies can plan and implement training for their

	Level	Description
Agency System Issues	I. Memory	The learner can recall facts, definitions, procedures, actions and behaviors. He/she can identify, define and describe.
Structure	II. Understanding	The learner has a grasp of concepts, ideas, procedures and techniques. Can explain, compare and justify.
Biblical View Development Self-Awareness	III. Application	The learner can use the concepts, ideas, techniques, in standard situations. Can use or apply things in the prescribed way.
Personal Growth Problem Solving Cross-cultural Communication	IV. Transfer	From all the concepts, ideas, procedures and techniques learned, can select the one most appropriate to a new, non-standard situation. Can modify or create new theories, ideas, or tools or cope with unique situations where there are not standard answers.

Figure 14: Levels of Learning

own staffs that is thoroughly developmental in nature, they offer little hope that they can realistically assist poor communities with any knowledge or expertise that is biblically developmental. Consistency between training approaches and ministry programs is one vital indicator of a Christian development agency's maturity in development assistance.

Relational vs. Institutional

Field training must also focus on the relational dimension of development ministry, not merely the institutional demands and procedures. The ability to interact with people in a different culture and build significant relationships is not something that comes naturally to staff members. It must be learned. Several critical assumptions must be developed by the field development worker for this to succeed. First, a basic belief in the people's worth and potential is essential. Not only must the field worker recognize that community members can contribute something to their own development, but they must be willing to learn from them as well. They must be willing to place themself in a learning posture.

Whether expatriate or national, many field workers have a problem in overcoming the "quick-fix" technical view that they know everything and have all the answers. This attitude hinders developing a relationship that involves respect, interest, equality, and a willingness to learn.

Paulo Freire says the proper approach is a "horizontal relationship" between persons engaged in a "joint search" that occurs within a context that is "loving, humble, hopeful, trusting, and critical" (1973:45). According to Freire, a full understanding of one's situation must emerge for people to solve problems in their experience. This understanding can be realized through the process of *dialogue*.

A critical task of field training must be to equip staff to ask questions and stimulate dialogue with the community members among whom they work. The ability to ask appropriate questions at the right time and to demonstrate a genuine interest and acceptance are essential ingredients of the dialogue process. The natural result of this developed skill is a growing awareness of other's points of view and an increased understanding and appreciation of other cultures.

International Faculty-Facilitators vs. Using Only Outsiders

The Lake Wale's agencies identified at least three distinct advantages in using a variety of *international* faculty and facilitators in their events. *Inter*-national means a mix of local, regional and/or "outside" the region internationalists as resource persons.

Advantages of Outsiders

The first advantage is the "stretch" factor, where participants are exposed to resource specialists from outside their usual frame of reference, and who have skills and experience in other regions and countries. A greater potential exists for stretching their perspective, enlarging their skills, and extending their experiences vicariously.

Secondly, outsiders bring a richness of diversity. Hearing from faculty from other agencies, other countries, or who have been trained in other disciplines, enriches the experience of field workers. Diverse gifts, insights, approaches, and styles can help staff understand more of God's intentions for communities by modeling for them the range of resources God has provided for the task. Finally, hearing from and having to work with faculty from cultures outside one's own provides practice in accepting and adjusting to cultural differences. To the extent that the training process itself can present diversity and alternative approaches, the staff will be better equipped to accept and creatively handle diversity as they confront it in communities.

Faculty Selection Criteria

The *criteria* by which training agencies select prospective faculty-facilitators is crucial. Several important lessons have surfaced over the last few years of experience in holding mobile training workshops of one-, two-, and three-weeks duration. The facilitators must have 1) proven competence in at least one area of development assistance; 2) a breadth of international development experience to enhance flexibility in adapting to a particular audience; 3) sensitivity to change and be able to adapt. Experience shows that seminary lecturers, for example, will tend to lecture even in a local workshop; and 4) proven experience and skill in facilitating the learning process and feel comfortable in that role. Not every hands-on practitioner is an able facilitator of the discovery process with others. Similarly, not every facilitator is equally sophisticated in his understanding of what is going on in the teaching-learning process to be able to comment on it as it is taking place.

Therefore, if there is to be a "training the trainer" component to field training, the facilitator must be able to facilitate the learning of participants, but also to stand back and talk about what and why they are doing what they are doing.

Only resource people with shared Christian value commitments and a developing theology will be able to lead staff in the critical reflection and integration discussions that are so vital to evangelical "theologizing" on development among the poor. Experienced faculty who can pull disparate threads of reflection together from diverse discussion and help learners weave a coherent pattern of meaning for themselves, colored with fresh insights from personal experience and wisdom, are invaluable resources to the field training process.

MAP's Richard Crespo adds this observation on the importance of the facilitator in the development education process:

> The quality of relationship between the facilitator and the learners is more important than the techniques that a facilitator uses. And facilitators can use a variety of means for developing relationships. However, the more that relationships are established in accordance to traditional or indigenous means, the process will become more natural and effective (1987:3).

Two important steps are often neglected in selecting and using outside resource persons. The first is taking adequate time before the event to *orient* the outside faculty to the local setting, the lingo, policies, and procedures of the host agency. More than one expensive training session has been sabotaged by an incoming guest speaker who obviously had no working knowledge of the way in which the agency was conducting their ministry. The more exposure and experience faculty have with the agency's ministry, the greater will be their ability to relate to the nitty-gritty problems and hang-ups facing staff.

Debriefing Faculty

A final step in using international faculty is to plan adequate time for *debriefing* the training experience with them. They need this decompression and guided reflection as much as you do. They are given the chance to get their observations and evaluations off their chest while they are still vividly fresh. Faculty members have a chance to glean from their experience and wisdom additional insight about how to improve their training in the future. In case there were problems during the training, de-briefing in a spirit of love can serve as "damage control" for both parties.

Integrated Evaluation vs. Fragmented Review

There is more than one way to evaluate a training event. Tragically, some are not evaluated at all. Worse yet, management often makes fragmented critical reviews without adequate or accurate data. From mini-evaluation forms completed on every module during an event or evening discussions with participants or a steering committee, to a final evaluation questionnaire passed out at the conclusion of the workshop, gathering participant feedback on the usefulness of the training is a vital first step to measuring training effectiveness.

In addition to evaluating the crucial dimensions of every training event, evaluation should also be conducted for the entire training process. Only by tracking staff performance over time, in relation to training received, can management determine if training is helpful: Is it making a difference in the service provided? Only by measuring the impact of training can you link evaluative feedback into the follow-up process with supervisors or managers.

Evaluation is also important as a means of accountability—to staff, to management, to communities, and to constituents. Most significantly, evaluation provides a means for equipping staff for self-development and personal growth reflection. Linked to biblical principles of accountability and stewardship, encouraging periodic evaluation, or modeling consistent evaluation of all training, sends a message to staff that the agency takes personal growth and development seriously. Rather than imposing it from the top, management can model it from within by engaging in regular self-reflection and personal evaluation. Linking training to performance demands intentionally designing evaluation mechanisms into the training process.

DIFFERENCES FOR TRAINING BETWEEN RELIEF AND DEVELOPMENT WORKERS

Differences in training for relief and development are inherent in the nature of differences between the two tasks. The task job or goal of accomplishing relief is very different from that of development. For a broader description of training for relief, see Doug Millham's chapter entitled "Training for Relief in Development."

SUMMARY AND RECOMMENDATIONS

Training relief and development workers in the Two-Thirds World for Christian wholistic ministry is a complex task. Seven non-negotiable "givens" were discussed which are critical to training effectiveness. When training is carefully need-based, it tends to be functional, practical, and relevant to the workers' reality. When it is experiential and action-oriented, staff are equipped with knowledge, attitudes, and skills which make an immediate difference in communities. When it is biblically-grounded and contextualized, it opens the door to evangelism and to the lost and human development that only the Gospel can bring. This type of training operates best when it is owned by and accountable to field management and not left floating somewhere in the clouds of "nice to do" activities. Training for Christian ministry is most powerful when it incorporates a Holy Spirit-empowered, facilitative teaching style which encourages human growth and development, rather than an authoritarian style which relies on position and external authority.

Curriculum planners must make six crucial "choices" in designing development assistance education. A nonformal approach to field training is, at once, more flexible than the schooling approach and more developmentally appropriate to the task of equipping Christian men and women with understanding the community development assistance process. This type of training will be more people-centered and relational, and it will utilize a variety of local, regional, and international faculty-facilitators to stretch participants' awareness and skills. For on-going nonformal education to be the most effective, it must be integrally linked into the management planning process and be evaluated regularly to measure impact on staff performance.

Having described in some detail what is currently taking place around the world in field training among Christian relief and development agencies, there are several areas in which methods could be improved or new approaches taken. The following are *recommendations* for four crucial activities to improve field training of Christian relief and development workers.

More Thorough Preparation of Development Workers.

The preparatory orientation for new staff discussed above should set the primary values, develop the skills, and provide the needed understandings to begin to cope with the real world of ministry and provide the basic pattern for continued learning.

On-going field training must continually prepare staff for continuing change, development, and education. Unless field training develops the capacity to change one's skills and understanding to keep pace with contextual realities, education is faulty (Ward, 1987:200).

More Cooperation vs. Separation

Time is short, and resources are too limited for Christian relief and development agencies to not commit themselves to more rigorous and disciplined cooperation in implementing the training function.

There must be intentional cooperation between the community, churches, and agencies in the region for wholistic development to be truly effective. Closer cooperation would include networking human resources, sharing of facilities, coming together for prayer, needs assessment, and careful long-range planning. With the increasing stress on limited finances, likeminded evangelical agencies would do well to plan long-range regional training strategies which would broker key resource people, share curriculum and expertise, inform of patterns of training and evaluation, and make what were formerly one-organization training events into cooperative ventures among local partner churches, missions, and development agencies.

More Networking Among Trainers

Possibly, the central reason for lack of cooperative training efforts at the present time, is the lack of existing networks among persons responsible for training and an overarching commitment to cooperation among these churches and Christian agencies to share limited educational resources. If there is more of a will to cooperate, based on principle rather than contingency, there could be found a way!

Networking must be explored as a tool to assist in the following training tasks: 1) as a means of curriculum development: faculty and facilitators sharing instructional strategies that work, 2) as a tool for trainers in development education: intentional networking of national and regional technical resource people. This networking would speed both indigenization and the de-centralization process, 3) for cross-fertilization of trainers and technical specialists between fields, regions, and agencies/churches, and 4) as a tool for community organizing: equipping community workers with understandings and skills in networking a community to implement development.

More Effective Equipping for Evangelism

Most evangelical relief and development agencies prominently publicize their goals and efforts to evangelize unreached peoples while assisting that community's holistic development. Yet this evangelization remains the cutting-edge issue which demands the most prayer, research, and learning from one another in the decade ahead. Christian development efforts still struggle to keep evangelistic planning a vital component in their development activities. We know all about how evangelism and social responsibility are *partners*, how development can be a *bridge* for evangelism, and how social activity is a *consequence* of evangelism (LCWE/WEF 1983:21–24); but, we still have trouble implementing all we know.

The following suggestions may serve in a variety of contents. First, effective local practitioners of evangelism in development must be identified and incorporated in future training if our community development efforts are to remain in the forefront of Christian mission, especially in restricted access countries.

Second, national field staff should be considered "home missionaries" and better equipped with skills in personal evangelism, in people-group thinking, and in planning evangelistic planning strategies with communities and churches. They must be constantly equipped and encouraged to be lifestyle witnesses wherever they minister.

Third, field staff must be better equipped to serve as church growth and evangelistic consultants to pastors and church leaders with whom they work. They must be comfortable and knowledgeable to act as *resource linkers*—linking churches with resources to support and assist them in their nurturing and equipping tasks.

Finally, more careful attention needs to be given to the interrelationship between evangelistic outreach, church growth, and leadership training.

When Christian community development efforts reap increasing spiritual harvests among resistant peoples in the decade ahead, churches and agencies will desperately need a Holy Spirit-led, cooperative, research-based strategy for conserving the fruit of the harvest in a responsible way. In the spirit of the Lake Wales Consultations, may Christian agencies begin planning now for more effective cooperative training of their relief and development staff in the Two-Thirds World. If we expect God to move mightily, then we need to plan expectantly and realistically to set in place participative approaches to community-based, mobile training workshops.

---

[1]For a fuller description of how to approach contextualizing training see the chapter on contextualizing training by Elliston, Hoke and Voorhies.

[2]Asbury Theological Seminary, Azusa Pacific University, Biola University, Eastern College, Fuller Theological Seminary, Seattle Pacific University, and Trinity Evangelical Divinity School are but a few of the schools known to the authors who offer extension courses in Community Development or have faculty ready to teach in related areas.

14

Options for Training

Edgar J. Elliston

THE VARIETY OF KINDS OF JOBS to be done, competencies to be achieved, or kinds of relief and development workers to be developed suggest different educational approaches. Many developmental or educational approaches already exist both in agency and educational institutional training models.

Three different modes of education combine to provide a wide variety of specific training models. Each model approach to education carries both strengths and some inherent weaknesses. The weakness of a given mode may be minimized by combining elements of the other two modes.

The three modes of education include *formal, nonformal and informal education. Formal education* is associated with schools and schooling. It aims at certificates and diplomas. It has long learning cycles. Its strengths and/or weaknesses are seen in how one values the development of theory, inflexibility, relatively higher costs, long cycle programs, external control, limited local or immediate relevance, restricted accessibility, and largely pedagogically-based methods of instruction.

Nonformal or development education provides planned learning outside school contexts. Seminars, conferences, workshops, some apprenticeship models, and some extension models fit into this genre.

EDGAR J. ELLISTON serves as assistant professor of leadership selection and training in the school of World Mission at Fuller Theological Seminary. In that role he coordinates the Development Concentration.

Nonformal education (NFE) generally has shorter cycles of learning and is more contextually relevant than formal education. NFE generally costs less and can flex to meet the needs of the learners and their communities. It is often criticized for a lack of theory and equivalence to formal education. NFE leaders face the continuing pressure to formalize, institutionalize, regularize, and upgrade their programs to be more costly, less flexible, and often less relevant.

Informal education emerges from the less structured or unplanned interactions one has in social settings. Informal education provides the way one learns many of the most influential components of his life. Worldview, with its interpretative and projective perspectives, values, and languages, are all learned informally in our interactions with people. While unplanned by definition, informal education is always possible to facilitate. Its costs are generally not even considered. It is relevant to the immediate situation, and it builds values. It always supplements both formal and nonformal programs. However, it may either serve to affirm or discredit the other forms of education.

While the structuring of informal education will likely result in nonformal education by definition, if we are conscious of our influence, we can facilitate the direction and influence of much of the informal education in which we participate.

The three modes of education can be mixed with varying effects. An appropriate balance of these three modes can be projected for each kind of leader's training, if basic questions are answered about purpose, context, resources, control, content, values, and the like. The particular balance, then, can be worked out in a variety of appropriate and specific training models.

Each of the three modes of education tends to produce predictable outcomes—especially as the educational form moves toward the paradigmatic "ideal." One can predict that a person who completes a formal education program will tend to value hierarchical structures, theory, schooling types of institutions, and a pedagogical approach to education. He will expect to have little voice in the control of the educational process and will accept the high cost. The person whose education has included a significant influence from nonformal education will likely favor more functional learning, which is delivered in shorter cycles, at a lower cost, and at a place and time which are accessible to the most suitable learners. He will expect an education to be more change-oriented. The learner will expect a higher level of participation in decision-making.

The person whose education has come primarily through an informal mode will likely be closely tied into the local traditions and culture, but he may not be able to explain the "why" of his position. Knowledge, skills, and attitudes will fit the social structure of which he is a part. These principles would fit either a person in a "traditional" society who has not been to school or a person in a complex society who has been to school and entered a vocational situation in which the "organizational culture" was not taught in a planned way, but through informal relational serendipitous ways.

When one begins to think of training options for relief and development workers, both the number and diversity of the programs may overwhelm even the most expectant person. We have seen from the previous Lake Wales research report prepared by Doug Millham that many Christian colleges, universities, and seminaries in the U. S. teach relief and development courses. Additionally, virtually every relief and development agency has planned training programs for their staff and for the communities they serve in their field operations. Not only do most relief and development agencies and Christian institutions of higher learning offer training, but so do a number of larger missions. Outside of the Christian community, universities and secular agencies offer a much wider range of relief and development training opportunities. Often, however, their value base is questionable.

With the bewildering array of options ranging from a Ph.D. in the sociology of development at Cornell University to a two-day workshop in Nakuru, Kenya to a three-year apprenticeship in Cochabamba, Bolivia, we are faced with both the confusing plethora of options and the gnawing fear that maybe none of the options fits our specific need.

How can we look at the training options in a way which will allow us to explain what they are and what they do, and predict their outcomes and determine whether they fit our needs or not?

Three paradigmatic categories serve first, to classify these programs and then, to predict their outcomes: formal, nonformal, and informal. When each is described as a paradigmatic form (theoretical model), the contrasts related to purpose, costs, control, results, deliver system, timing, and so on, clearly emerge. Those contrasts emerge in figure 15. Many educational institutions, relief and development agencies, and missions have recognized that often, any one of these three basic educational approaches by itself is either inadequate, inappropriate, irrelevant, too costly, counter-developmental, or just plainly dysfunctional. Others have recognized that the dysfunctions of one mode can be treated by a balance with the other two modes. The establishing of an appropriate balance, however, is like any issue of balance. It must be contextually conditioned. Whether one speaks of the balancing of a tight rope walker or an ecological balance in a Vermont lake. The context determines the appropriate conditions, criteria, and behaviors.

RELATIONSHIPS AMONG THE THREE MODES OF EDUCATION

Now let us look briefly at these three educational modes to see their typical characteristics and their relative strengths and weaknesses. Simkins (1977) has provided a basic framework for contrasting formal education and nonformal education. I have modified his description somewhat and added the contrastive characteristics of informal education.

The following figure suggests both contrasts and commonalities among these three modes of education. Each mode may be paired with another and then contrasted with the other one. Informal and formal education both tend to be stabilizing. Informal education is stabilizing in terms of relationships, while formal education is stabilizing in terms of institutionalization. Both contrast with nonformal education, which tends to be change oriented. Nonformal and informal education both tend to be functional, whereas formal education tends to be theoretical. Formal and nonformal education are both deliberate or planned, whereas informal education is not planned or deliberately structured. The paradigmatic model of any of the three may not be ideal for a given learning situation. In most cases some balance is desirable. A balanced approach, which draws on the strengths of each mode, can be contextually developed. In a given context, a variety of forms which draw on each of the paradigmatic models is likely to provide the optimum learning experiences (see Elliston, 1986:15).

The wise educator or relief and development worker will immediately see several implications of these descriptions:
1. Any one of the basic modes is, by itself, inadequate in the overall picture.
2. A balance among the three modes is needed to take advantage of the strengths of each one and to compensate for the weaknesses accompanying the other two.
3. Given a certain kind of relief and development worker for an educational program, in order to be optimally effective, the balance

Formal	Nonformal	Informal
	PURPOSES	
Long-term and general	Short-term and specific	Immediate and Specific
Credential Based	Noncredential Based	Life task related
	TIMING	
Long cycle	Short cycle	Noncyclic, continuous
Preparatory	Recurrent	Intermittent
Full-time	Part-time	Occasional
	CONTENT	
Shows sequence, continuity and integration over multiple units	Shows sequence continuity and integration over single units	Nonsequential, no continuity, not integrated
Input centered	Output centered	Context centered
Standardized	Individualized	Individualized
Academic	Practical	Serendipitous
	DELIVERY SYSTEM	
Institution based	Environment based	Relationship based
Isolated	Community related	Person related
Rigidly structured	Flexibly structured	Structured within daily life experiences
Teacher centered	Learner centered	Interpersonal centered
	CONTROL	
Externally controlled	Self-governing	Not controlled
Hierarchical	Democratic	Egalitarian
	SELECTION	
Clientele determined by entry requirements	Entry requirements determined by clientele	Entry based on relationships, not academic achievement
	COSTS	
Resource intensive	Resource saving	Resource saving—often resources not used
	RELEVANCE	
Relevant to generalized nonspecific future situations	Relevant to immediate context	May or may not be relevant
Child oriented	Adult oriented	Nonage specific

Figure 15: Comparison of Forms of Education
(see Simkins, 1977; Elliston, 1986:12–14)

Formal	Nonformal	Informal
ADVANTAGES		
Generalized futuristic preparation	Specific present preparation	May focus on specific and immediate needs
Develops institutions involved	Develops both communities and individuals involved	Develops relationships
Provides theoretical base	Provides experiential base	Provides relational base
Accredited by outsiders	Accredited by insiders	Not accredited
	Low cost	No or low cost
LIMITATIONS		
May be culturally economically and educationally dislocative; expensive in finances, personnel, time, material; may be immediately irrelevant	May lack theoretical base; may not be relevant in a different situation. Learning time for comparable content and skills may be longer than formal approach	Difficult to assure learning of specified content, skills or attitudes. Accountability difficult to include

Figure 15: Comparison of Forms of Education
(Continued)

of the three modes of education have to be tailored for that worker and for the context in which he works.

4. Before a balance can be established for a given situation, several questions must be answered. These include questions about the purpose, resources available, who the learners are to be, where and what is the context in which they will work, the timing in terms of the length of the total learning cycle, in terms of the learners' career paths, and in terms of the daily, weekly, monthly, or annual living or work cycles.

5. Given the changing and diverse world in which we live, any "balanced model" developed in one time and place will need to be re-cycled whenever the applicational context changes. Over a period of time, a program will have to change in the same place. Also, whenever transplanted to a new place, the educational program should adjust accordingly.

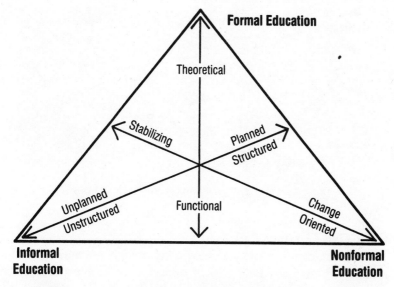

Figure 16: Contrasting the Three Modes of Education

CURRICULAR COMPONENTS

Fred Holland, drawing on the thinking of Ted Ward and Sam Rowan, has given us another model which may help us see four important curricular components for the development of relief and development workers. Each of these four component parts interactively contributes to the other three and to the overall learning or development of the individual (see figure 17). The figure is obviously based on Ward's and Rowan's Split Rail Fence Analogy, but adds to it the dimension of spiritual formation (see Holland, 1978).

The parts of the analogy include the following elements:

1. *Rail #1: Input*
   The relief and development worker certainly needs the cognitive input or informational base on which to begin to work. One can identify many things that the relief and development worker needs to know.

2. *Rail #2: Ministry Experience*
   The relief and development worker needs to have experience, in order to address the matter of skill development. The experience provides a referent for his learning, as well as a strong motivational base.

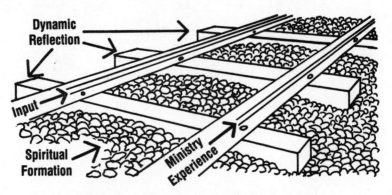

Figure 17: Holland's Two-Track Analogy

3. *Cross-Ties: Dynamic Reflection*
The dynamic reflection enables the integration between the informational base and the ministry experience. The process of the reflection stimulates, not only application, but evaluation as well.

4. *Roadbed: Spiritual Formation*
The spiritual formation serves as the base on which all else rests. The spiritual formation provides the value, worldview, and being base, both for the learning and ministry. The insistence on the establishment of a strong spiritual formation base provides one of the key distinctives of the Christian relief and development worker. Beginning from a different value base, the other functions of the inputs, dynamic reflection, and field experience will all be received, perceived, and acted upon differently.

Holland's Two-Track Analogy facilitates our considering the balance among these four essential elements. If any one of the four is missing or over-emphasized, the whole enterprise will suffer. Without the information, the worker will flounder. Without the experience, the theory and information will seem irrelevant. Without the reflection, the learning of the new information may not be applied in an optimal way to the ministry. Finally, without a dynamically growing spiritual base, the whole lifestyle, ethics, values, and direction of the enterprise will likely go awry.

Summary
The appropriate training model for a given relief and development worker should be selected (or developed) on the bases of the following concerns:
1. The purpose of the task to be done.

2. The people who are expected to be the workers (learners).
3. A balance of the three modes of education, as it fits the context, resources, and value bases, should be established.
4. A balance among the inputs, experience, dynamic reflection, and field experience is essential.

CAREER PATHS

One must look at the modes of education and curricular components in the light of the career path of the learner. One can argue for the individuality of a given career path, but as is the case for most human behavior, career paths follow observable patterns. Curricula can be tailored to fit these patterns.

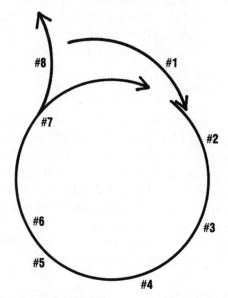

1. Entry into career training
2. Beginning orientation and work in career track
3. Completion of initial orientation on field
4. Full responsibility assumed
5. Achieved skill proficiency—reached growth plateau
6. Begun continuing education for improving work skills
7. Decision to continue in same job—job stability
8. Re-tooling for new job

Figure 18: Career Path

The kind of training which is appropriate for a given relief and development worker depends on where he is on his career path. One's place on the career path will condition decisions related to the basic modal approach as well as the specific issues of purpose, delivery system, timing, content, control, and costs.

A career path may be viewed as a cyclical process with an optional exit (see figure 18). One's career may simply make one life-long pass through the cycle without changing jobs. More commonly re-cycling occurs with a progression through a series of jobs and their re-training cycles.

One can relate training to the various stages along the career path. Each of these kinds of training may have a somewhat different mix of formal, nonformal, or informal education as the purpose for the training differs. The various stages of the career path may also be described in terms of their relationship to the service. The education at these different stages may be classified as pre-service, in-service, interrupted service, or a-service education.

Pre-Service Education

Before entry into a specific relief and development career, a candidate is expected to have completed the minimal requirements for that particular career path. If one considers a Type I leader or relief and development worker, that pre-service education may be as minimal as being a functional enculturated adult in a local community with no formal requirements. Or, the requirement may require such a narrow and highly trained speciality as an orthopedic surgeon to work in a hospital surgical department. The competency required will condition the pre-service training models.

In-Service Education

In-service education generally focuses on skill improvement and keeping the worker current, both with advances in knowledge and techniques. In-service education may also focus on attitude development and motivation.

Since in-service training occurs while the worker is employed, it faces time, delivery system, purpose, and other constraints. The worker cannot leave work for any extended period, so the delivery system and timing have to be adjusted to fit. Often the training focuses on a specific issue; therefore, a given training cycle is likely to be relatively brief. Nonformal education generally serves as the dominant mode of in-service education.

In-service education nearly always has a large informal training component. If this mode is brought into focus and its educational power recognized, it can greatly facilitate learning.

Formal education may also play an important role. However, the courses one would take as in-service studies are often scheduled outside the normal work hours. The learning cycles may be extended with few courses being taken. Or, what would normally be a "formal" course in an educational institution, takes on the function of a nonformal course in which the learner or the community he serves decides on the "courses" to take, the time to take them, and is generally less concerned about a certificate. Educational institutions frequently design these kinds of courses with the in-service learner in mind.

Interrupted Service Education

With interrupted service education, a person breaks into his career to pursue further training. This kind of training frequently focuses on formal education in which a full time concentrated effort can be directed toward a specific learning goal. Very often this kind of interrupted service education marks a transition time along the career path.

The attention given to informal education and nonformal education in this kind of education is generally notably less than in the pre- or in-service education. While the informal education may not be in focus, it may be the more important and the more powerful in its influence. As the person is looking for a change in his career path, the modeling of the leaders or teachers to whom the learner is giving attention will have a powerful effect.

A-Service Education

Some educational experiences simply do not correlate with stages along one's career path. They may be either directly related or may only indirectly relate to the job at hand. These kinds of training may fit in any of the three basic modes.

One's interest in a hobby or an unrelated career, for example, may motivate the learning of wide bodies of knowledge, developing highly technical skills, or developing a significant shift in one's values and worldview. Any one of these kinds of learning will likely impinge on one's job performance in his career.

TYPICAL TRAINING MODELS

Each of the educational modes presents a range of training options, and within any given effective model, one is likely to find some elements of each of these modes. Effectiveness almost demands that each of the modes be brought into a balance for the given context, learners, purpose, and other variables.

One can chart formal, nonformal, and informal education in another way which may help one understand his relationships. If one considers educational programs on the basis of structure, it may be possible to see them on a single continuum, with formal education at one extreme and informal at the other, and nonformal education in-between with indiscrete boundaries.

Formal Models

Schools, institutes, colleges, universities, and seminaries offer a wide variety of formal training models. In some cases, individual relief and development courses are simply isolated elective courses which fit into a diploma or degree program. Often, with these courses, the field experience component is limited. However, some institutions have well-integrated programs which include either on-site intern programs or simulations to supplement the classroom teaching. Wheaton's HNGR Program and Warner Southern's HEART Program fit into this genre. Both programs fit into a degree-based curriculum.

Formal training models are among the easiest to identify because they are tied to established institutions. They are nearly always aimed at certificates, diplomas, or degrees. The time commitment often stretches over several years. While some flexibility may be present in terms of the scheduling and the place of learning, the sponsoring institution controls the curriculum by deciding the content, contact hours, class format, learning experiences, evaluation, location, and the like.

Figure 19: Formal-Nonformal-Informal Continuum

Nonformal Models

Relief and development agencies, missions, churches, and occasionally, educational institutions offer nonformal education models. These models are typically shorter cycle and not certificate- or degree-based. Seminars, conferences, and workshops typically fall within this genre. Such training programs as offered by Missionary Internship and Food for the Hungry's Rancho La Argentina in Mexico fit this genre. These programs may stretch over a few days or several months. On-site workshops and seminars conducted by scores of agencies and churches are nearly always nonformal.

These nonformal models generally focus on developing or improving functionality in a given set of skills or operations. The teaching methods frequently are andragogical in nature. The content of the teaching may focus on skills or may include a significant theoretical component. Nonformal programs flourish because of their lower cost, greater flexibility, and relevance.

Informal Models

Informal training models are the most common, but are the least often identified as being educational. Informal learning accompanies every formal and nonformal learning context. It occurs in the daily social interactions of people. While it is powerful in its effects, it is generally characterized by a low level of accountability on the part of the learner. Mentoring, imitation modeling, and some apprenticeship models fit into this genre. Informal education opportunities are continuous in a given situation. The processes, structures, and relational interactions all contribute to the informal educational experiences one has. One learns his first language, his worldview and most values informally. Informal learning can be significantly enhanced by reflection, which moves it toward a nonformal mode.

The learner's "position" on his career path and the purpose of the training both contribute to the training goals and purposes. The resources available for the training and the purposes for the training contribute to the decision making about the structuring or facilitating of the learning experiences in formal, nonformal, or informal education. The structuring of the learning experiences should allow the learners to have opportunities to practice what they are expected to learn in relevant ways, which also provide satisfaction and encouragement. The practice should provide feedback about the results in a way by which the learner can improve his behavior through additional practice. The educational designer should construct the learning experiences so they are appropriate to the learners' present learning level, their learning styles, and the context in which they will apply the learning. Care should be taken to avoid irrelevancies—either what the learners already know or what is not needed in their work context. The learning program designer will recognize the wide variety of learning experiences available for use. The wise instructional designer will also seek to select and organize them in a way which balances them within the three modes and generates interest. The structuring of both the formal and nonformal learning cycles or units will similarly employ the values of continuity, sequence, and integration.

15

Training for Relief
in Development

Douglas E. Millham

For He will deliver the needy who cry out,
the afflicted who have no one to help . . .

Psalm 72:12

OVER THE PAST SEVERAL DECADES, the number of Christian agencies and organizations which are involved in the practice of relief and development has steadily increased. Although experience will prove that these two arenas most certainly overlap at significant points, relief is not development, and development is not relief. Development workers often engage in relief operations. Relief workers, hopefully, carry out relief activities in developmental ways which lead to further development. While related, relief and development work does not lead to one profession, but two. Academically, they are separate, but the essential links are too often vague. Training in the field of emergency relief has yet to fully emerge as a recognized entity. Few, if any, pure relief training models exist, outside of internal agency models. And this undoubtedly contributes to the blurring of the two fields.

This chapter first presents a model of training, designed to provide a basic foundation of understanding for those leaders of relief planning or operations. It is a model developed in a joint effort of Fuller Theological Seminary and World Vision International.

DOUGLAS E. MILLHAM served in Somalia and Thailand in refugee ministries for World Vision International. Currently, he is director of World Vision's cross-cultural exchange program, a mission mobilization and training process for local congregations. He is an ordained Presbyterian minister.

Secondly, it distinguishes the manner in which emergency relief is a predictable and foreseeable interruption of ongoing development activities. "Relief *and* development" gives way to relief *in* development as a far more descriptive title. This chapter also shows emergency relief as a distinctive field, requiring unique strategies for the training of men and women who will lead.

For those who will be both planning and implementing relief responses, however, the options for training in this field are extremely limited. As we will see, very few curriculum models exist in the United States. This chapter presents one of those models, and the reader is encouraged to expand the simple foundations of this model, to challenge the premises, and to break much needed ground in the field of relief curricula. Improvements in this training model will be easy to make, and if it stimulates additional efforts in the training of relief leadership, then a greater good will most certainly be served.

WHAT IS RELIEF TRAINING?

At least two types of training serve the field of emergency relief. The first could be called skill or technical training which concerns local relief workers facing operational issues related to physical intervention and assistance at the local relief site. Contingency planning at this level frequently is non-existent, and the relief response is often, at best, a frantic exercise in the coupling of any available or obtainable resources with the existent immediate needs.

The second type of training could be called leadership training and will be the focus of this model. This type of training is focused upon the expansion of planning and decision-making capabilities of relief agency leaders.

Its topics will concern broader understanding of the definition and causes of disaster; the effects of outside intervention upon victim communities; vulnerability of the poor, and the effects of disaster on development; theological and biblical foundations for disaster mitigation; a historical view of evangelical relief and development; differences between natural- and human-caused disasters; and most importantly of all, it will concern the prevention of disasters altogether.

The model curriculum presented in this study will focus upon this second type of training, which emphasizes the broader issues. It will be dependent upon a learning environment which draws upon the experience and expertise of the participants, and in which the teacher is more of a facilitator of creative thinking than a repository of facts and information.

IS THERE A DEMONSTRATED NEED?

There is, by any measure, an overwhelming opportunity for the development of training curriculum in the area of emergency relief. The last decade has seen a global expansion of the evangelical community into the ministries of international relief in a magnitude unprecedented in history. The end of the Vietnam war, combined with severe drought and suffering in East Africa along with other highly visible events, brought intense media coverage to disaster situations. The response of the evangelical community was overwhelming. Today more than 250 agencies exist in North America alone, born out of a desire to meet human need and alleviate suffering.[1]

This growth is not surprising given the age in which we live, the availability of resources, and the accessibility of virtually every corner of the globe on very short notice. The result has often been a proliferation of groups and individuals rushing headlong into emergency situations without planning or preparation. A few days later they have left, having contributed little and possibly having caused great long-term disruption.

Donors' needs were met, agency needs were met, some relief needs were met, but, quite possibly, the affected community was more severely destabilized by the outpouring of inappropriate materials or the flood of uncoordinated workers with seemingly unlimited budgets.

In the past few years, however, more and more agencies, educational institutions, and individuals are recognizing the urgent need to develop intentional processes for equipping and training Christian leaders for relief. One such agency is World Vision, which recognized, through its work with both Vietnam boat-people and African drought in the mid-1970s, that Christian stewardship, not to mention effectiveness on the field, dictated that major efforts be made to transfer lessons learned from the past into strategies for intervention for the future. No doubt, by now many other agencies are similarly investing in training for emergency relief.

However, many agencies still lump all relief and development training together under one umbrella, much in the same way that they call themselves "relief and development" agencies, using the phrase as a generic heading for all sorts of international ministry among the poor. Secondly, many agencies in this field have not clearly separated the two

254 CHRISTIAN RELIEF AND DEVELOPMENT

structurally, and in practice the same workers who labor in development are automatically expected to be capable of relief responses. This unlikely assumption has caused many agencies to find themselves operating in publicly visible relief arenas with leadership poorly trained or untrained in the primary concepts of relief.

A PERSONAL JOURNEY INTO RELIEF TRAINING

After returning to the United States in 1985 from four years of refugee service overseas, I decided to try and find a course in emergency relief so I could analyze all the things I had done wrong and to learn about all the things I should have done right. My cross-cultural preparation had been the best available to short-term Christian workers; although, no one, it appeared, had any background to prepare us for what was ahead. We learned by doing and gained wisdom as we gained experience dealing with challenging and diverse situations in Africa and Asia.

It seemed natural to find the best courses available in relief theory and practice and to sharpen my skills with new insights. To my absolute surprise, I could not locate a single accredited course. I looked at catalogues, called all the educational and training institutions I could think of, and could not find a single course with a focus in emergency relief. One year later, while conducting a survey for the Lake Wales Consultation, my suspicions were confirmed. From the more than seven hundred Christian institutions of higher education contacted, not one responded as offering a course in relief. There are, of course, many courses in development which cover a vast array of subcategories.

There were courses in economic development, community development, wholistic development, theology of development, anthropology of development, and many more. Presumably, some of these dealt with relief as well. Nowhere, however, could a focus be found fully upon relief, although it is a topic of such considerable interest to the Christian public. Beyond this lack of accredited courses, it was discovered that, of the more than two hundred relief and development agencies surveyed, very few even offered internal training programs in relief.

What makes the impact of this discovery more startling is the astounding amount of money which has been spent in the delivery of emergency relief around the world by those same agencies. One source estimates more than one billion dollars has passed through the hands of the ten leading Christian agencies since 1975.[2] And yet, there existed no formal course specifically for the preparation of individuals for relief leadership located among the hundreds of Christian evangelical educational institutions which produce many of the leaders in these agencies.

In an attempt to fill this void, Fuller Theological Seminary created a forum for the pilot test of a graduate course entitled "Relief in Development." Thirty-six individuals representing six nations and more than twenty different relief organizations, mission agencies, and denominations converged on this two-week intensive course. I was privileged to serve as the facilitator for this course which drew so many people with extensive field experience. The atmosphere was very creative and enthusiastic. This course appears to have been a timely response to the growing involvement of the evangelical community in the expanding ministries of international relief.[3]

The balance of this chapter provides an overview of this course in the hope that this model will serve as a stimulus to many schools and individuals to take what has been done and expand it. There are many persons in this field far more qualified than I to handle such a task. Such training is urgently needed if we are to achieve excellence in the meeting of human need on a global scale.

OVERVIEW OF THE COURSE

Designed in cooperation with World Vision, the course "Relief in Development" was created to provide a forum for the study of the complex field of international emergency relief and its implications for Christian witness and ministry. While structured primarily for the person with operational and/or administrative responsibilities, this course also provides an orientation to emergency planning and implementation for future relief personnel, as well as a thorough introduction to the field for the general student. There were no official prerequisites for the course, but some knowledge of international relief or development was helpful.

It was the intent of the course to blend the academic environment of Fuller Theological Seminary with the global relief and development experience of World Vision. It was hoped that such a cooperative effort would support and strengthen the many agencies and organizations who serve in this field, while serving as a model for interdenominational, interagency cooperation.

During the ten, four-hour classroom sessions, participants were exposed in depth to the planning and implementation methodologies of World Vision and also interacted with professionals from the relief community. A biblical basis for intervention in disaster situations was presented as a foundation for the study. Relief and development agencies were assessed, and philosophies concerning the transition from relief to development were examined. Particular emphasis was placed on the implications for wholistic ministry throughout the entire process of relief management. Case studies, available training videos, and the participants' own field experiences were integrated into this course offering. No textbook currently exists which provides a focus on a Christian response to training in emergency relief. However, an excellent book by Frederick C. Cuny was found and utilized as the text for this course. It is entitled *Disasters and Development*, published by Oxford University Press, 1983. Secondary sources include *Natural Disasters: Acts of God or Acts of Man?*, by Anders Wijkman (published by Earthscan: International Institute for Environment and Development; Washington, D.C., 1984); and *Handbook for Emergencies*, United Nations High Commissioner for Refugees (UNHCR, Geneva, 1982).

OUTLINE OF THE COURSE

The Fuller Seminary/World Vision course, "Relief in Development," was designed to provide a forum for the exchange and interaction between field-experienced participants. As a stimulus for discussion, a number of key topics were presented, either through lecture, video, case studies, or evaluation of student projects descriptive of their individual experiences in relief management. A listing of these topics and a summary of our focus in each area will follow.

What Is the Goal of Relief Training at This Level?

This course had as its primary goal the attainment of several learning objectives.
1. To learn the basic theological and philosophical principles which provide the foundation for wholistic relief and development ministry.
2. To acquire essential knowledge about key operational issues, such as the role of the church in relief situations, the relationship of relief to development, and issues of prevention.
3. To understand the complex causes of both natural and human-caused disaster, especially as they relate to the poor.

4. To develop essential knowledge and skills necessary to produce a contingency plan for disaster preparedness.

What Is Relief?

Emergency relief is a very evocative term. It suggests images of suffering on a large scale, and heightens global awareness to the point where emotion spills over into active responses of many types.

One definition used by World Vision is that relief is the urgent provision of resources to reduce suffering resulting from a natural or man-made disaster. In short, this will usually require the provision of emergency aid. It is, by its very nature, immediate, temporary, and prolonged only when self-reliance is impossible.

In the United States alone, there are more than two hundred fifty Christian agencies and organizations specializing in relief and development in virtually every country on earth. The types of programs and their effects are as diverse as the organizations themselves. Catholic and Protestant, conservative and liberal, evangelistic in focus or socially concerned, government subsidized and privately endowed—these are amazingly diverse organizations and so are the experience and skill levels of their leadership in the area of relief. Their definitions of the term *relief* also vary widely.

It is important to note that this lack of coordination and common focus among agencies can often create a second, and very unfortunate, situation. For survivors of a natural disaster, a second disaster may also be looming. The very aid intended to help them recover may be provided in such a way that it actually impedes recovery, causes further economic hardship, and renders the society less able to cope with the next disaster.

What Is Rehabilitation?

In many ways, rehabilitation is an archaic term. Traditional definitions of relief call attention to an objective of "restoring a community to its predisaster conditions." This objective was often achieved through a process called "rehabilitation." The folly of this definition is, of course, that it was precisely those "redisaster conditions" which most likely turned a natural phenomenon into a disaster.

Why, for example, does the same hurricane which causes no loss of life and little property damage in Florida destroy entire villages with huge loss of life in Haiti? The answer is obvious! Florida has, through its stringent building codes and efficient prediction and response technology, created "predisaster conditions" which greatly limit damage. Haiti, as in the case of many poor societies, can provide none of that for its people. Caught with no warning and protected by flimsy structures at best, entire populations become exceedingly vulnerable. To restore those people to their former state is to condemn them to repeated disasters with no end.

A new concept must be developed which not only restores the former levels, but rectifies the conditions that brought about the disaster.

What Is Development?

Referring again to World Vision's basic definitions, development is defined as a process enabling a community to provide for its own needs, beyond former levels, with dignity and justice. In short, it is the improved capacity of a community to meet its needs. Development must be indigenous, comprehensive, long-term, and aimed for improved self-reliance.

This process of enabling a community to provide for its own needs virtually requires a relief contingency plan. Since it is the poor who suffer most, relief leaders must address the question of how to reduce poverty, and thus reduce vulnerability to disaster, while placing disaster response within the context of development. Reducing the vulnerability of the poor is a development issue, and the awareness of disaster causation should become an opportunity to aid in overall development processes.

Early relief efforts by aid organizations suffered from a basic conceptual failure to link disasters with development. The concept of disasters as separate events requiring aid response of medical and material aid was not entirely accurate and led to efforts that were not only very ineffective, but in cases counterproductive. Relief agencies tended to view disasters solely as emergencies. Today, with an awareness of the interrelatedness of relief within the total context of development and with advanced contingency planning and leadership training, relief is viewed more realistically as a predictable interruption of ongoing development processes.

What Constitutes a Disaster?

Cuny defines a disaster, as "an event that causes a temporary break in the normal life of a community." He goes on to note:

The time between the disaster occurrence and the point at which normal activities are re-established is considered the recovery time. The goal of both governmental and nongovernmental agencies is to reduce this time (1983:197).

The term *disaster* conveys the idea of great tragedy, loss of life and property, but is this idea a broad enough understanding of the term? Perhaps. The goal is not so much to find the right answers just now, but simply to begin understanding the right questions.

Many natural phenomena cannot be predicted, nor can many of the human-created problems that affect the poor. However, most assuredly it is very easy to predict that whenever certain physical conditions are present, such as unsafe housing, poor soil or water management, and the like, then given the first major convergence of phenomena with these conditions, a disaster is certain to follow.

What's the point? Disasters cannot be predicted, but they can surely be widely prevented if those working in the ongoing process of development are trained to look for and reduce the vulnerability of the poor to disaster, as well as to see the urgent need to plan ahead for disaster response and relief long before it occurs. This is not only a prescription for local development workers, but also for those in the global management of relief organizations. To their credit, many major relief and development agencies have taken a proactive role in relief training at local, regional, and international levels.[4]

What Causes Disasters?

James A. Cogswell, writing in the *International Bulletin of Missionary Research*, notes the fascination of the Western media with symptoms of disaster rather than causes. And we, the agencies who depend upon that same media to provide us with pliable donors and the source of income they represent, are frequently too busy in our response to carefully study, let alone work to solve, the root causes. He writes:

> Hear me clearly. I am not saying that "relief" and "development" are bad words. Rather, they are inadequate words, for they do not penetrate to the deeper level of reality that underlies the hunger and poverty of the third world—the level of systemic injustice (April 1987:74).

This is no small topic. It is vastly greater than I have space or ability to deal with here. Suffice to say that the study of relief in development must have as a primary goal the intensive self-examination of our historic relief responses. We must recognize that they do not occur in an isolated vacuum which much of media would have us believe.

Rather, those of us in relief leadership must be compelled to rise above our traditional reactive methods and plan boldly, not only for the *intervention* of relief in development, but far beyond that at the same time. The ultimate goal for Christians in this line of work must be to *eliminate*, as much as possible, the root causes. However, only trained eyes can see them—eyes that have been opened to the source of suffering at its deepest roots and ears that have been opened to the enormity of disaster that befalls the poor.

The plain reality is that poor people are the most frequent victims of disasters and are especially vulnerable to natural and political catastrophes. Disasters may exacerbate poverty or reverse the progress of the poor in achieving self-reliance. So it becomes increasingly important to more fully understand the causes of disaster and to bring justice and love to bear on their eradication. It is not enough merely to achieve an efficient or effective response.

Again, we must try to carefully ask the right questions before we jump ahead with our expedient answers. For example, in a disaster of the same magnitude, three thousand deaths will occur in one poor country while only five hundred in another. How can this be? While both were disasters in the traditional definition of the term, the poor country may take years longer to recover, if ever, from the event. The effects of the "disaster," which came and passed in the other country, will remain in its aftereffects for years in the other. Is the responsibility fulfilled when wealthy societies restore communities to their previous levels of poverty, or is there a deeper issue here? As Cogswell goes on,

> . . . there must be a readiness to wrestle with principalities and powers. While working on micro-structures through development programs, we must address the macro-structures which perpetuate and deepen human poverty and misery, and which undercut all the good intentions of relief and development (1987:76).

How Can Disasters Be Avoided or Their Effects Be Mitigated?

Whether natural, such as earthquakes and floods, or human-caused, such as refugee situations and hunger, disasters are occurring constantly around the world. In our age of global information, we are increasingly more aware of disasters when they strike, but only vaguely aware that most disasters are preventable. Natural phenomena themselves, such as earthquakes and floods, are, of course, not preventable. However, the physical, social, and environmental conditions which turn a natural phenomena into a human disaster are undoubtedly preventable.

Cardboard shacks set precariously on a riverbank will most certainly wash away with the first severe flooding. Fire in an overcrowded slum will, without question, affect the lives and property of an entire community. However, homes constructed of strong materials and safely located will prevent the natural event from becoming catastrophic. Which is the more effective, not to mention Christlike, course of action for the Christian relief and development community—reactive intervention to repair the loss of property and comfort for the irreparable loss of life or learning the methods of proactive prevention that can dramatically reduce losses of all types?

What Constitutes a Contingency Plan?

A contingency plan is basically an outline of alternative strategies and appropriate tasks designed to achieve previously established objectives in response to sudden, but anticipated, change.

The goal of a contingency plan is to maximize the effectiveness of an organization's response to crisis, avoiding wasted resources, time, and money. A major result will be the reduction of confusion, indecision, and wasted effort.

Contingency plans must be clear, simple, flexible, and above all, usable in each different context. All individuals affected should be consulted in the design and implementation of contingency plans. The final details should be agreed upon by all involved. These plans then will become the practical, hands-on field procedures for responding to emergency disaster situations.

The key to relief is to address needs *before* the disaster occurs. These actions must be taken within the community, the government, and the church. In the absence of this preparation, enormous waste and duplication will most certainly occur. Nothing is so frustrating as to be in a disaster situation not knowing what to do; or worse, knowing what to do, but having no resources. As a result, this type of planning is essential.

Basic elements of a contingency plan could include:
1. *Predisaster preparedness* includes the identification of local, regional, and/or global trends and patterns. Historical patterns can

be studied and the impact of likely probabilities anticipated. Appropriate prevention measures can be recommended and implemented.

2. *Alert, verification.* The alternative responses are triggered by an early-warning, early-alert information system. News media sources are of particular assistance, as are the various early warning organizations.

3. *Project planning and design.* Response strategies can be outlined and modified, continually monitoring changing conditions of various kinds.

4. *Project management phase,* where goals are carried out. This phase includes implementation of chosen disaster plans, monitoring of various response indicators, and evaluation of both participants and recipients of this strategy.

5. *Community restoration* requires awareness of factors that contributed to disaster and a commitment to eliminate these whenever possible.

6. *Transition or termination* occurs where the aid was adequate, and everyone agrees it is time to move on.

7. *Evaluation.* Evaluate performance under real-life conditions, and modify plans accordingly. Disseminate lessons learned throughout system and to other agencies. Encourage appropriate decision-making based on the evaluation.

Nothing is mysterious about contingency planning. It is simply an analysis of previous disasters which affected the given area, the planning for alternative responses by the agency, and decisions about how it will meet situations in the future. It has as its key objectives:

1. To assist in identifying communities vulnerable to future disasters.

2. To assist in identifying appropriate mitigation protection and prevention measures in coordination with vulnerable communities.

3. To assist in anticipating consequences of future disasters, and developing appropriate advance strategies to efficiently manage relief, reconstruction, and development responses to emergency situations.

4. To assist in identifying specific needs in field staff training.[5]

Toward a Uniquely Christian and Biblical Approach

Training in emergency relief must stress the uniqueness of our Christian response. In order to stress that uniqueness, we must first be sure that we have one. What distinguishes our response from that of non-Christian agencies?

A Christian response to acute human suffering is not optional. Jesus came with great compassion and brought a message of "relief" for the poor and the needy. The topic of emergency relief is not a debate between "evangelism" and "social action." It is a matter at the heart of the kingdom of God striking at the core of who we are as Christians in the one church of Jesus Christ responding to situations of human need. The Gospel of Luke records a vivid illustration of this truth:

> The scroll of the prophet Isaiah was handed to him. Unrolling it, he found the place where it is written: "The Spirit of the Lord is on me, because he has anointed me to preach the good news to the poor. He has sent me to proclaim freedom for the prisoners, and recovery of sight for the blind, to release the oppressed, to proclaim the year of the Lord's favor."
> Then he rolled up the scroll, gave it back to the attendant and sat down. The eyes of everyone in the synagogue were fastened on him, and he began by saying to them, "Today this scripture is fulfilled in your hearing" (Luke 4:17).

In order to restore health to people's lives, God intervenes into our world with the gospel. The gospel provides an integrated approach to meeting the needs of all humanity.

We are living in a world of increasing struggle for most people on earth, a struggle against daily grinding poverty that can become absolutely overwhelming. These same people deserve to know the God who cares, who intervenes.

Isaiah predicted that there would be a day of renewal and restoration in the future. In that day many would be brought back to wholeness and allowed to experience life. They would hear the good news and find relief and rehabilitation to newness of circumstances and life. It would involve both the spiritual and the physical circumstances.

Jesus, hundreds of years later, selected this Spirit-led prediction to be the heart of his ministry. In the synagogue of Nazareth, he openly declared that he would begin the process, and that it was being fulfilled in their very hearing. Relief from the tragedy of life involves the total person. It is not just from war, natural disaster, or tragedy. It is also to a new life that is abundant; and although it certainly may be difficult, it will provide a meaning previously undreamed of. Thus, tragedy can bring a better change when properly handled and done in a Christian spirit.

The kingdom of God can bring about a renewal of relationships, a restoration of home and family life, and an establishment of more

264 CHRISTIAN RELIEF AND DEVELOPMENT

just circumstances for personal living. And, it must bring justice and hope for the hopelessly poor and oppressed. The kingdom of God can do that. All of us in this profession can participate, by God's grace, in bringing the kingdom of God to bear on the world's needs. God wants to heal, restore, and set free all men and women to godly, healthy lives. The kingdom has come when peoples' most urgent physical needs are met, and when they also hear and respond to God's voice. The first time many people will hear his voice or see his handiwork will come through the lives of those serving in emergency relief settings.

We are God's people. We are part of the body of Christ, and we are his hands and feet and voice. The information and skills obtained in the study of a Christian response to relief in development are not just for our own knowledge and career development, but also so that we can transfer this information to others who, likewise, may need to know this information in order to save and restore life in God's name.

Relief and development involves not only physical and organizational skills, but more importantly, spiritual and moral qualities of life in those of us whom God has called to serve others in the name of Christ. God has intervened in history. The method he has chosen is through Jesus Christ, and we are the means God will use to complete the task of reaching a very hurting world in his name. World Vision International's president, Tom Houston, speaking on the subject of a Theology of Relief, has noted that relief work must be, of course, humanitarian, but not exclusively so. For Christians, it is the love of the neighbor for Christ's sake that engages us in disaster relief. And this, as Jesus said, is an outflow of our primary love for God. Secondly, relief is done in the context of what God is doing to take the good news of Jesus Christ to all the peoples.[6]

With these as the primary objectives of the Christian relief leader, several key values and goals emerge, according to Houston:

1. Our engagement in disaster relief must be efficient and effective, meeting real needs in a God-honoring way.
2. Our relief efforts must be done with genuine care and compassion and total respect for the people and their culture.
3. The lifestyle and manner of our people must be evidence that the good news is true.
4. There should not be any attempt to proselytize, capitalize on tragedy, or to discriminate in distribution of supplies.
5. Our explanations and verbalization of the Christian message need

to be adapted to the degree of knowledge of and favorable attitude to Jesus Christ in the context where we work.

6. We should always be thinking about the long-term effects on the people in their journey toward Jesus Christ, and act now to encourage their progress in the future.

A uniquely Christian and biblical approach to relief will require uniquely Christian and biblical relief leadership. This much is perfectly clear. Fearless, confident, competent witnesses for the Lord, firmly rooted in the gospel of Jesus Christ and established in prayer—these are the characteristics of the person whom God will use to fulfil his plans and purposes among the poor.

SUMMARY

Other chapters in this book define development from a Christian perspective, broadening the perspective from this chapter. Relief is not ever distinct from development. Development is an ongoing process which, when natural or human-caused phenomena converge upon it, may indeed be severely interrupted, requiring an emergency intervention.

Whenever preparation is not adequate to prevent these phenomena, a disaster frequently occurs. What follows, invariably, will be a relief effort of some scale, always locally, and frequently regionally or globally. If this is the usual scenario, then planning relief must best be seen as an integral and inevitable element of the development process. And the key to planning rests in the programs of training of individual leaders and workers.

Relief *in* development means relief training and preparation are essential as a fully predictable component of ongoing development programs. Yet, emergency relief does not take place apart from the ongoing developmental processes that exist in virtually every community on earth, whether intentionally designed or naturally occurring. This is why, once again, we choose the descriptive phrase, relief *in* development as a title for this course.

Relief *or* development is not a good philosophical foundation for strategic planning; it places the two fields in opposition. Rather, my choice for a clear descriptive title for a strategy of training in emergency relief leadership remains relief *in* development. This choice more accurately describes a unique component of Christian mission, which is at once separate, yet interdependent upon development. Relief becomes viewed as a predictable event, one for which planning can take place in any development setting. Relief becomes not merely the reactive intervention of a sudden disaster, but rather an extremely likely possibility among any vulnerable population for which preparation is possible. It becomes an inevitable and foreseeable interruption in virtually any development process, so much so that development workers can plan their responses in advance. Planning leads to the development of resources, to the accumulation of skills and training, and training ultimately leads to a state of preparation. Such a process will greatly reduce both the immediate impact of the causes of disasters as well as their long-range impact on development. But it will illuminate the physical, social, and environmental factors which frequently make the difference between a crisis becoming a disaster, or its passing with little societal disruption or loss of life.

CONCLUSION

Without a doubt, this model curriculum is first generation. It is, at best, a starting point for much-needed dialogue on the causes and solutions to disasters and our Christian response. Many more educational institutions need to look seriously at initiating courses of their own, so that quality research and reflection can begin to take place on a national and international level. The goal must be a more informed and enlightened leadership emerging in the field of relief, so that planning processes and decision-making skills will guide the church and its response to a very needy world in a much more effective and appropriate manner.

Some issues are going to come into focus in this present decade. First of all is the need for a strategy for interagency cooperation and coordination. The image is fresh of dozens upon dozens of United States agencies descending upon Mexico City a few years ago, each expending vast amounts of resources and funds, duplicating the efforts of the other. Leadership training in relief will need to stress the importance of networking, of sharing limited resources, and of exploring the possibilities of decentralized, regional training programs which will benefit far greater numbers of people worldwide.

Secondly, there will be the continual emergence of training needs for non-Western relief specialists. From these leaders, we in the West should learn vastly more than we do from one another, since it is a fact of history and geography that these individuals will have had significantly more experience in disaster response than most of the rest of us.

My prayer is that educators who study these words will be more firmly compelled and stimulated to expand this field of leadership training and preparation to far deeper levels with far-reaching results.

---

[1]On October 13, 1985, leaders of mission agencies and Christian educational institutions met on the campus of Warner Southern College in Lake Wales, Florida, to examine the issue of training and preparation of Christian workers for relief and development. The Lake Wales Consultation, as that meeting came to be known, now meets annually for this purpose. As a result of that gathering, a research task force was formed, which I headed, to attempt a comprehensive understanding of the present situation in North America in the area of training. Survey questions were developed and sent to 218 relief and development agencies and 702 schools, from which the Lake Wales reference manual was produced. This manual, produced by World Vision, is divided into two main sections. The first major section (Candidate Profiles) surveys the desired characteristics of personnel sought by relief and development agencies, and includes data concerning numbers of short-term personnel associated with that agency. The second major section (Schools) outlines the training resources available in various Christian educational and training institutions surveyed.

[2]Mission consultant Marv Bowers has completed considerable research in this area, and cites the annual reports of the top ten Christian relief and development agencies as the source for his statistics.

[3]Under the direction of Professor Edgar J. Elliston, I had the privilege of co-instructing this course with Ron Maines of MAF. Ron formerly served as Director of Relief for World Vision International.

[4]World Vision has designed and held regional seminars for the preparation and training of relief managers in each country in its system. Significant amounts of training materials have been translated into Spanish for use in Latin American regional countries.

[5]World Vision training materials on contingency planning have been written by several very capable and highly experienced relief experts, among whom are Paul Jones, Ron Maines, and Randy Strash.

[6]For complete text of this speech, see "The Biblical Context for Relief Ministries," by Tom Houston (available in print or video); December 16, 1985.

16

Advocating for Women in Development

Evelyn Jensen

International development has traditionally occurred in the male world. When groups in industrialized nations . . . attempt to work toward change in the "Third World," men have worked with men to solve male-defined problems related to poverty, low productivity, and other symptoms of existence at the periphery of the world economy. Men define the problems, establish the channels, and direct the resources— knowledge, money, and personnel (Flora, 1983:89).

FLORA'S STATEMENT SOUNDS very strong, and yet the research that has been done since 1970 shows that indeed women have been essentially left out of the planning, executing, and lastly the benefits of many western based development projects. One reason is because, generally speaking, the cognitive and experiential training of development workers has not included an emphasis on the particular needs of women in the Two-Thirds World. The purpose of this chapter is to present some ideas regarding women in development that should be part of the training curriculum of development workers. The chapter is divided into three major sections: (1) a discussion of the goals and purposes of a training course focusing on the needs of women in development; (2) a presentation of five core issues which should be included in such a course; and (3) some suggestions for course activities and/or projects that would increase the learning experience of the students.

EVELYN JENSEN serves as the director of doctoral programs with the School of World Mission at Fuller Theological Seminary. Formerly a missionary in Ecuador with Christian Missionary Alliance, she also serves as the associate pastor in a Mennonite Church in Los Angeles where she works with abused women and women who have substance-abuse problems.

A HISTORICAL SURVEY

Initially, it would be good to give a brief review of how women's concerns in international development programs first were articulated and then slowly implemented in the last two decades. Ester Boserup in her classic book, *Women's Role in Economic Development* (1970), presented for the first time a new perspective on economic development and its relation to the real world of women. She clearly illustrated that the previous development projects had discriminated against women and children, which in turn essentially brought failure to the whole project. Little by little her ideas were accepted by development agencies. By 1974, not only had agencies begun to rethink their development projects, but also to give consideration to having women on the decision-making boards of the agencies and at other administrative levels.

> Projects of a different genre came to the fore, oriented not necessarily toward immediate profitability, but rather toward development of "human capital" and thus ultimately toward profitability . . . The purposes were usually twofold: to increase the productivity of female work, thus increasing income, and to increase "human capital" by way of education, training, skill acquisition, improved health (Bernard, 1987:44, 45).

The Decade for Women of 1975–1985 sponsored by the United Nations continued to raise awareness of the plight of women and children in the undeveloped nations of the world. The delegates to the International Women's Year Conference held in Mexico City in 1975 drafted and adopted the document called "World Plan of Action." That same year, the General Assembly of the United Nations (a total of 133 nations) adopted the World Plan of Action, which initiated many pro-women changes in governments around the world, and declared that 1976–1985 would be the U.N. World Decade for Women. During the 1980s, the amount of academic literature related to women's issues in development has steadily increased. Indeed, it is now time for Christian development workers to be more aware of and committed to the special needs of women around the world.

PURPOSES AND GOALS OF THE CURRICULUM

A course for training development workers regarding the special needs of women, by nature, must be an inter-disciplinary study. Early in the planning of such a course, it must be decided whether the course will be introductory in content or intentionally directed towards development workers who already have field experience. The suggestions presented in this paper are based on the supposition that the students have not had field experience as yet. The general purpose of the course would be to raise the students' level of awareness in regard to the real world in which women live. Indeed, awareness raising is a key word throughout the entire study. The cognitive and affective goals and objectives would be as follows.

Cognitive Goals and Objectives

From an educator's point of view, what is presented here needs to be refined and redefined according to the specific needs of the students. However, keeping in mind that qualification, the general goals and objectives of the course would be:

1. To examine, in a general way, the social situation of women around the world in terms of their education, work place, health care, and political situation. To know, in a specific way, the social situation of women in a specific geographical area—preferably that area of the world to which the student will be assigned.
2. To be able to apply development principles and theories to the needs of women in such a way that it is truly a benefit for women, from women's points of view.
3. To understand more clearly the gender roles and traits of men and women in the society to which the student will be going. This understanding includes the ability to define the gender roles and traits, as well as be able to see how they are perpetuated from generation to generation.
4. To investigate the family systems in which women in various cultures find themselves and to discover the specific needs of the women within these family systems.
5. To understand how various religious systems support and perpetuate the subordination of women and the implications of this for Christian development workers.
6. To understand, in a general way, the growing influence of the international feminist movement.

Affective Goals and Objectives

It is hoped, that in such an academic course students would not only process cognitively large amounts of new information, but that they would also be changed in terms of their attitudes, values and worldview. Such a course has great potential for challenging not only sexism but also racism, ethnocentrism and classism (Stitzel, et al, 1985:34). Some of the affective goals and objectives might include:

1. That students would not only be aware of the needs of women in various parts of the world, but that they would be committed to meeting the needs of women in their real world.
2. That students would move increasingly towards a non-sexist worldview. This means, that not only would the students be able to verbalize and organize their actions around non-sexist values, but that they would internalize non-sexist values to the point that these values become part of their whole being and character.

In planning a course which stresses women in development, the question often arises: "Should feminist perspectives be integrated into existing class material on development, or should feminist perspectives be presented as a separate class?" The solution to this dilemma is probably a both/and approach rather than an either/or approach. In the total training curriculum of development workers, feminist issues should be both *integrated* into every class on development and also be specifically emphasized in *separate* classes. The professor is the key person in avoiding two principal dangers. When feminist issues are integrated into the existing curriculum, the professor must be fully familiar with all the issues and literature so that they can be continually and consistently woven into the existing material without becoming absorbed into, subordinated by, or dissolved by masculine perspectives. However, when feminist issues are presented in a separate class, the professor must continually and consistently work towards highlighting feminist issues in a wholistic perspective for the enrichment of all of humanity, both men and women.

CORE ISSUES

In order for students to be better equipped for meeting the needs of women in development, the following core issues need to be part of the curriculum: the diversity of the social realities of women around the world in terms of their work, education, health, and political situations; gender roles and traits; religion; family issues; and the international feminist movement known to some as the "Feminist Enlightenment" (Sivard, 1985; Bernard, 1987).

Diversity of Women's Social Realities

Approximately 2.5 billion female human beings live on this globe. Some are western women, but most are non-western; some are old, but many are young; some are rich, but the majority are poor; some are white-skinned, while most are women of color. General statements about them belies the wide range of varieties in their social situations, roles, and status. The danger is that women become faceless or invisible in generalizations. Therefore, it is important to expose students early, not only to the global trends of women's diversity, but also to the diversities of women's lives in specific geographical areas. The following four themes serve as the basis of such a study.

The Work Place

Much of the work done by women, both in the past and present, goes unnoticed and unpaid. The long hours that women work at bearing and caring for children, growing and providing food for the family, maintaining clean and healthy environments for the family often go unappreciated by the family. This work is not counted among the productive activities of the society. It is unpaid and not calculated into the economic balance of the society, and yet it undergirds of the whole society. "Many [women] carry triple work loads; in their household, labor force, and reproductive roles. Rural women often average an 18-hour day" (Sivard, 1985:11). Those women who are working in the paid labor force are usually found in the low paying, low status service jobs with longer worker hours and very few fringe benefits. In most countries around the world, a large gap still remains between the men's wages as compared to women's wages in equally skilled jobs. In summary, students need to understand the real situation of women's work and how different it is from men's work.

Education

In recent times, the field of education is where the most advances and open doors have appeared for women. Yet deficiencies there still glare at us. In many countries, laws require all children go to at least primary school. However, in many developing countries "almost sixty percent of girls ages 5–19 are not in school" (Sivard, 1985:11). Also for girls, drop-out rates and absenteeism rates are higher. Possibly because in many societies the girls are needed at home to help with the work, while the boys are given priority in receiving education.

One way of measuring the level of basic education is to examine the national literacy rates. Generally, literacy rates have increased around the world for both men and women. However, a large gap still remains between the literacy rates of men and women. In developed countries, the literacy gender gap is slight; however, in developing countries the literacy gender gap increases markedly. A positive correlation exists between female literacy rates and national income.

> Low literacy rates for women, as well as broad sex differentials, have a common denominator in poverty. At least 60 percent of the 500 million women who are unable to read and write live in countries where the average per capita income in 1980 was below $300. In many of these countries, especially in Africa and Asia, four out of five women over 25 years of age have never had any schooling at all (Sivard, 1985:19).

The lack of basic education not only prevents women from developing all their intellectual faculties, it also strongly influences how women's self-images, abilities, and ambitions are shaped. Thus, we see it is important that development workers understand the importance of womens' education.

Health

Women have always been concerned with family health matters. In fact, they are the major informal providers of health care for all societies. One way of measuring women's health is by observing the life expectancy statistics. The life expectancy of women in the developed nations ranges between seventy to seventy-five years as compared to as low as forty to fifty years in developing nations (Sivard, 1985:36, 37). "Studies show a strong correlation between women's life expectancy and per capita GNP in the developed countries and stronger than between men's life expectancy and GNP" (Sivard, 1985:24).

One of the factors affecting health and longevity of women is malnutrition. Of course, both men and women can be malnourished, but "evidence both in social custom and in surveys [show] that malnutrition occurs disproportionately among girls and women" (Sivard, 1985:25). Nutritional anemia is a severe health problem for women in developing nations, especially during their child-bearing years. If the mothers are malnourished, the children born to them will be malnourished also. Thus begins a vicious cycle of malnutrition and other problems that go along with malnutrition (low energy, low productivity, poverty, and reducted learning abilities).

Early age pregnancies, frequent pregnancies, and short birth intervals all contribute to added stress on women's health reserves. In spite of women's reproductive role, it seems that men occupy more of the available hospital beds than women (Sivard, 1985:27). Even though women have been the health providers throughout history, only recently have governments begun to realize that caring for the individual woman's health is a key in providing and promoting good general health for the whole nation. Likewise, development workers need to be committed to women's personal health care and thus benefit the whole community.

Government and Laws

When development workers enter a country, they should be aware of the laws that govern the people. And particularly, if they are going to effectively advocate for women, they must understand the laws regarding women. These laws include women's right to vote, their legal rights in terms of marriage and family, legal rights of ownership, pay scales and labor laws, and religious laws. Since the Decade for Women (1975–1985) promoted by the United Nations, many nations have instituted new laws which work towards equality of men and women. However, that does not mean that these laws are really in practice at the grass-roots level.

Gender Roles and Traits

Gender roles and traits are other core curricular issues for development workers. Hierarchy and patriarchy would appear to be almost universal principles of social organization. Indeed, it would seem that subordination is a key word in understanding the relationships between men and women. In spite of this, the question must be asked, "Is it true to say that subordination of women to men is a universal given?" And, if it is true, "why" is it so? The causes of this subordination are very complex and must be approached from various perspectives. An interdisciplinary approach provides the best way to look at the theories of gender subordination.

For instance, sociologists suggest that the causes of sexual subordination are centered around the theories of production and economics,

276 CHRISTIAN RELIEF AND DEVELOPMENT

the roles women may or may not play in the labor force, and their roles or lack of them in the fields of power and politics. If women are never allowed into the work force, nor are permitted economic control of their lives and their world, they will always be in subordination to those who do control—namely men. These very important theories demand consideration.

From another viewpoint, anthropologists suggest that the reason behind female subordination is related to the sexual roles, mores, and cultural values placed upon women. The values and meaning placed upon giving birth, mothering, and families are different in every culture. In other words, even though a woman might have good earning power, if her work or her person are not appropriated as a high cultural value, the possibility or probability remains that she will still be viewed as being inferior. However, in another society the highest cultural values may center around the family and children, in which case, the very fact that women are given the cultural task (or a certain division of labor) of caring for the family may indicate that a high value is placed on women and their work.

In western societies, especially, the academic discipline of psychology has done much research in the area of gender subordination. It has centered around such issues as the concept of a personal identity, female ego development, and roles within the family system. Cross-cultural psychology is revealing new insights about women and how they function psychologically in non-western cultural situations.

In non-western societies, the worldview of the people usually centers around the religion of the people. In several of the world religions, the teachings and practices strictly enforce the subordination of women. The inferior status of women is considered to be the norm of the universe and the way God intended it to be. Religious belief systems then become the root cause of establishing and maintaining subordination of women to men.

Feminist historians suggest that one of the important factors in maintaining female subordination is that historical studies have been done by men and basically about men from a decidedly male perspective. In the process, women's stories and their contributions have never been told. This neglect explains how women become invisible in the society. Therefore, as each new generation of females is born they lack positive and prominent feminine models and are gradually socialized into believing that their story is not important enough to be heard. In this way, women continue as very necessary and useful to the society but invisible and thus inferior.

All of these perspectives provide a viewpoint from which to delineate the causes of subordination. Each perspective presents certain truths about the feminine social reality. Even with this cursory review, it can be seen that the causes of apparent female subordination around the world are very complex issues.

Another way of conceptualizing the issue of gender roles and traits is to think of the female world and male world in terms of integration or separation. Each culture has formal and informal ways of dividing up their sexually based worlds. The most obvious, of course, is the sexual division of labor which many believe grows out of the biological differences whereby women bear and care for the offspring. This division automatically requires women to be confined to the private sphere. Men then are assigned the public sphere (see Boserup, 1970; Bernard, 1987). Many studies have shown that the separation between men and women is evident not only in the economic and biological fields, but that it can also be seen in the linguistic and spatial fields. In some societies, for instance, men and women may speak a different dialect of the same language. Space, who occupies it, and how it is used has, for a long time, been an important concept for anthropologists and sociologists. Space also takes on psychological, social, and even moral values.

> As a result of these physical, psychological, and social separating processes, a host of cultural prescriptions, proscriptions, and expectations arise which constitute a reality of incalculable power to guide, shape, and control—that is, to "genderize"—behavior. So taken for granted are the walls of the world that surround each individual that they are rarely noticed and even more rarely breached (Bernard, 1987:26).

Why is all this important? In order for development workers to be adequate advocates for women in the Third World, they must be able to conceptualize, analyze, and appreciate both the male and female worlds in a given culture. Sometimes development projects will need to be designed and executed separately for women, while in other situations, projects can be sexually integrated. Development workers must be sensitive to the gender roles and traits of women, and all that entails in any cultural situation.

RELIGIONS

In non-western cultures, religious doctrines and practices often powerfully influence the assumptions and values in the other segments of the culture, such as the politics, government laws, family life, and male-female relationships. For instance, at the present time the ideology of Islam strongly influences the various government laws of Arab countries. The major world religions, including Christianity, profoundly affect the relationships between men and women. Religion is also a key factor in the perpetuation of the gender attitudes and values from one generation to another. In order for development workers to understand the male and female worlds in a given culture, and how they relate to each other, it would be important that they do some research into the doctrines and practices of the religions of that area. Included also in this study would be the myths, rituals, and symbols of the religion. Christianity, and particularly the teachings of Jesus, advocates for the dignity of women in every aspect of life. Jesus, in his relationships to women, did not conform to the attitudes and values of the surrounding Jewish culture. Instead, he chose to relate to women in ways that affirmed them in all their capacities. Christian development workers are called to follow in the steps of their Leader.

FAMILY ISSUES

The family is the third area of primary concern for a development curriculum. The lives of women revolve around their families much more so than for men. Therefore, if development workers intend to be effective advocates for women, they must be concerned about the family systems to which the women belong.

No one doubts that modernization and urbanization trends are two social forces that have deeply affected the Third World. Family systems have also been profoundly affected by these world movements. "Modernization of agriculture has often altered the balance between the sexes, increasing women's dependent status, as well as their work load" (Sivard, 1985:17). The "trickle down" concept of economic equality has not been fulfilled for women. Rather, there has been increased poverty for women. Even in prosperous nations, "two out of three adults living below the poverty level in 1983 were women; one elderly woman in six was poor; one in every two poor families was headed by a woman" (Sivard, 1985:16). This process has been called the "feminization of poverty." Since women are the primary, and often the only caretakers of children, it means that an increasing segment of society finds themselves engulfed in the cycle of poverty. Rural Third World women particularly are vulnerable to poverty.

> Overworked, undertrained, often undernourished and illiterate, they have limited chances to enter the cash economy, although they account for more than half the food produced in the Third World, and for as much as 90 percent of the family food supply of rural Africa (Sivard, 1985:16, 17).

Another reason why women are increasingly poor is because more frequently they are left with the complete support of the children. "Women are the sole breadwinners in one-fourth to one-third of the families in the world. The number of women-headed families is rapidly increasing" (Sivard, 1985:11). Much of the aid to Third World nations of the past has been provided to Third World nations with the underlying assumptions that the social structure of these nations was based on a male as the head of the household and as the main producer. That assumption is very ethnocentric and male oriented. In the process, women have been marginalized and have not received the long term benefits of the aid.

As is obvious, feminization of poverty impacts the whole family, but especially the women and children. Much more attention must be given to the needs of the total family system in development projects.

Feminist Enlightenment

Some think that the women's movement is a phenomenon found only in the western world. Jessie Bernard (1987:109–122) presents a very convincing case to show that the feminism has moved around the world emerging into "a kind of global feminine consciousness" (1987:36). Bernard calls this global process of feminine consciousness raising the "Feminist Enlightenment." She likens the Feminist Enlightenment to the French Enlightenment of the eighteenth century.

> This movement [the Feminist movement] emerged about two centuries after an eighteenth century intellectual movement which came to be known as the French Enlightenment (because France was its source and center) arose and cast its rays far and wide, even as far as the Russian Empire. This movement gave the western intellectual world a new view of its history; it rejected the old status quo, especially its old authority structure, and installed one based on reason, on science. In

these respects the twentieth-century Feminist Enlightenment resembled it in many ways (Bernard, 1987:109, 110).

An important impetus behind feminism has been the research done by women about the realities of the female world.

> With training, they developed the skills for asking their own questions, mapping their own reality, formulating their own paradigms, making their own interpretations, for handling their own archives and documentation. In brief, for using the tools of research to make their own discoveries about themselves, who they were, what they did. It was, indeed, a female counterpart of the French Enlightenment. Like that one, it was also casting its beams in many dark corners. This research push was one of the most important aspects—as antecedent and as consequence—of this Feminist Enlightenment. It was a long step toward female empowerment (Bernard, 1987:122).

Why is the concept of Feminist Enlightenment important? If development workers are going to be effective advocates for women in development projects, their own consciousness must be raised in regard to the conceptualizations, ideologies, and movements of global feminism.

In summary, five core issues of a training course for development workers have been presented, centering around the special needs of the women who are the recipients of development projects. The first core issue is to study the diversity of women's social realities. This diversity includes women's work place, women's education, women's health, and government laws related to women. The second core issue is that of gender roles and traits. The third core issue centers around the religious environment in which women find themselves. The fourth core issue deals with the needs of women in various kinds of family systems. The fifth core issue introduces the growing Feminist Enlightenment. The next section presents ideas on how to make the teaching of these core issues more interesting.

PROJECTS AND ACTIVITIES

As mentioned in the first section, the most important general purpose of this course is raising awareness of the needs of women around the world. Before planning the learning activities, the teaching team will need to develop a bibliography about women in development. Excellent sources for bibliographic information are Kathleen Stuadt (1986) and Irene Tinker, et al (1976). The kinds of learning projects and activities which promote awareness raising stimulate the students to have a high level of participation and interaction. Some ideas that might be implemented in the classroom include task forces, case studies, interviews, films, videos, and/or slide presentations.

Task Forces

The first core issue—the Diversity of Women's Social Realities—constitutes the major portion of the class material. When the global trends of women's realities are presented, the lecture method can be utilized. It is also important that students have a more detailed and in-depth picture of what is going on in a specific geographical area of the world. One way of developing a clear picture of one area is to divide the students into study groups or "task forces." The first "task" of the task force would be to do a detailed study of a certain part of the world and then make a report to the whole class. The task force would investigate and describe the real world of women using the headings presented in the previous section: women's work, education, health, and political situations. A second responsibility of the task force would be to develop a hypothetical development project in which they would demonstrate how women's needs could be met. This hypothetical project could include the specific design of the project, implementation of the project and also evaluation of the project.

Case Studies

Another method of understanding the real world of women would be to analyze the published descriptions of different types of development projects from around the world. This approach would not only raise awareness in students, but it would also help them develop sound analytical skills. Some of the questions that might be asked include: Did this project meet the real needs of women and children, as well as the needs of men? In light of the social realities of that given situation, was there equitable distribution of economic benefits of the project? Or, did the project increase the number of women and children living in subsistence conditions? Did the project promote and support family integration or family disintegration? Were women left with greater financial, emotional, and spiritual burdens to bear? Was the gospel presented in such a way that personal, as well as spiritual, needs were met? Was a wholistic gospel presented? Did the proclamation of the gospel free and empower women, as well as men, to be all that God intended them to be? Another resource for understanding the real world of women would be to study and analyze various ethnographies.

Interviews

If the training center of development workers is fortunate enough to be located where there is a variety of ethnic groups and international students, it would be well to invite such people to the class to be interviewed. It is always good for students, as well as outsiders, to interact with insiders of another cultural situation.

Films, Videos, Slide Presentations

Part of the preparatory work of the professor of the class would be to investigate the audio-visual materials available that deal specifically with women in development. Check the university library, the public library, and development and aid agencies that might be located in your area for any audio-visual presentations.

This chapter has presented the goals and objectives of a course which emphasizes the needs of women in development, including five core issues of the course content and several learning activities. May your class be challenged with the tremendous social and personal needs of women around the world. May each student own their responsibility to be advocates for women in the Two-Thirds World.

17

Training for Community Health Evangelism

Stanley Rowland

FLORENCE NANTAKA FROM BUMASIFWA, Uganda was in her Community Health Evangelism (CHE) training class with twenty-two other CHE volunteers. As she sat in class, she thought about the training and how different it was from any other training she had ever experienced.

Most people in the class were villagers like herself who had only a primary school education. They sat in a circle instead of rows. They could all see each other, which made each one feel what he had to say was just as important as anyone else. No teacher stood in front lecturing to them.

Most classes started with a drama done by other students. This drama presented a real problem in the village. Then the trainer asked the CHE volunteers sitting around the circle what they saw, what they thought the problem was, and what they could do about solving the problem. Sometimes the CHE volunteers suggested ideas which were incorrect or only partially true, but the teacher never ridiculed them. He gently corrected them. Most of the answers, however, came from the group of CHE volunteers themselves.

After they discussed the problem, Florence and the other CHE volunteers actually put into practice what they had learned in the discussion. Sometimes they worked together to protect a spring so

STANLEY ROWLAND serves as the director of the community health evangelism program with a Campus Crusade/Life Ministries in Nairobi, Kenya.

their village could have clean drinking water. Sometimes they made a special drink to give their children when they had diarrhea.

After this activity as a review, they practiced how to use a little picture book on the topic. This picture book reviewed the cause of the problem, how they could treat it at home, when they needed to go to a doctor because the problem was too serious, and when to treat at home. The picture book also showed how the problem could be prevented.

They used this picture book to share what they had learned with their neighbors and friends when they visited in homes. These picture books were used for both physical health and spiritual health topics.

The other exciting thing was the spiritual teaching. For every topic about physical health, they covered a topic about spiritual health. They learned how they could know Christ in a personal way and how He could control their lives moment by moment. Then they learned how they could tell this exciting news to others. Many of the trainees committed their lives to Christ for the first time.

When the spiritual teaching was tied into the teaching on physical health, changes in the village began to be seen. People were more healthy both physically and spiritually.

CAMPUS CRUSADE HEALTH BACKGROUND

Life Ministry Africa (Campus Crusade for Christ) has been operating several hospitals and clinics since 1978. In 1980, we established our first rural Community Health Evangelism (CHE) program. In all these projects we have an aggressive evangelism and discipleship ministry. We have had twelve CHE teams working in seventeen African projects and have trained over four hundred CHE volunteers. We anticipate having seventy-five CHE teams in place in the next seven years.

The following underlying philosophy permeates all of our work:
1. The health services should be viewed as a servant to the spiritual ministry.
2. Success of the Christian health endeavor should be measured more by discipleship than patient case load. However, both are integrated and must be measured.
3. Evangelism and discipleship need to be intimately interwoven into the practice of health and should emanate from the personal ministries of the health personnel rather than through an appointed chaplain or evangelist.

4. A sufficient number of staff should be supplied so they can operate as a team in both the spiritual and health aspects of the ministry.
5. All the Christian staff and workers should receive initial and refresher training in spiritual skills of evangelism and discipleship. This training is especially important for doctors because they must be seen as pacesetters and not as "too busy for spiritual ministry."
6. Overall success of a health strategy should be measured in terms of multiplication, i.e. everything that is taught should be transferable to others who can, in turn, teach it to still others who will teach it to others.

Community Health Evangelism as a ministry of LIFE Ministry has the expressed purpose of helping people prevent disease, promoting good health, and living an abundant Christian life. This purpose is accomplished by the training of local villagers (chosen by community health committees) in development and spiritual truth. The CHE volunteers pass on what they have learned to their neighbors, who in turn pass what they have learned on to others.

The training covers such topics as water purification, sanitation, agriculture, nutrition, maternal and child care, care of the ill in the home, and prevention of disease. Spiritual topics cover how to be sure you are a Christian, how to tell others about Jesus, how to live under God's control, how to study the Bible as well as how to lead Bible study groups.

GROUPS MAKING UP A CHE PROGRAM

In establishing a CHE program we have involved three different groups. Each group plays a significant role and cannot be ignored. They include: the training team, community health committee, and the CHE volunteers.

Training Team

The training team initiates the program. This team generally comes from outside the area. Two to four people serve on each training team with a combination of the following skills: nursing, public health, teaching, agriculture, nutrition, water development, and sanitation.

The training team is a mixture of expatriates and nationals. The nationals come from the church in which the program is being developed. The approach facilitates the church's having a financial and moral commitment to the program.

Community Health Committee

The CHE program is integrated around community health committees which are chosen primarily from Christians. However, these committees may include other community opinion leaders. They remain, however, church-based.

The members of the Community Health Committee are mature, well-respected people who represent different segments of the community. They choose the CHE volunteers, plan, organize, supervise, and evaluate the program on a day-to-day basis. The CHE volunteers report to the committee.

CHE Volunteers

The Community Health program focuses mostly on the Community Evangelism volunteer. The CHE volunteers are chosen from their villages to undergo training and to help meet their neighbors' physical and spiritual needs.

As volunteers, their job is to put into practice what they have learned. They promote good health, prevent disease, and model an abundant Christian life. They do evangelism and discipleship with individuals and groups in order to saturate their area for Christ.

They regularly visit their neighbors sharing the spiritual and physical truths they have learned. They also initiate and coordinate local community self-help projects. They are encouraged to teach in such a way that what they teach to others will be taught by them to others also.

CHE PROGRAM OVERVIEW

A team of three or four trainers work with the local church in the community to assess their needs and to establish community health committees. These committees choose CHE volunteers who have a local village education. The training team's skills can be any combination of nursing, public health, agriculture, sanitation, nutrition, social work, and/or teaching.

A group of fifteen to twenty CHE trainees from five to eight areas within walking distance of the training locale come for training.

Training sessions are usually conducted two days per week, three to four hours each day. Forty to fifty training days are necessary for graduation. Half of each training day is spent on teaching community health subjects and the other half is spent on spiritual subjects. All teaching aims to be transferable so that the people being trained will be able to teach others who in turn can teach others.

The CHE trainees share what they have learned in their community by means of story-telling, discussions, and example. Their main roles are teaching in the homes, assisting in community health projects, and having a spiritual ministry. A part-time CHE worker can work with up to four hundred people.

The program works better if the CHE workers are volunteers, but the Community Health Committee may decide to give some remuneration. If so, it is the community's responsibility to provide the funds.

The CHE program is begun in one area then sequentially expanded into adjacent areas. Additional workers are then trained in the original area in order to obtain a better ratio of CHE volunteers to the population. The community provides the training facilities, food, and a nominal training fee.

The goal is for each initial training team to be replaced by three to six national CHE volunteers chosen from those CHE volunteers who were trained by the outside team. These local training teams will expand the program into adjacent areas.

As much as possible, funding for the individual project comes from the local community. However, where local resources are insufficient, funds may be solicited from agencies especially interested in community health. Outside funds may be useful for "pump priming."

CHE STRATEGY

The establishment of a CHE program requires three major elements. CHE has two parallel tracks: the internal ministry and the external ministry. Both tracks are laid on a strong foundation of training and materials.

Internal Ministry

Two to four Campus Crusade/Church projects are established as models in a country where the CHE programs are utilized. These projects provide models for other organizations to see how CHE works. Campus Crusade supplies half of each project training team, and the church provides the other half.

External Ministry

The external ministry establishes training programs to train other organizations in how they can establish their own integrated community health and evangelism programs. These programs are called "Training of Trainers" (TOTs).

Foundational Training of Trainers and Materials

Equipping the training teams is needed for the establishment of, first, a program and then a movement. Creation of awareness for the CHE concept is aided by speaking at conferences, writing articles, and a book on the subject.

Materials such as lesson plans for CHE volunteers, committees and trainers, picture books on physical and spiritual topics, and teaching pictures for the CHE volunteers are provided. These diverse materials are necessary if the CHE concepts are to be multiplied through others.

INTEGRATION OF EVANGELISM/DISCIPLESHIP AND COMMUNITY HEALTH

We are commanded in Luke 10:27 to love God totally and to love our neighbors as ourselves. If we love our neighbors as ourselves, we will truly be concerned with both their physical and spiritual welfare.

When Jesus sent out his twelve disciples to minister to others, he commanded them preach the good news of the kingdom and to heal the sick. They were to give freely just as they had been given. Jesus was concerned about the whole person. He healed the sick as he preached and taught. As Christians, we too must be concerned for the well-being of the whole person. This concern involves meeting both physical and spiritual needs.

CHE is concerned with both the physical and spiritual needs of people. They go together. Humans are whole beings and cannot be separated into compartments.

Our intent is to have an integrated program of evangelism, discipleship, and community health. We have found that it is easy to say

"Let us have a program that integrates both physical and spiritual truths," but it is very difficult to implement such a combination.

We attempt to integrate a spiritual ministry into a health program by looking for "changed, transformed lives" in both the physical and spiritual sense. Transformed lives come from inward changes because of the love of Jesus Christ. These inward changes lead to physical changes in individuals, followed by changes in their families, then in their communities, and ultimately, changed societies. These inward changes come before the outward change.

We begin with a training team made up of mature, born-again Christians. If the training team members are not more mature Christians, then it is impossible to model what is expected of others.

The training team has the common objective of integrating a spiritual ministry into their health work, thereby dealing with the whole person. They must be like-minded. If they are not, then others are confused and do not know which example to follow.

Aggressive evangelism and discipleship serve for spiritual multiplication. The training team must know how to personally share their faith in Christ and how to do follow-up of new believers. It is good if all go through the same training so that what is taught to others will be consistent.

The training team must be able to teach in such a way that their knowledge and skills are transferable and multipliable. What the staff teaches must be taught by those they have taught, who will teach what they have learned to others. We enhance this transfer of knowledge and skill through the use of "Picture Books" on both physical and spiritual topics.

During home visiting, the trainers model what is expected of the CHE volunteers in health teaching. In addition they model aggressive evangelism, follow-up, and discipleship.

We seek to spend as much time in evangelism and discipleship as we do in physical subjects. We make time to do evangelism, follow-up, and discipleship and are not satisfied with only meeting physical needs. This type of commitment shows both components are important.

All personnel do both physical and spiritual work and teaching. It is not good for one person to concentrate on physical and another on spiritual needs. To specialize in one aspect implies to the trainee that physical and spiritual are to be separate. This weakens an integrated approach.

An important outcome of the program is the active involvement of people in Bible studies called New Life Groups. The people who are trained first lead these groups. As the members in their groups grow spiritually, they begin to lead their own Bible studies. The content of these group studies aims at evangelism and discipleship which encourages the members to put what they have learned into use.

We create enthusiasm and build momentum through the use of large scale outreaches. These momentum builders in evangelism are the "Jesus" film and "I Found It" campaigns. These two approaches create excitement and enthusiasm, as well as give people the opportunity to make many evangelistic contacts in a short time.

We expect and inspect for spiritual integration. If we do not expect spiritual change in peoples' lives, then all we may see is some temporary physical change. If we expect spiritual changes, then we should expect to see that these changes are taking place. As we see spiritual changes taking place, excitement and momentum grows.

MEETING CHE TRAINING NEEDS

All of the people we seek to teach are adults. As adults and Christians, they differ from typical students in terms of experience, motivation, readiness to learn, and relationships in their communities. These contrasts require an educational approach tailored for African adults. Table 3 describes some of the key distinctives of our approach to the adult Africans with whom we work.

TRAINING COURSES AND MATERIALS

Life Ministry's two track strategy of Internal and External ministry is built on a strong foundation of training and materials. The CHE program has three constituencies who need training: the training team, the local committees, and the CHE volunteers. Standard training packages are now available for each constituency.

Trainers' Three-Phase Training (TOT)

A three-phase training program was developed to instruct the training teams. Most of LIFE Ministry's expatriate trainers come with limited work experience and exposure to Africa. This three-phase training establishes a common foundation so all trainers will have the same frame of reference. From it, the trainers begin a program based on the experience and knowledge gained from previous projects.

The three-phase training process is designed with several months between each phase in order for trainees to practice what they have learned. The recommended time between Phases I and II is six to nine months, and four to nine months between Phases II and III.

Phase I

Phase I focuses on development philosophy and the initiation of a CHE program. Spiritually, the emphasis is on evangelism. We present LIFE Ministry's basic messages on the Christian life, and we teach the trainees how to use the Picture Book, the Four Spiritual Laws and the Jesus film.

Phase II

The second phase focuses on developing teaching materials, methods, and curriculum. Spiritually, the emphasis is on follow-up through the use of the follow-up Picture Booklets. Their content reviews the basic messages of the materials studied in Phase I.

Phase III

The third phase focuses on evaluation, project expansion or multiplication, and project management. Spiritually, the emphasis is on discipleship.

Twenty four lesson plans for each of the three phases have been developed. They are now in use in many training programs across the continent of Africa.

To date, we have trained about five hundred workers in seventy-five non-LIFE Ministry projects who have established their own integrated community health and evangelism programs. Our desire is to be involved in training in over six hundred such projects in the next seven years.

Committee Training

A six-day, three-to-four-hour-per-day training curriculum is used to train village committees. Initially, we did not train the committees, and as a result, we discovered they did not understand their role. They viewed the program as something from the outside and had little commitment to it.

Function	Inward Christian Transformation
Aim	Change individuals who change others thus changing society from within.
Strategy	Changed people who are taught so concepts are transferable, multipliable, and reproducable. The individual inward change causes outward change which affects others.
Intention toward	FREEDOM through Christ. Inward change which shows itself in outward change.
General approach	GOD-CENTERED. There are absolutes to learn, but learners participate in their learning.
Effect on people & community	TRANSFORMING. Helps people find ways to gain more control over their lives under God's control.
How students & people are viewed	Basically *active* under God. Able to take charge and become self-reliant. As God's children, they have ultimate worth. Responsible when treated with respect and as equals.
What the students feel about the teacher	TRUST based on God's Word and seeing changed lives spiritually and physically.
Who decides what should be learned	Instructors and students work together with the community, but there are absolutes to be learned which include spiritual ones.
Teaching methods	Open-ended dialogue in which some answers come from class's experience, but there are some absolutes on which learning is based. Role plays, dramas, and a relating to own life experiences.
Main way of learning	ACTIVE. Everyone is a contributor. Learning through doing and discussion, as well as modeling by trainers through home visits, practicing what is learned.
Flow of knowledge and ideas	Back and forth between student and teachers and also between students.
Area for studying	LIFE. The classroom is life itself, as verified by God's Word and practiced in homes.

TABLE 3: CHRISTIAN ADULT LEARNING GUIDELINES

Function	Inward Christian Transformation
Class size	15–20 in a large group but often broken into small groups of five to seven people for discussion.
Important subjects or concepts covered	–Community development integrated approach. –Dignity obtained through Christ. –Self-reliance under God. –Being an example (modeling what has been learned). –Health topics. –God's Word and how it relates to life. –Use of local resources. –Teaching skills. –Innovation.
How the class sits	Class sits in a circle so all are at the same level and can see each other. No one is superior to another. This fosters discussion and inter-change.
Attendance	Students come because they want to and the learning related to their lives; what they have to offer is accepted in the class.
Group interaction	COOPERATIVE. Students help each other. Those who are quicker assist others. Techniques and games to open teaching methods with the students seeing what is expected of them from trainers.
Purpose of exams	To see if ideas are clearly expressed and if the teaching method works. No grades. The faster help the slower.
Evaluation	Simple and continual by community, students and staff. The purpose is to improve what is happening.
After Training	Students are encouraged to work hard to keep learning and given supportive assistance. Diploma.
Accountablilty	The person is accountable to the community under God's direction.

TABLE 3: CHRISTIAN ADULT LEARNING GUIDELINES
(Continued)

We discovered when we trained the committee first, the members began to take more responsibility and leadership and chose to be trained as the CHE volunteers. We also provided ongoing committee training.

The committee training materials are based on the trainer's Phase I training. Lesson plans are available for this curriculum and answer the following questions: What is community and what is development? What is a CHE program and how does it work? How does the committee form and govern itself? What is the role of the CHE volunteer? How can/should we plan? Spiritually, the committee members are exposed to our basic evangelism messages.

CHE Volunteer Training

As new projects started, we saw the need to standardize our training. Lesson plans were developed and then used by the individual projects. They then submitted additions, deletions, and changes which were incorporated into the lesson plans. Additional topics are being added regularly. No one team uses all the topics in our "Training Manual," but chooses those topics which meet the needs of the community. Currently, the training manual has sixty-five physical lesson plans and fifty spiritual lesson plans (see the CHE Topic List).

Through our TOT's, all our trainers have now been exposed to the adult education principles which emphasize that teaching should be learner-centered. This approach draws upon the knowledge of the learner through problem-posing situations which are used to start discussions.

Lesson Plans

Lesson plans are designed to present the physical and spiritual lessons in ways that use a high degree of learner participation which will aid the learner. Each lesson plan is designed in four columns:

KNOWLEDGE   SKILL AND ATTITUDE   METHOD   EVALUATION

First, we present the KNOWLEDGE which the learner needs in order to do a good job. Second, the SKILL AND ATTITUDE desired on the part of the learner is specified. Third, teaching METHODS are given which will help the teacher, such as starter codes, role plays, stories, and pictures. We also list the materials that are needed for the lesson. Fourth, we describe how to EVALUATE the effectiveness of the lesson. The CHE volunteer lessons on diseases are presented in a set sequence with a lesson plan for each of the following:

- What causes the disease?
- How to treat at home
- What are the symptoms for professional medical help?
- How to prevent the disease

Picture Booklets

Picture books have proven to be helpful in decreasing the fear CHE volunteers had of sharing something new. The picture booklets were developed for non-readers as a result of the success of the "Four Spiritual Laws Picture Book" for non-readers. The "Picture Book 4 Laws" was modeled after the "Four Spiritual Laws" for readers.

The first picture booklets on health and spiritual topics had no words and used stick figures. They were used for three years and proved to be successful. We later re-drew the booklets and added words to provide more guidance for the CHE volunteers. Since then, the booklets have been redone with additional topics.

The booklets are used as a review of the teaching on a given topic, such as Worms. They follow the same sequence as did the individual lessons on the topic. The CHE trainees then practice using the booklet with each other. They are given an assignment to share the booklet with at least three of their neighbors.

We have found the above training techniques and materials to be very useful in the development of a community health evangelism project.

CHE RESULTS

We have been greatly encouraged and helped by the recorded results of some of our early CHE projects. As an example at Buhugu, Uganda out of twelve people chosen by the community for training, only three had an initial personal commitment to Jesus Christ. However, by the completion of the four-month training cycle, all twelve could testify to a personal relationship with the Lord.

Additionally, over a two-year period, the Buhugu CHE volunteers have personally introduced more than one thousand persons to Christ. At one time in 1985, the Buhugu CHE volunteers were conducting thirty-two Bible studies involving 285 people. Of those 285 people, twenty started their own evangelistic Bible studies which involved an additional one hundred people.

In terms of physical and social results, local trainees and workers from ten villages involved in the Buhugu project have protected forty springs and built an eight-mile gravity-fed water system that serves more than ten thousand people. Measles has been reduced by 40 percent, and deaths due to diarrhea have decreased by 30 percent.

The people started a number of individual projects such as bee keeping, seedling tree nurseries, ponds for raising fish, improvements in many home garden plots from which they derive most of their staple food.

During a period of political unrest in Uganda in 1985, it was necessary to withdraw the expatriate CHE training teams just as several new projects were either training their village committees or training the first groups of CHE volunteers. Three of these projects were less than one year old.

When the expatriate training team returned eight months later, they found the communities were ready to start where they had left off and some had continued in a limited way on their own. This desire was especially encouraging, because at that time nearly all progress in Uganda was at a standstill, due to the turmoil in the country.

It often requires a number of years for a project to become self-reliant; however, the Buhugu clinic continued to function on its own throughout that time.

In 1981, a project was begun in western Kenya in conjunction with the Africa Inland Church. After a group of fifteen CHE volunteers were trained, we realized the people were not taking any initiative, but were expecting the training team to carry the entire burden.

A decision was made to withdraw from the project and wait for the community to take action. Thirty months later, some church leaders from that area requested that we provide more training. We then discovered that 30 percent of the original people trained were still doing home visiting and sharing the CHE concepts with their neighbors without any encouragement from the training team.

In another area, a woman trained as a CHE moved with her husband to a village some distance from their original home. At the new location, she found the community in need of health care. So on her own initiative, she organized a community health evangelism training program. She trained thirty CHE volunteers and has since trained five of them to be trainers in order that the community health concepts could be carried into adjacent areas.

We feel these examples speak for the results of what can happen when people catch a vision and under God's direction, begin to take responsibility for their own health care and protection.

18

Tentmaking, the Layperson, and Your Mission Agency
A Plea for Integration in Missions Strategy

C. Richard Staub, Jr.

WITH THE RELEASE OF *Today's Tentmakers* in 1979, J. Christy Wilson breathed new life into the term "tentmaking." The book inspired a lively discussion in churches and mission agencies across America. Wilson portrayed tentmaking as one solution to the dilemma of evangelizing "restricted access countries." Via his or her secular occupation, a tentmaker could enter over seventy countries that now refuse missionary visas. Tentmaking provides a way to reach the 3.5 billion people who live in those restricted countries. The apostle Paul was cited as a biblical practitioner of tentmaking. William Carey and others were cited as recent historical examples. Some touted the economic advantages of a "self-supported" tentmaker over the high cost of the "traditional" missionary.

Access to "closed countries" is biblically and historically based and cost-effective. Like the proverbial Toyota: who could ask for anything more?

Today, eight years after *Today's Tentmakers* first appeared, tentmaking still has its committed advocates. Books have been written,

C. RICHARD STAUB is president of Global Resources, an international placement and consulting firm. He previously served as executive director of Intercristo and Tentmaker's International.

new organizations have been spawned, and the Lausanne Committee for World Evangelization has added an official Tentmaking Task Force to its Strategy Working Group. But some mission leaders have raised serious questions about tentmaking and are very cautiously considering the part tentmaking and lay people are to play in their mission's future.

I would like to see more mission agencies take advantage of the benefits that tentmaking can offer as a strategy to help their missionaries enter restricted-access countries and as a way of capitalizing on the growing interest of lay people in world missions. I will touch on four subjects relevant to any mission agency interested in establishing a tentmaking policy or program.

WHAT IS A TENTMAKER?

This basic question has become a watershed issue, a wall of partition between advocates and adversaries of tentmaking. A recent convocation in Wheaton received the following responses to that question: "Any dedicated Christian who lives and works overseas and who uses his secular calling as an opportunity to give personal witness to Jesus Christ." "Witnessing for Christ while productively employed abroad." "The tentmaker is a missionary in terms of commitment, but is fully self-supporting." "The tentmaker is a fully prepared missionary, accountable to a mission board, mandated to plant a church, who uses an occupational cover to enter a restricted-access country."

These examples show that some define tentmaking by referring to the source of one's income, others see it as a mere strategic accommodation to a changing visa situation. All agree that it includes witness for Jesus Christ, but others feel it must include church planting. "Why is there such a wide range of definitions?" The answer is very simple: The term "tentmaking" is being used to describe two concurrent, yet very different movements God is stimulating towards the year two thousand.

In *mission circles*, tentmaking describes a strategy for penetrating restricted-access countries with fully trained missionaries. It answers the question, "How can we get our missionaries in there?" As Greg Livingston says in the film, *Operation Tentmaker*, "the Great Commission does not say 'go ye into all the world and preach the Gospel except where you cannot get a missionary visa.'" Tentmaking is a way to get in and stay in restricted-access countries.

Among *lay people*, tentmaking describes the integration of occupation (job for pay) and vocation (work done to fulfill God's agenda on earth). It is a concept that emerged when the church began to reemphasize the role of the lay person in ministry and missions. Sermons were preached describing the role of the pastor-teacher as an equipper of the laity so the laity could do the "work of the ministry." It became popular to discuss the priesthood of all believers. Just as Lausanne appointed a tentmaking task force, it also appointed a Senior Associate for Lay Ministry. Inter-Varsity developed a Marketplace conference focusing on lay people in the marketplace as a companion to its Urbana conference. Lay people praying for China suddenly discovered that they might be the answer to their own prayers when China swung its door open for teachers and businesspeople from the West.

Both uses of the term tentmaking are important. Unfortunately, many see the two as mutually exclusive, and dismiss one or the other as illegitimate. Thus, you hear the lay person saying that the missionary using the occupation as a "cover" is not really a tentmaker, because he or she does not really have a job. Likewise, missions have been heard to dismiss the lay person's use of the term because the lay person working abroad is not "equipped to plant a church." It seems to me such a dichotomy will cause us to miss the remarkable and rich possibilities God has created in our day.

Fortunately the same person's pen inspired both groups' use of the term tentmaking. Certainly, if anyone can help bridge the laity and the missions agency it is the Apostle Paul! In one man we have the consummate missionary and at the same time the champion of the mobilized and equipped laity.

Paul's use of the term tentmaking is instructive for us today. He made tents occupationally and was also involved in vocation (see Acts 18:3-4). His reason for this dual approach is touched on in 1 Corinthians 9. Three conclusions emerge from this passage about Paul's brand of tentmaking: 1) Paul did not have to make tents. He could have accepted income from the church, but he chose not to do so (1 Corinthians 9:14-15). 2) Paul refused money from the church for a strategic reason (1 Corinthians 9:11-12). 3) Paul chose tentmaking, not just as a means of support, but as a strategy at a particular point in his ministry. Paul was a Christian who intentionally used his occupation strategically to facilitate his ministry.

This leads me to a working definition of a tentmaker as a Christian who intentionally uses an occupation strategically to facilitate his or her ministry. This definition fits both the missionary who uses an occupational cover to enter a restricted-access country *and* the lay person who uses his or her occupation to support ministry vocation.

By embracing what God is doing in missions and in the laity, we can seize remarkable new opportunities. I believe God is bringing these two streams into one as we approach the turn of the century.

THE BENEFITS OF TENTMAKING

Tentmaking offers significant benefits to the missions agency or church.

Entry into Restricted Access Countries

Your mission can enter restricted-access countries. With over seventy countries now closed and over 3 billion people living in these countries, we must find ways to get in! Tentmaking is one way. In just three short years, Tentmakers International has placed tentmakers in over fifty countries including twenty-eight restricted-access countries. It can be done!

Recruitment of an Enlarged Workforce

Your mission can recruit an enlarged workforce. Right now over three million Americans live abroad. It is estimated that over two hundred thousand of those are evangelical Christians. Meanwhile, more than sixty thousand North American missionaries live abroad. Think of the potential of linking our professional missionaries with lay witnesses who desire to be used by God in their international posts. The largest workforce in American history, the babyboomers, have highly marketable skills and a growing awareness of the global community. What a windfall awaits the mission agencies that discover how to recruit and harness that talent and energy!

Deployment of a Strategic Workforce

Your mission can deploy a strategic workforce. Many lay people working abroad are in strategic and important posts. They sometimes have diplomatic pouch privileges. They often have hiring authority and could possibly retain one of your "undercover" missionaries in a managerial post. In some countries, the very best way to reach certain influential groups is to work among them.

A recent research project by George Otis, Jr., of Issachar reports that the Mormons implemented a strategic "tentmaking" plan fifteen years ago. Why? By placing Mormons in diplomatic posts and key businesses worldwide, they have influenced entire nations towards Mormonism. While we debate definitions of tentmaking, the Mormons are doing it!

Recruitment of a Funded Workforce

Your mission can recruit a funded workforce. While I do not see the economic benefit as the most important one, most tentmakers are able to provide some or all of their financial support. If they go with a large corporation their training, travel, and other expenses are fully covered. With the number of missions concerned about the shrinking donor dollar and rising costs of missions work, the tentmaker can spell R-E-L-I-E-F!

Model a Fuller View of the Church

Your mission will model a fuller view of the church in North America. Recently, a secular journalist reported on the Catholic Church's Maryknoll lay missions program. He was discussing a friend's recent decision to go overseas as a Maryknoll missionary. In an attempt to understand why his friend would make such a decision, he talked with the vicar general of the Maryknolls. The vicar explained to him that "The value of bringing lay people into the mission program ultimately lies in the completeness it brings." The vicar went on to explain, "We know that the clergy are not a complete representation of the U.S. missionary program."

Get on the Crest of the Wave

Your mission can get on the crest of the wave. There is no question that an increasing number of missions are getting involved in tentmaking programs suitable to their own situations. With the number of missions facing visa restrictions, shortages of candidates, and funding problems, tentmaking is offering some solutions. Some missions are beginning to see their handling of the tentmaking movement as analogous to IBM's strategic mishandling of Apple computer. In the early days of Apple, IBM doubted that the home computer phenomenon was significant. IBM even tried to dismiss Apple's computer by declaring that it was not really a computer at all, but rather a faddish toy. Only too late did IBM realize that Apple was to become the major force in the industry. "Big Blue" has been struggling to catch up ever since. If this lay tentmaking movement is here to stay, the established missions agencies that keep pace may be those that take it seriously and adapt to the new realities.

PROBLEMS WITH TENTMAKING

Many agencies have not incorporated tentmaking into their plans because they are concerned that the problems of tentmaking outweigh the benefits. The following issues keep recurring in the tentmaking debate.

Accountability

The tentmaker has a dual responsibility both to the mission and to his or her employer. This fact is especially true with the lay tentmaker. Will these tentmakers be loyal and accountable to your mission?

Preparation

Most lay tentmakers have devoted themselves to a career path completely different from that prescribed by your mission for missionary service. This is especially true of specialized training required of church planting missionaries. How much preparation will you require of the lay tentmaker? Who will oversee it? Who is equipped to prepare lay people? The problem may not be as severe as you may fear. Don Hamilton of TMQ Research has found that effective tentmakers take their responsibility for preparation very seriously and are highly motivated to learn all they can before going international.

Conversely, most of your missionaries will need preparation that will make them "marketable" for the business, government, and educational jobs that provide entry to restricted-access countries. Where will they get it?

Time for Ministry

How can a person work all day and still have time for ministry? Some ministry is enhanced by the workplace relationships. The

Japanese businessman is an example of a "people group" for which the job provides the ideal entree for ministry. Nevertheless, the job will absorb time and energy usually reserved for more direct "ministry" activities. How will your mission manage these new variables?

Placing the Tentmaker

How will you find job openings for the people you want to place? How will you target geographic regions? What will you do to help your missionaries interview for jobs that may not seem to build on their educational and work experience? One mission wanted to try a modest experiment with tentmaking and announced this plan in their magazine. They were overwhelmed with the response from lay people in their constituency who wanted to serve with them. What will you do with constituents who do not fit your missionary profile, yet whom you do not want to alienate?

On-field Supervision

How will your tentmaker missionaries and lay tentmakers relate to your regular missionary staff? How will you maintain contact and accountability with your worker in restricted-access countries? Who will coordinate ministry strategies?

Policy Issues

What will you tell your constituency about your tentmaking program? What will you tell the government in the countries you intend to enter with tentmakers? How will you deal with salary differentials? Will you limit your program to restricted-access countries, or will you coordinate lay tentmakers' activities as a complement to your missionaries in open countries? Are you concerned that you will lose your pool of deputation candidates? What about policies covering the ethics of deception? How will your tentmakers answer questions regarding why they are living and working in the restricted-access country? What will the role of the tentmaker's local church be in the tentmaking endeavor? This becomes especially important with the lay tentmaker. What about the trend towards teams of tentmakers?

Despite the benefits of tentmaking, the problems I have just outlined make many mission agencies hesitant to integrate tentmaking programs into their plans. If God is behind the resurgent interest of the lay person in missions, and if geopolitical trends are going to increasingly restrict your mission's activities in the very countries you want to reach, this hesitation could cause you to miss the remarkable opportunity God created. Furthermore, without the involvement of missions agencies, the lay tentmaking movement will move ahead without the benefit of your years of experience in world missions. This too would be tragic, because, as Ralph Winter has said, "The mission society is the only kind of organization which 2,000 years of Christian experience assures us is able effectively to go beyond normal mono-cultural evangelism and reach cross-culturally to the vast proportion of those who do not yet know Jesus Christ as Lord and Savior."

Without your mission's involvement in tentmaking, your mission will lose a strategic opportunity, and the lay-tentmaking movement will miss out on what you bring it. Is there not a way to join these forces in order to accomplish the common goal of world evangelization?

NEXT STEPS

Given the several compelling reasons for going the tentmaking route, several steps await the church or agency to initiate this ancient approach.

View as a Continuum

View tentmaking as a continuum, not an either/or. Tentmaking can strengthen a more complete model for world missions in two ways. Both require looking at the continuum of work and workers required to accomplish our task.

The Work

Paul talks about a process involved in reaping our harvest (planting, watering, growing, laying the foundation, building).

The Workers

Paul also makes it clear that no one person will be responsible for the whole process. Paul plants, and Apollos waters. Paul describes this as an interdependent process in which we accomplish the continuum of God's work with workers who have different gifts. Crucial to

Paul's argument was his statement that, "No part of the body can say to another part of the body, I have no need of you."

It appears that a hierarchical view of God's work has crept into our thinking about world missions. We look at the role of lay people as a lesser role than the "higher calling" of the church planter or "professional" missionary. In essence, we tell anyone less than a fully trained church planter, "I have no need of you." This view keeps us from developing integrated strategies that coordinate the efforts of the whole continuum of workers required to effectively accomplish the whole continuum of God's work. What would happen if your mission designed strategies that broadened your place in the continuum?

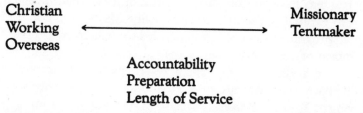

While the Christian lay person differs from the missionary in many ways, such as, accountability, preparation and length of service, the tentmaker can play a vital role in the continuum of evangelism. The tentmaker can be effective in meeting non-Christian co-workers and planting a seed of evangelism. At the appropriate time, the tentmaker could pass these contacts on to the missionary whose gifts equip him for a different aspect of ministry in the continuum. As it now stands, the two ends of this continuum often fail to benefit from each other's unique contribution. Mission agencies could coordinate the efforts of Christians working overseas and missionary tentmakers.

Find Your Mission's Niche

A mission does not need to rush headlong into new tentmaking programs. One can, however, begin to identify the kind of tentmaking program that would fit both the mission's and personal needs. Three questions can help you define your program.

What Aspect of Tentmaking Fits Your Mission?

If you have a particular region as a target for activity and that region is closing its borders to missionaries, then your first experiment with tentmaking may be limited to placing regular missionaries in tentmaking types of assignments.

What Aspect of Tentmaking Fits Opportunities?

One must look at the needs or opportunities already identified in your planning. A person may see a need for more recruits or ways of mobilizing more recruits at a lower cost. You may see an opportunity to enter a certain country by mobilizing new kinds of recruits.

What Kind of Program Fits Your Resources?

You may have an extensive network of in-house lay professionals who are eager to go work internationally. Maybe you could offer a training program that could be expanded to include lay people. Some percentage of your constituency may already be living and working abroad. An audit of these human resources may indicate that you already have the makings of a prototype program without really knowing it. Your mission has a wealth of recruiting, screening, preparation, and on-field management programs that could be adapted to build new programs.

You may find you need outside resources. Tentmaker's International and other agencies are committed to serving your mission and its needs. Through TI's ACCESS program you can get unlimited access to our comprehensive data base of international jobs. TI developed a *Tentmaker Resource Guide* listing hundreds of resources that you as mission agencies have recommended for training the tentmaker. TI also offers a film and other materials you can use to develop your own tentmaking program. The Mid-West Center for World Missions now features a Tentmaker Training Center. ACMC (Association of Church Mission Committees) stands ready to work with churches in preparing lay people and churches in partnership with you for world missions. Never before have so many resources been available to link mission agencies and lay people for world evangelization.

There is no question that introducing tentmaking will also introduce change. Managing that change in a way that produces the desired results will require great ingenuity. The missions that are seeing positive results have certain features in common.

Select a champion to lead the movement. New projects require a special kind of leader. In business, the new product or service is assigned to a "champion." This person "champions" the new concept to make it more accepted. The individual selected for this role must be experienced in your ministry and must command respect of the key people at every level of the organization. The individual must also be totally committed to the importance and value of tentmaking. This commitment is what will motivate the person to overcome the resistance that accompanies any change.

A new project like this will require agreed-upon objectives that are specific and measurable. The plan moves tentmaking from a concept for discussion to a program ready for implementation. In planning, you can address the problems of tentmaking. You can set the parameters of the program. Set policy that will allow tentmaking to mesh well with your current programs and policies. You will also establish a budget for the program that not only sets limits, but also releases the resources necessary to subsidize and launch a new endeavor.

A lot of criticism directed at tentmaking is due to "overpromising" in the early stages of its introduction. People come to expect more than tentmaking can produce. Going slowly and setting reasonable goals will let your ministry grow into a tentmaking program. This "evolutionary" approach beats the "revolutionary" in building new programs. Communicating clearly allows the whole organization to come to grips with the complex transitions inevitable with change.

Identifying problems and solving them must be part of developing your new program. Furthermore, we will all benefit if we can develop networks for sharing the success and failures of our tentmaking experiments.

Cleo Chook, veteran tentmaker, recently said, "The need is there for tentmaking; the opportunities have never been greater." With this in mind, I trust we will forge new cooperative ventures, and I hope they will involve your mission in tentmaking.

19

Evaluating Training for Christian Social Transformation

Edgar J. Elliston

OLE KUTENGALA STOOD TO SPEAK. As the senior age grade leader for the ruling elders of the Ildamat sub-tribe of the Maasai, his standing led to a hushed expectancy both among the gathered church leaders and missionaries. The two-year drought had been the topic of discussion through the whole series of meetings over several days. For a people whose livelihood depended on meat and milk, the drought appeared to be driving them toward a famine. Now when he stood leaning on his walking stick, his words took on an added significance, "*Metii kule!*" "There is no milk! We must act now."

"No milk" to the Maasai meant empty shelves in the markets to the city dwellers. Indeed, the situation was serious. Tens of thousands of animals had already died.

The ensuing project led to the regular feeding of more than twenty thousand people in food-for-work projects. Famine was stayed. The people not only survived, they built churches, roads, schools, clinics, airstrips, water catchments, and other development projects. Community structures were strengthened, and a new Christian community confidence was born.

After Ole Kutengala said, "There is no milk," the Maasai elders identified the key issues to decision making with the missionaries. These issues then provided the impetus for three kinds of immediate

EDGAR J. ELLISTON serves as assistant professor of leadership selection and training in the School of World Mission at Fuller Theological Seminary. In that role he coordinates the Development Concentration.

evaluation and suggested the need for a fourth. With each kind of evaluation came training implications. The context required a carefully detailed survey so that from the needs, specific goals and objectives could be identified. Resources needed to be identified so that the organization and structuring of the responses could be done. Looking at the process of carrying out the program aided in making the required procedural decisions for implementation and quality control. With the goals and objectives in mind, the base for examining the results to aid in making the recycling decisions was laid.

Training implications emerged from each kind of evaluation. As we looked at the context, the goals for training—orienting—equipping the local men who would supervise the local food-for-work projects became clear. As resources were assessed (time, available people, finances, transportation facilities, milling facilities, food supplies), the decisions were made for organizing the orientation program. As the food-for-work program began, ongoing process evaluation provided useful insight for the continuing training of the local supervisors. After the program was completed, it was then possible to evaluate the results in the light of previously identified values and criteria to make recycling decisions. Some parts of the orientation were obviously of little use and could be dropped. Other components simply needed a little fine tuning and could be continued. The evaluation of the results provided the essential information for these decisions.

Evaluation may serve the whole decision-making process. An evaluation also serves to inform in the setting of goals and objectives. It may provide useful information for making decisions about structuring or organizing. Procedural and control decisions find supportive information from evaluation. Finally, as one evaluates the outcomes of a training program, useful information for the recycling decisions of continuation, termination, or modification can be made. Whether one looks at the overall program or just the training component, evaluation may be useful.

The curricular development process involves a series of decisions about the learners, goals, objectives, educational structures, learning experiences, processes of education, recycling, and many more. To make wise decisions, useful information is required all along the way. The process of securing, analyzing, and presenting this information is all part of evaluation.

NEED FOR EVALUATION

"Training problems" for development workers often arise regardless of the wisdom of the developers or their commitment to design and implement appropriate curricula. These problems arise because of the changing learner's situation, and changes in the instructors. The successful curriculum developer recognizes these problems and works through them with the constituencies involved by making and implementing appropriate decisions.

Established curricula often suffer from institutionalization or a hardening of the categories. Inflexible curricula often drift into irrelevance. The complaint of an educator may, in fact, be realized: "The wrong people teach the wrong learners in the wrong way in the wrong structure at the wrong time to do the wrong things wrongly." If no change is implemented in the curriculum, the students and communities being served will soon suffer from growing irrelevance in the training.

Eye-clouding inflexibility often blinds the curriculum worker's use of evaluation. Evaluation, which may provide useful information for making decisions at every stage of the curricula process, is too often relegated to a position of "We'll evaluate if we have resources left and if anyone really wants to know what we've done."

Even development educators often develop patterns of thinking and habits of design which mirror the educational programs in which they were trained. One tends to assign positive values to his own perspectives and experience. Without deliberately seeking to depreciate another's point of view, this narrow egocentric perspective may lead into many kinds of educational or training problems.

While a person cannot predict the specific results of a given educational program, if the processes used in design, the objectives, the resources, the structure, and educational process are known, then the overall results can be generally anticipated.

Effective decision-making, which addresses these issues, depends heavily upon the kinds of information which are provided through the evaluative process. The fact that problems can always be expected simply serves to underscore the need for evaluation.

USEFULNESS OF EVALUATION

Evaluation of the context to be served can provide the needed information for setting purposes, goals, and objectives. An evaluation of the resources available can help one decide about appropriate structures. An evaluation of the process provides useful information about implementation and control. An evaluation of the results can help greatly in making decisions that lead into modification, termination, or continuing the program as it is. The cyclic nature of evaluation suggests that it may be initiated at any stage of development and processed through the other stages.

THE EVALUATION PROCESS

Two kinds of information must be clarified before the evaluation process can begin. First, the values related to the enterprise need to be identified. The setting of values comes from outside of the immediate evaluation process. These values may come from any of the basic disciplinary perspectives mentioned in the first part of this book, such as theology, or from the community being served.

The second kind of information which needs to be specified before the appropriate evaluation can be done is the kinds of decisions which have to be made. Once the decisions to be made are clearly in mind, then the appropriate evaluation research can be designed.

Four kinds of decisions have already been noted. Stufflebeam places them in a comprehensive picture in the following matrix:

	Intended	Actual
Ends	Planning decisions supported by context evaluation to determine objectives	Recycling decisions supported by product evaluation to judge and react to attainments
Means	Structuring decisions supported by input evaluation to design procedures	Implementing decisions supported by process evaluation to utilize control and refine procedures

Figure 20: Types of Decisions and Corresponding Evaluation (Adapted from Stufflebeam, 1973:133–135)

The following matrix suggests some of the kinds of values which may be brought to bear on each of the domains (context, inputs, produce, and process).

	Intended	Actual
Ends	**CONTEXT/OBJECTIVES** Objectives should be culturally, biblically, educationally and developmentally appropriate. Objectives should affirm values of local culture, including learning styles and leadership styles.	**PRODUCT** "Graduates" should function effectively as Christian development workers. They should demonstrate: continued growth in spiritual formation, skill proficiency in leadership, and ability to apply new experience to improving their leadership.
Means	**INPUTS** Educational structure should be appropriate to the purpose and goals, indigenous culture and resources which are local and renewable. Foreign subsidies (money, personnel, teaching materials) should only be accepted in an established disengagement program.	**PROCESS** Learning/instruction process should be culturally appropriate using known teaching, learning styles and learning experiences. Sequence, continuity and integration should be present in indigenous terms.

Figure 21: Suggestive Value Matrix

Stufflebeam's definition of evaluation suggests three steps including: "the *processes of delineating, obtaining, and providing* useful information for judging decision alternatives" (1973:129). In the following scheme described by Ward and Dettoni, the delineation is description. The obtaining of the data compares with Ward and Dettoni's measurement and assessment. Stufflebeam does not show how values apply in the process as do Ward and Dettoni. Ward and Dettoni assume that the evaluation will then be provided to the appropriate decision-makers as is suggested by Stufflebeam's final step. The final step for the evaluator is to provide the information which results from the obtaining process in a usable form to the decision-makers. One simply needs to present the data which is relevant to the problem at hand in a form which is appropriate both to the context and for the decision-makers. Raw data is seldom useful for decision makers. Data must be assessed, analyzed, and prioritized in a valid way.

	Context Evaluation	Input Evaluation	Process Evaluation	Product Evaluation
OBJECTIVE	To define the *operating context*, to identify and assess *needs* and *opportunities* in the context, and to diagnose *problems* underlying the *needs and opportunities*.	To identify and assess *system capabilities*, available input *strategies*, and designs for implementing the strategies.	To identify or predict, in process, *defects* in the procedural design or its implementation, to provide information for the pre-programmed decisions and to maintain a record of *procedural events and activities*.	To relate *outcome information* objectives and to context, input, and process information.
METHOD	By describing the context; by comparing actual and intended inputs and outputs; by comparing probable and possible system performance; and by analyzing possible causes of discrepancies between actualities and intentions.	By describing and analyzing available human and material resources, solution strategies, and procedural designs for relevance, feasibility and economy in the course of action to be taken.	By monitoring the activity's potential procedural barriers and remaining alert to unanticipated ones, by obtaining specified information for programmed decisions, and describing the actual process.	By defining operationally and measuring criteria associated with the objectives, by comparing these measurements with predetermined standards or comparative bases, and by interpreting the outcomes in terms of recorded context, input and process information.
RELATION TO DECISION-MAKING IN THE CHANGE PROCESS	For deciding upon the *setting* to be served, the *goals* associated with meeting needs or using opportunities, and the *objectives* associated with solving problems, i.e. for *planning* needed changes.	For selecting *sources of support*, solution *strategies*, and procedural designs, i.e. for *structuring* change activities.	For *implementing* and *refining the program design and procedure*, i.e. for effecting process control.	For deciding to *continue, terminate, modify*, or *refocus* a change activity, and for linking the activity to other major phases of the change process, i.e. for recycling change activities.

Figure 22: Stufflebeam's Evaluation Model (Adapted from Stufflebeam, 1973:139)

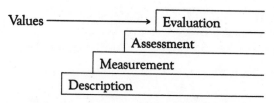

Figure 23: Evaluative Operations
(Adapted from Ward and Dettoni, 1974:209)

Ward and Dettoni summarize the process of evaluation in four successive stages.

Description

In the above figure, we see the sequence beginning with description. "The description of phenomena to be evaluated is a necessary first step" (1974:209). These descriptions may be verbal, graphic, or pictorial. The first step is the description of the "problem" or the decision to be made.

Measurement

The next stage is measurement, or obtaining the appropriate information. In most cases, the descriptions will need to be measured or quantified for a comparative analysis. Whatever it is that is being evaluated should be measured. Maybe it is the number of graduates. Maybe it's scores on examinations. Maybe it is something that relates to attitude development. Perhaps, it is a measurement of spiritual formation. If there is to be an evaluation, there needs to be measurement. Ward and Dettoni describe measurements as "expressions of the descriptions in numerical terms" (1974:209).

To appropriately measure the issues at hand an appropriate kind of research methodology must be initiated. This stage in the evaluation process is the obtaining of the data. As one considers a design for obtaining the data, the questions of validity and reliability arise. Validity concerns relate to asking the appropriate questions or the right questions and collecting relevant data. Reliability issues relate to the consistency of the results of the research.

Many times development workers will be expected to learn another language. An "evaluation" is often required. However, the evaluation often may not be valid. The development worker is expected to learn to both speak and hear the new language with understanding. If the testing (measurement) is only done with written/visual means (written exams), the results may be reliable (consistent), but they will not be valid because written exams do not test either speaking or listening fluency. A more valid test would require speaking and listening in a "real" context.

Assessment

Assessment, the third step on the evaluation ladder, is "a comparison of two or more measures" (Ward and Dettoni, 1974:209). A single measurement is seldom adequate in an evaluative process. Successive scores of an individual, scores of several individuals, or measures of other variables normally must be compared and assessed. It is usually at this point where statistics are used in the analyzing of the data.

Evaluation—Assignment of Values

Evaluation, the fourth step, is "the process of putting a value judgment on the conclusions of an assessment" (Ward and Dettoni, 1974:209). Evaluation is "judgment of the worth or importance of an empirical finding" (Ward and Dettoni, 1974:209). When a person says "this decision *ought* to be made," it reveals a prior value. The whole process of decision-making stands on the prior establishment of values. The establishment of values clearly lies outside of the process of evaluation. In Ward and Dettoni's model, the statement of values lies outside of the process which begins with description and moves on through measurement, assessment, and evaluation.

Often, this establishment of values is not understood in the evaluation process. Values are established outside of the research process which treats a given problem at a given time.

VALUE ESTABLISHMENT

Values should be brought to bear in the evaluation process for the development of curricula for social transformation workers from the basic disciplinary perspectives identified earlier in this book. Each of these foundational perspectives provides a set of complementary values to consider. Values from history, theology, anthropology, sociology, missiology, economics, development theory, and education combine to provide a comprehensive set of values, which affect every stage of the curricular process. How one perceives and employs these values will affect the view of the present situation and the future. It will affect the three sets of primary relationships (with God, with others, and with the environment) which will, in turn, affect the whole training process. It will affect the setting of the purposes, goals, and objectives. It will affect the perception and structuring of the resources for training. It will affect the implementation and control of the training procedures. And, it will affect one's responses to the training outcomes.

The identification, clarification, and/or setting of one's value base profoundly affects not only the evaluative process, but the impact both *on* and *of* the development workers who are affected by the training. One never works in or from a "value-free" setting. One's values, even if unexpressed, are a part of one's worldview, as well as a part of the worldview(s) of the other constituencies involved.

Values from Theology

Theological values undergird much of the equipping of Christian development workers. Values emerging from the great biblical themes such as the kingdom of God, covenant, creation, redemption, reconciliation, and stewardship all carry implications not only for equipping, but functioning in social transformation as well.

From the scriptures, we find both the evangelistic and cultural mandates to which Christians are committed. Theology also provides guidance about the processes on the way to the goals. From theology, we see the importance of continual growth toward spiritual maturity in the process of spiritual formation. We can also see the value bases for the primary relationship with God and the resulting relationships with others and the environment.

Values from Anthropology

From anthropology, we value the expectations and cultural values of the community being served. As long as these client community values do not go counter to biblical teaching, then they should be upheld and affirmed. They may be used in the evaluation process. For example, among the Maa speaking peoples of Kenya and Tanzania, the value of *enkanyit*, that is, respect or worthiness, should be a part of any instruction or evaluation of Christian social transformation workers. It is a key value within the culture. It should be a value that is used in evaluating curriculum as it is designed, as instruction is proceeding, and in terms of how the leaders function after they have completed their training.

Values from Education

Education provides another set of values for the development of curriculum. Different modes of education, namely formal, nonformal, and informal, reflect different value bases. Andragogical and pedagogical approaches to education suggest two other sets of contrastive values. To work toward a "balance" suggests a value position. As one looks at these different modes, each one has its own set of values, and each one has its own set of forms. Each one may be balanced by considering the context and the purpose of education in that context. One can derive from the study of education certain values which ought to be employed in evaluation. In addition to the modes and the different perspectives of education, other values which relate to attitude development, to task analyses, and to organizing learning experiences have been identified. For example, learning experiences should show continuity, should show sequence, and should be integrated. These values should be true in formal education and nonformal education. To the extent that they can be encouraged in informal education, they should be encouraged there as well. Another educational value we have noted is that the structure, process, and content should all be perceived as presenting the same messages.

Values from Leadership Theory

Leadership theory provides another set of values which ought to be considered. One important set of values is that the leadership style of the leader should be appropriate for the kind of group which the leader is seeking to lead. We have seen that the leader is one who is part of a transactional context with the group he is leading. Values that come from this perspective might suggest that the training of leaders ought to include training of the leader in the context where he is to serve. Other values might include the support of local leadership values that relate to the use of power, appropriate leadership styles, status, and role matches and the like.

Values from Development Theory

Several different kinds of values emerge from development theory. For example, participation values demand attention. The principal value, perhaps, would be stated in this way: the community to be served by the graduates should participate in the establishment of the curriculum. Or, another value might say: leader trainees should participate at every stage possible from planning, from implementing the instruction to evaluation in the curricula process.

Values from Missiology

Missiology raises the issues of the *missio Dei* as they are worked out in the balance of the cultural mandate and the evangelistic mandate in the Kingdom of God. The Christian development worker must continue to remember that even though they are not members of a church planting or evangelistic mission or under the supervision of a church, they remain accountable to God in the kingdom. Christian workers are not separated by which commands they may obey. Gifts and callings differ, but God's purpose remains the same. He expects the same obedience toward his goal of all his workers, whether they be called development workers or church planting missionaries.

The great mandates and revealed values of the scriptures provide a rich base on which to evaluate one's motivation, methods, and goals. They provide the key values in evaluating the outcomes in terms of relationships with God, with one's neighbors, and with the environment. Missiology takes the mission of God seriously and provides the values for the Christian development worker to evaluate every part of the development work.

Values from Other Domains

Values from other domains such as political science, economics, sociology, and communications may also bear on the evaluation process for curriculum design implementation and evaluation. These domains suggest the breadth from which values should be derived before initiating the evaluation process. However, for the Christian development worker, the revealed values from Scripture take priority over contemporary views in these social and behavioral sciences.

CONSTRAINTS TO EVALUATION

Several constraints restrict implementating evaluation. Some people misunderstand the purpose of evaluation. Others do not have clear values on which to make judgments. In other cases, invalid or unreliable measurements may be used.

Evaluation Misconceptions

Unfortunately, many people see evaluation simply as an extension of the grading process from their own schooling experience. While grades and grading may well be useful in evaluation, they provide only a small piece of the picture. They may provide a serious threat to the process of evaluation. Seeing evaluation as grading often brings a threatening image in the person's mind, because he does not want to be graded. This problem may be treated by looking again at the purpose of evaluation, at the process of evaluation, and at the people who should participate in the evaluation. By looking at the purpose of evaluation, one can see that it is to provide useful information for decision making. If the person has decisions that need to be made, then evaluation can supply useful information for those decisions. If a person participates in the evaluation in the delineation of the problem, perhaps in the obtaining of the data, the threat will be diminished. However, if the decision-maker participates in the evaluation part, that is, the assignment of values, and then brings this evaluation to bear in the decision making, then this misconception and the constraint that it brings can be overcome.

Unclear Values

Sometimes evaluation is requested when the values which are to be employed are unclear. If the values are unclear, it is impossible to assign a valuation to the assessed data for decision making. The establishment of values is generally not the task of the evaluator, but rather the task of the administrator. These values must be established in advance of the description/delineation of the decisions and certainly before data are collected. These values help to determine what information will indeed be valid.

Invalid Research

Another set of problems which constrains evaluation centers around an invalid research methodology. The problem may not be defined—that is, what is to be evaluated may not be described or delineated to use the terms of Stufflebeam, Ward and Dettoni. After identifying the issue *valid* data must be collected.

The questions which are raised to collect data to answer the problem must be the right questions. They must be appropriate. If, for example, one is to judge the effectiveness of a social transformation training program, it may be less important to know the number of graduates than it is to know the number of graduates who are indeed functioning as the kind of development leaders that they were intended to be. If an institution has five hundred graduates and 90 percent of them have entered government service as clerks, leaving only fifty as part-time social transformation leaders and part-time taxi drivers, the question of how many graduates the program has would not be as important as what are the graduates doing. How are they serving the churches? It is crucial that the right questions be asked.

Not every evaluation problem requires a high level of sophisticated research and statistical techniques. However, the design must be appropriate for the questions being asked and the problems being addressed.

EVALUATION SUMMARY

Evaluation provides a useful means by which information can be given to Christian social transformation decision-makers. The process of evaluation can be facilitated by the participation of the people who are making the decisions. Participation all the way along is important in the identification of the problems to be addressed or the decisions to be made. By identifying the way that the information will be collected. By checking to see that the values that will be brought to bear are agreed upon and by the assigning of the values to the analyzed data.

One should be careful in evaluation about providing information for the appropriate people to make decisions. While this chapter has not dealt with the administrative issues in evaluation, it should be noted that those making the decisions and implementing the decisions should be the same ones who are receiving the information from the evaluation. For example, if the people who are making decisions are the learners, then they are the ones who should receive the information. If the people who are to benefit and make the decisions from the evaluation are the instructors, then the instructors should participate in the evaluation and decision-making.

Bibliography

Agency for International Development
  1982   *Partnership in International Development with Private and Voluntary Organizations* (Washington, D.C.: Agency for International Development).
Aikman, David
  1978   "Cambodia: An Experiment in Genocide," *Time* (July 31, p. 39–40).
Ajemian, Robert
  1981   "Zealous Lord of a Vast Domain," *Time* (March 30, p. 27).
Allen, Roland
  1960   *Mission Methods: Saint Paul's or Ours?* (London: World Dominion Press).
Anderson, Gerald H.
  1961   *The Theology of the Christian Mission* (Nashville: Abingdon Press).
Anderson, Ray S.
  1986   *Minding God's Business* (Grand Rapids: Eerdmans).
Arensberg, C. M. and A. H. Niehoff
  1971   *Introducing Social Change: A Manual for Community Development*, Second edition (New York: Aldine).
Asian Theological Association
  1983   *1983 Directory and Survey of Theological Schools* (Taiwan: Asian Theological Association).
Association of Theological Schools
  1979   *Voyage, Vision and Venture* (Dayton, Oh.:ATS.). A report from the Task Force on Spiritual Development.
Avevalo, F.
           "The Theology of Inculturation," *East Asian Pastoral Review* (19:245–246).
Barnet, Richard J. and Ronald Muller·
  1974   *Global Reach: The Power of the Multinational Corporations* (New York: Simon and Schuster).
Barrett, David B.
  1982   *World Christian Encyclopedia* (New York: Oxford University Press).
  1983   "Silver and God Have I None: Church of the Poor or Church of the Rich?" *International Bulletin of Missionary Research* (7:4:146–152, October).
Barth, Karl
  1936   *The Doctrine of the Word of God* (Edinburgh: T. and T. Clark).
  1961   *The Humanity of God* (London: Collins).
Barton, Laura, Wayne Bragg, and Eugene B. Shultz, Jr.
  1988   "From Subsistence to Market Economy: Food in Times of Stress in Southern Guanacaste Province, Costa Rica" (proceedings of

the Fourteenth Annual Third World Conference, April 7–9;
Third World Conference Foundation, P.O. Box 53110, Chicago,
IL 60653).

Baumol, William J. and Alan S. Blindes
1979   *Economics Principles and Policy* (New York: Harcourt Brace
Jovanovich).

Beaver, R. Pierce
1980   *American Protestant Women in Mission* (Grand Rapids: Eerdmans).

Beeftu, Alemu
1973   *Field Staff Training for Development in East Africa: A Case Study
in One PVO* (unpublished Ph.D. dissertation, Michigan State University).

Belcher, Forest, R. H. Wilson and James Pearson
1971   *A Manual on Forming National Training and Development
Organizations* (Madison: American Society for Training and Development).

Bellah, Robert
1985   *Tokugawa Religion* (New York: The Free Press).

Bennett, A.
1973   *Reflections on Community Development Education* (Orono, Calif.:
The Northeast Regional Extension Public Affairs Committee).

Bennis, Warren G.
1969   *The Planning of Change* (New York: Holt, Rinehart, and Winston).

Berkouwer, G. C.
1954   *The Person of Christ* (Grand Rapids: Eerdmans).

Bernard, Jessie
1987   *The Female World From a Global Perspective* (Indianapolis: Indiana
University Press).

Block, J. H.
1971   *Mastery Learning Theory and Practice* (New York: Holt, Rinehart
and Winston).
1974   *Mastery Learning in Classroom Instruction* (New York: Macmillan).

Bloom, Benjamin, et al
1971   *Taxonomy of Educational Objectives, Handbooks I and II* (Longman, U.K.: David McKay Co., U.S.).
1981   *Evaluation to Improve Learning* (New York: McGraw-Hill Book
Company).

Boff, L.
1978   *Jesus Christ Liberator: A Critical Christology for Our Times* (Maryknoll: Orbis).

Book of Common Prayer
1979   The Episcopal Church (New York: The Church Hymnal Corporation).

Boorstin, Daniel J.
  1983   *The Discoverers: A History of Man's Search to Know His World and Himself* (New York: Vintage Books).
Bosch, David J.
  1979   *A Spirituality of the Road* (Scottdale, Penn.: Herald Press).
  1980   *Witness to the World: The Christian Mission in Theological Perspective* (Atlanta: John Knox Press).
  1987   "Toward Evangelism in Context," in Vinay Samuel and Christopher Sugden (eds.) *The Church in Response to Human Need* (Grand Rapids: Eerdmans. pp. 180–192).
Boserup, Ester
  1970   *Women's Role in Economic Development* (New York: St. Martin's Press).
Bowen, Earle
  1984   "The Learning Styles of African Students" (Ph.D. dissertation, Florida State University).
Braaten, E. E.
  1977   *The Flamming Center: A Theology of the Christian Mission* (Philadelphia: Fortress Press).
Bragg, Wayne G.
  1976   *Nonformal Education and Social Change in Brazil: The Role of Projeto Rondon in National Integration* (Ann Arbor: University Microfilms).
  1987   "From Development to Transformation," in Vinay Samuel and Christopher Sugden (eds.) *The Church in Response to Human Need* (Grand Rapids: Eerdmans. pp. 20–51).
  1988a "The Ethics of International Development: An Alternative Approach" (Proceedings of the Fourteenth Annual Third World Conference, April 7–9; Third World Conference Foundation, P.O. Box 53110, Chicago, IL 60653).
Bragg, Wayne G., Alejandro Martinez, and Eugene B. Shultz Jr.
  1988   "Estrategia Para Nuevas Empresas Agricolas en Centroamerica: Desarrollo del Jicaro en Nicaragua" (presented at the 34th Annual Meeting of the Central American Cooperative Program for the Improvement of Food Plants, San José, Costa Rica, March 21–25).
Bready, John W.
  1942   *This Freedom Whence* (New York: American Tract Society).
Brewster, E. Thomas and Elizabeth S.
  1984a *Bonding and the Missionary Task* (Pasadena: Lingua House).
  1984b *Language Learning Is Communication—Is Ministry!* (Pasadena: Lingua House).
Bridges, Jerry
  1978   *The Pursuit of Holiness* (Colorado Springs: Navpress).

Brislin, Richard W.
    1986   *Intercultural Interactions* (Beverly Hills: Sage).
Brookfield, Stephen
    1986   *Understanding and Facilitating Adult Learning* (San Francisco: Jossey Bass).
Buhlmann, W.
    1978   *The Coming of the Third Church* (Maryknoll: Orbis).
Cannon, William
    1960   *History of Christianity in the Middle Ages* (Nashville: Abingdon).
Carrol, John B.
    1970   "Problems of Measurement Related to the Concept of Learning for Mastery" reprinted in J. H. Block, *Mastery Learning Theory and Practice* (pp. 29–46).
Candy, Philip C.
    1981   *Mirrors of the Mind: Personal Construct Theory in the Training of Adult Educators* (University of Manchester Monographs).
Carstairs, G. M.
    1955   "Medicine and Faith in Rural Rajasthan," in B. D. Paul (ed.) *Health, Culture and Community* (New York: Russell Sage Foundation).
Casse, Pierre
    1979   *Training for the Cross-Cultural Mind* (second edition, Washington, D.C.: Society for Intercultural Education, Training and Research).
    1982   *Training for the Multicultural Manager* (Washington, D.C.: SETAR).
CEPAD Report
    1988   "Baptists Reject 'Tainted' Funds for Managua Hospital" (Alton Conference Center, 32867 SE Highway 211, Eagle Creek, OR 97022, July–August).
Chang, Lit-sen
    1969   *Zen-Existentialism: The Spiritual Decline of the West* (Phillipsburg, N.J.: Presbyterian and Reformed Publishing Co.).
Charlton, Sue Ellen M.
    1984   *Women in Third World Development* (Boulder, Colo.: Westview).
Cherupallikat, Justinian O.F.M. CAP.
    1975   *Witness Potential of Evangelical Poverty in India* (Switzerland: Nouvelle Revue de Science Missionaire).
Clinton, J. Robert
    1982   "Preparing Instructional Objectives" (Pasadena: School of World Mission, unpublished Programmed Instructional and Information Mapped Module for use in ML 561 Programmed Instruction Class).
    1984a   *Leadership Emergence Patterns: A Self-Study Manual for Evaluating Leadership Selection Processes* (Altadena: Barnabas Resources).
    1984b   *Leadership Training Models: A Self-Study Manual for Evaluating Training* (Altadena: Barnabas Resources).
    1984c   *Leadership Training Models* (Altadena: Barnabas Associates).

1985a *Spiritual Gifts* (Alberta, Canada: Horizon House Publishers).
1985b *Leadership Training Models: Reader* (Altadena: Barnabas Resources).
1985c *ML 531 Leadership Training Models Syllabus* (Pasadena: School of World Mission, unpublished course syllabus).
1986 *ML 530 Leadership Emergence Patterns Syllabus* (Pasadena: School of World Mission, unpublished course syllabus).

Cockburn, Alexander
1988 "Beat the Devil," *The Nation* (247:13:446–447, November 7).

Conn, Harvie and Samuel Rowen
1983 *Missions and Theological Education in Perspective* (Farmington, Mich: Associates of Urbanus).

Costas, Orlando E.
1974a "Evangelism and the Gospel of Salvation," *International Review of Mission* (63:249:33, January).
1974b *The Church and Its Mission: A Shattering Critique from the Third World* (Wheaton: Tyndale).

Craig, Robert (ed.)
1976 *Training and Development Handbook* (New York: McGraw-Hill).

Crespo, Richard
1987 "Effective Field Training," Personal interview with Stephen Hoke.

CRESR
1982 *Evangelism and Social Responsibility: An Evangelical Commitment* (Lausanne Occasional Paper 21, John R. W. Stott (ed.), Wheaton: Lausanne Committee/World Evangelical Fellowship).

Cropley, A. J. and R. H. Dave.
1978 *Lifelong Education and the Training of Treachers* (New York: Pergamon Press/UNESCO).

Cunningham, Fred B.
1982 *A Presbyterian Program of Spiritual Formation for Candidates for Ministry; Need, Theory and Practice* (unpublished D. Min. Project for Louisville Presbyterian Seminary).

Curley, Michael D. and Richard E. Gift
1985 "Investment Incentives and Rural Conflict: The Case of South Vietnam," *The Journal of Developing Areas* (20:50, October).

D'Abreo, Desmond A.
1983 *From Development Worker to Activist* (Mangalore: DEEDS, Lower Bendur, Karnatakaa 574002, India).

Daloz, Laurent
1986 *Effective Teaching and Mentoring* (San Francisco: Jossey Bass).

Davis, Ivor K.
1981 *Instructional Technique* (New York: McGraw-Hill).

Davis, Robert H., Lawrence T. Alexander, and Stephen L. Yelon
1974 *Learning System Design—An Approach to the Improvement of Instruction* (New York: McGraw-Hill).

Davis, Sheldon H.
  1977 *Victims of the Miracle: Development and the Indians of Brazil* (London: Cambridge University Press).
Dawson, David
  1982 *Equipping the Saints*, 4 Volumes (Greenville, Texas, ETS Ministry).
Dayton, Edward R.
  1987 "Social Transformation: The Mission of God," in Vinay Samuel and Christopher Sugden (eds.) *The Church in Response to Human Need* (Grand Rapids: Eerdmans. pp. 52–61).
Declaración a la Iglesia Cristiana de América Latina
  1988 "A Declaration by the First Workshop on Rural Development and the Environment." San José, Costa Rica (Copies: Dr. Rolando Mendoze, Programa de Educatión Ambiental, Universidad Estatal a Distancia, Aptdo. 1017, 2050 San Pedro de Montes de Oca, Costa Rica, July 9–17).
DeLamotte, Roy
  1980 "Can Blacks Escape the Mainstream?" *Christian Century* (97:9:277, March 12).
Dennis, James S.
  1899 *Christian Missions and Social Progress: A Sociological Study of Foreign Missions* (New York: Fleming H. Revell, 3 vols. 1887, 1899, 1906).
DeSherbinin, M. J.
  1982 *1981 World Refugee Survey* (New York: United States Committee for Refugees).
Dobyns, Henry, Carlos Medrano and Mario Vasquez
  1966 "A Contagious Experiment," in Arthur H. Niehoff (ed.) *A Casebook of Social Change* (Chicago: Aldine).
Dolan, Edwin G.
  1980 *Basic Economics* (second edition, Hinsdale, Ill.: The Dryden Press).
Dollar, Harold
  1978 "Lawrence Kohlberg's Theory of Moral Development a Discussion" (unpublished paper, Fuller Theological Seminary, School of World Mission).
Douglas, J. D. (ed.)
  1974 *The New Bible Dictionary* (Grand Rapids: Eerdmans).
  1975 *Let the Earth Hear His Voice* (Minneapolis: World Wide Publishers).
Downey, Raymur J.
  1982 "In-service Ministerial Formation: The Perspective of Jesus' Training Methodology" (unpublished paper, Fuller Theological Seminary, School of World Mission)..
Draves, William A.
  1984 *How to Teach Adults* (Manhattan, Kan.: Learning Resource Networks).

Drewery, Mary
  1979 *William Carey, A Biography* (Grand Rapids: Zondervan).
Dubose, Francis
  1978 *How Churches Grow in an Urban World* (Nashville: Broadman).
Dubose, Francis (ed.)
  1979 *Classics of Christian Missions* (Nashville: Broadman).
Dyrness, William A.
  1983 "The Kingdom Is Our Goal," *Together* (October–December, pp. 1–3, 39–40).
Edelman, Marc
  1985 "Extensive Land Use and the Logic of the Latifundio: A Case Study in Guanacaste Province, Costa Rica," *Human Ecology* (13:1:153–185).
Edwards, Tilden H. Jr.
  1980 "Spiritual Formation in Theological Education: Ferment and Challenge," *Theological Education* (17:1, Autumn).
Ellacuria, I.
  1976 *Freedom Made Flesh: The Mission of Christ and His Church* (Maryknoll: Orbis).
Elliston, Edgar J.
  1981 *Curriculum Foundations for Leadership Education in the Samburu Christian Community* (Ph.D. dissertation, Michigan State University).
  1984 "Maasai Leadership Education—An Emerging Process," *East African Journal of Evangelical Theology* (2:2:20–31).
  1986 "Designing Theological Education" (Address given to the Association of Professors of Mission, Chicago).
  1987 Interview with Lynn Samaan, May 28, 1986.
Elliston, Edgar J. and W. Michael Smith
  1976 "An Outline for Leadership Program Planning and Evaluation" (mimeographed paper).
EPOCA
  1987 *Central America: Roots of Environmental Destruction*, Green Paper Two (The Environmental Project on Central America, 13 Colombus Avenue, San Francisco, Calif. 94111).
Esayas, M.
  1981 *The Local Context as a Source of Evaluation of Mass Communication, Development, Education and Religion in Africa* (unpublished Ph.D. dissertation, Michigan State University).
Escobar, Samuel
  1970 *Christians and Social Responsibility, Latin America Evangelist* (Coral Gables: Latin America Mission, March).
Etlings, Arlen Wayne
  1975 *Characteristics of Facilitators: The Ecuador Project and Beyond*

(Amherst: Center for International Education, University of Massachusetts).

Evans, David R.
1981   *The Planning of Nonformal Education* (Paris: International Institute for Educational Planning).

Fiedler, Fred
1977   "The Trouble with Leadership Training Is That It Doesn't Train Leaders," in William R. Lassey and Richard R. Fernandez, *Leadership and Social Change* (La Jolla: University Associates), pp. 238–246.

Flanagan, Padraig (ed.)
1979   *A New Missionary Era* (Maryknoll: Orbis Books).

Flora, Cornelia Butler
"Incorporating Women into International Development Programs: The Political Phenomenology of a Private Foundation," in Kathleen and Jane Jaquette (eds.) *Women in Developing Countries: A Policy Focus* (New York: Naworth Press).

Ford, LeRoy
1978   *Design for Teaching and Training: A Self-Study Guide to Lesson Planning* (Nashville: Broadman Press).

Forman, C. W.
1974   "Is There a Missionary Message?" *Mission Trends No. 1* (Grand Rapids: Eerdmans).

Foster, Richard
1978   *Celebration of Discipline* (San Francisco: Harper and Row).

Fowler, James W.
1981   *Stages of Faith—The Psychology of Human Development and the Quest for Meaning* (San Francisco: Harper and Row).

Freire, Paulo
1973   *Education for Critical Consciousness* (New York: Seabury Press).
1985   *The Politics of Liberation* (South Hadley, Mass: Bergin and Garvey Publishers).
1986   *Pedogogy for Liberation* (South Hadley, Mass: Bergin and Garvey Publishers).

Frymann, Jeleta
1986   "The Movement: Charting the Rising Tide of Mission Interest," in *World Christian* 5:1 (January–February):25–28.

Gaestel, Robert
1986   Interview with Lynn Samaan: Center for Christian Spirituality, Church of the Angels (August 28).

Gagne, Robert
1974   *Essentials of Learning for Instruction* (Hinsdale, Ill.: The Dryden Press).

George, Susan
  1988 "Financing Ecocide in the Third World," *The Nation* (246:601–606, April 30).
Gerber, Virgil
  1980 *Discipling Through Theological Education by Extension* (Chicago: Moody Press).
Gibson, Tim
  1987 "Introduction," in Tim Gibson (ed.) *Stepping Out A Guide to Short-term Missions* (Monrovia: Short-term Missions Advocates, Inc.).
Gilpin, Clifford W.
  1979 *Issues in Nonformal Education and Training for Rural Development* (New York: World Bank).
Glasser, Arthur F.
  1974 "What is Mission Today?" in G. H. Anderson and T. F. Stransky (eds.) *Mission Trends No. 1* (Grand Rapids: Eerdmans).
Goodenough, Ward Hunt
  1963 *Cooperation in Change* (New York: Russell Sage Foundation).
Goulet, Denis
  1971 *The Cruel Choice: A New Concept in the Theory of Development* (Cambridge, Mass: Center for the Study of Development and Social Change).
Greenleaf, Robert K.
  1977 *Servant Leadership: A Journey Into the Nature of Legitimate Power and Greatness* (New York: Paulist Press).
Greenway, Roger
  1983 "Don't Be an Urban Missionary Unless . . . " *Evangelical Missionary Quarterly* (19:2:86–94, April).
Gregory, John Milton
  1917 *The Seven Laws of Teaching* (Grand Rapids: Baker).
Griffen, Karen W.
  1976 *The Incarnation: Christian Personhood and the Covenant Community* (M.A. Thesis, Fuller Theological Seminary).
Grigg, Viv
  1984 *Companion To the Poor* (Sutherland, Australia: Albatros Books).
Grounds, Vernon
  1969 *Evangelicals and Social Responsibility* (Scottsdale, Penn.: Herald Press).
Gudmunson, Lowell
  1983 *Hacendados, Politicos y Precaristas: La Ganadería y el Latifundio Guanacasteco, 1800–1950* (San José: Editorial Costa Rica).
Gutierrez, Gustavo
  1984 *We Drink from Our Own Wells: The Spiritual Journey of a People* (Maryknoll: Orbis Press).

Haines, J. H.
  1980 A World Without Hunger (Washington, D.C.: National Council of
        Churches, Church World Service).
Hanks, L. M. and J. R. Hanks
  1955 "Diptheria Immunization in a Thai Community," in B. D. Paul
        (ed.) Health, Culture and Community (New York: Russell Sage
        Foundation).
Hanneh, Ian
  1924 Monasticism (London: Allen and Unwin).
Harris, Mike
  1983 "An Analysis of an Apprenticeship Accountability Group" (un-
        published paper, Fuller Theological Seminary, School of World
        Mission).
Hastings, James (ed.)
  1959 Encyclopedia of Religion and Ethics, Vol. 6 and Vol. 11 (Edinburgh:
        T. and T. Clark Publishers).
Havelock, Ronald G.
  1973 Training for Change Agents (Ann Arbor: University of Michigan).
Haveman, L. J.
  1981 Non-governmental Organizations in International Development:
        Their History, Role and Opportunities (unpublished M.A. thesis,
        Michigan State University).
Hawthorne, Steve (ed.)
  1987 Stepping Out: A Guide to Short-term Missions (Monrovia: Short-
        term Missions Advocates, Inc.).
Hayter, Teresa
  1981 The Creation of World Poverty: An Alternative View to the Brandt
        Report (London: Pluto Press).
Henry, Carl F. H.
  1947 The Uneasy Conscience of Modern Fundamentalism (Grand Rapids:
        Eerdmans).
  1971 A Plea for Evangelical Demonstration (Grand Rapids: Baker).
Hearne, B.
  1980 "Christology and Inculturation" AFER, (22:335–341).
Heredero, J. M.
  1977 Rural Development and Social Change: An Experiment in Nonfor-
        mal Education (Columbia Mo.: South Asia Books).
Hestenes, Roberta
  1982 "Some Issues on Developing a Protestant Spirituality" (report, Fuller
        Theological Seminary, The Office of Christian Community).
Hicks, J.
  1987 "Christology in an Age of Religious Pluralism" Journal of Theology
        for Southern Africa (35:4–9).

Hiebert, Paul G.
1983 *Cultural Anthropology* (Grand Rapids: Baker).
1985 *Anthropological Insights for Missionaries* (Grand Rapids: Baker).
Hill, Peter J.
1987 "Analysis of the Market Economy: Strengths, Weaknesses and the Future" *Transformation* (4:3 and 4:41, June and September).
Hofstede, Geert
1980 "Motivation, Leadership and Organization: Do American Theories Apply Abroad?" *Organizational Dynamics* (Summer, pp. 42–63).
1987 "Megatrends in Missions" in *Direction* 16 (Spring):1.
Holland, Frederic
1978 *Theological Education in Context and Change* (D. Miss. dissertation, Fuller Theological Seminary).
Hollyday, Joyce
1986 "'You Shall Not Afflict . . . '" *Sojourners* (15:3:18–22, Spring).
Hoopes, David S. and Lippitt, Gordon L.
1978 *Helping Across Cultures* (Washington, D.C.:International Consultants Foundation).
Hutchinson, William R.
1987 *Errand to the World: American Protestant Thought and Foreign Missions* (Chicago: University of Chicago Press).
International Consultation on Simple Lifestyle
1980 *An Evangelical Commitment to Simple Lifestyle* (Colorado Springs: World Evangelical Fellowship).
International Consultation on Simple Lifestyle
1980 "Evangelicals Discuss Theology of Human Development" (Press release, Hoddeson, England, March 15).
Jegen, Mary Evelyn and Bruno V. Manno
1978 *The Earth is The Lord's* (New York: Paulist Press).
Jeng, Timothy
1982a "Evangelism Explosion Training Program Evaluation—LACC" (unpublished paper, Fuller Theological Seminary, School of World Mission).
1982b "Masterlife Discipleship Training (A report and an Evaluation of a Masterlife Workshop)" (Pasadena: SWM, unpublished paper).
Johnson, Arthur
1978 *The Battle for World Evangelism* (Wheaton: Tyndale).
Jorgensen, K.
1976 "Models of Communication in the New Testament" *Missiology* 4 (October):465–484.
Kahn, Herbert
1970 *The Year 2000: A Framework for Speculation on the Next 33 Years* (New York: Random House).

Kahn, Herman
  1982   *The Coming Room* (New York: Simon and Schuster).
Kemp, Jerrold
  1977   *Instructional Design* (Belmont, Calif.: David S. Lake Publishers).
Kia, Cyprian
  1987   Personal report to Paul Hiebert, Fuller Theological Seminary, School of World Mission.
Kime, James Richard
  1983   *The Incarnation in Missiological Education: Some Proposals for an Australian Curriculum* (D. Min. dissertation, Eastern Baptist Theological Seminary).
Kinnear, Angus
  1974   *Against the Tide* (Fort Washington, Penn.: Christian Literature Crusade).
Knowles, Malcolm
  1980   *The Modern Practice of Adult Education —From Pedagogy to Andragogy* (Chicago: Follett Publishing).
Knox, Alan B.
  1986   *Helping Adults Learn* (San Francisco: Jossey Bass).
Kohls, L. Robert
  1981   *Developing Intercultural Awareness* (Washington, D.C.: Society for Intercultural Education, Training, and Research).
Kolb, David A.
  1984   *Experiential Learning* (Englewood Cliffs: Prentice-Hall).
Kraft, Charles H.
  1979a *Christianity in Culture: A Study in Dynamic Biblical Theologizing in Cross-Cultural Perspective* (Maryknoll: Orbis).
  1979b *Communicating the Gospel God's Way* (Ashland, Ohio: Ashland Theological Seminary).
Krathwohl, David R. et al
  1964   *Taxonomy of Educational Objectives Affective Domain* (New York: McKay).
Kraybill, Donald B. and Phyllis Pellman Good (eds.)
  1982   *The Perils of Professionalism* (Scottsdale, Penn.: Herald Press).
Kuitse, A. C.
  1982   "Mission by Presence" (unpublished paper presented to the Mennonite Council for International Ministries, May 25).
Kuyper, Abraham
          Christianity and the Class Struggle (Grand Rapids: Piet Heirr Publishers).
  1983   *Lectures on Calvinism* (Grand Rapids: Eerdmans).
Laird, D.
  1985   *Approaches to Training and Development* (second edition, Reading, Mass: Addison-Wesley).

Lassy, William R. and Richard R. Fernandez
  1976 *Leadership and Social Change* (La Jolla: University Associates).
Lausanne Committee for World Evangelization
  1982 *Evangelism and Social Responsibility* (Grand Rapids Report No. 21, Monrovia: World Evangelical Fellowship).
  1983 *Evangelism and Social Responsibility* (Exeter: The Paternoster Press).
Lean, Geoffrey
  1980 "Conserving Earth's Web of Life," *The Observer* (London, March 9).
Lear, John
  1966 "Reaching the Heart of South America," in Arthur H. Niehoff (ed.) *A Casebook of Social Change* (Chicago: Aldine).
Lee, David Tai
  1983 *A Missionary Training Program for University Students in South Korea* (D. Miss. dissertation, Trinity Evangelical Divinity School).
Lee, John and Ronald Taylor
  1986 *Ravage in the Rain Forests, U.S. News and World Report* (March, 3161–62).
Leech, Kenneth
  1980 *True Prayer* (San Francisco: Harper and Row).
Levine, S. Joseph and Alemu Beeftu
  1987 "Improving Staff Training in Nonformal Education," *Together* (July–September, pp. 11–13).
Lind, Tim
  1978 *Biblical Obedience and Development* (Akron, Penn.: Mennonite Central Committee).
Long, Paul Brown
  1981 *Disciple The Nations: Training Brazilians for Inter-Cultural Missions* (Ph.D. dissertation, Fuller Theological Seminary).
Louth, Andrew
  1983 *The Origins of the Christian Mystical Tradition* (New York: Oxford University Press).
Lynton, Rolf P. and Udai Pareek
  1978 *Training for Development* (West Hartford, Calif.: Kumarian Press).
Macagba, Rufi A.
  1977 *A Managerial Approach to Relief and Development in Developing Countries* (unpublished manuscript).
Mager, Robert F.
  1962 *Preparing Instructional Objectives* (San Francisco: Fearon Press).
  1968 *Developing Attitude Toward Learning* (Belmont: Fearon Press).
  1972 *Goal Analysis* (Belmont: Fearon Press).
  1973 *Measuring Instructional Intent* (Belmont: Fearon Press).
Mager, Robert F. and Kenneth M. Beach, Jr.
  1967 *Developing Vocational Instruction* (Belmont: Fearon Publishers).

Magnuson, Ed
  1980   "The Poisoning of America," *Time* (September 22, pp. 58–69).
Maloney, George A. (ed.)
  1983   *Pilgrimage of the Heart: Treasury of Eastern Christian Spirituality* (San Francisco: Harper and Row).
MARC
  1982   *Directory: North American Protestant Schools of Missions* (Monrovia, Calif.: MARC).
Marsden, George
  1980   *Fundamentalism and American Culture: The Shaping of Twentieth Century Evangelicalism, 1870–1925* (New York: Oxford University Press).
Martin, Alvin
  1974   *Missiological Education: An Appraisal of the 1972–1974 Curriculum of the School of World Missions and Institute of Church Growth* (Pasadena: Fuller Theological Seminary, School of World Mission).
Maslow, Abraham
  1954   *Motivation and Personality* (New York: Harper and Row).
Mbiti, John S.
  1970   *African Religions and Philosophy* (Garden City, N.Y.: Anchor Books).
McGavran, Donald A.
  1969   "Five Kinds of Leaders" (a lecture presented at Columbia Bible College).
  1970   *Understanding Church Growth* (Grand Rapids: Eerdmans).
McKechnie, G. L. (ed.)
  1979   *Webster's New Twentieth Century Dictionary Unabridged* (2nd ed., William Collins Publishers).
McKenna, David
  1986   *Megatruth: The Church in the Age of Information* (San Bernardino, Calif: Here's Life Publishers).
McKinney, Lois
  1982   "Leadership: Key to the Growth of the Church," in Vergil Gerber (ed.) *Discipling Through Theological Education by Extension* (Chicago: Moody Press, pp. 179–191).
  1983   "Educational Planning for Cross-Cultural Ministries" (Wheaton: Wheaton Graduate School Course Syllabus and Course Notes).
  1983   "Social Factors in Learning" (Wheaton: Wheaton Graduate School Course Syllabus and Course Notes).
Mead, Frank S.
  1965   *Encyclopedia of Religious Quotations* (London: Peter Davis Ltd).
Metosalem, Castillo
  1975   *Missiological Education: A Proposed Curriculum for the Alliance Graduate School of Church Growth and Missions* (D. Miss. Dissertation, Fuller Theological Seminary).

Michaelson, Wes
1979 "Evangelicalism and Radical Discipleship," in *Evangelicalism and Anabaptism*, C. Norman Kraus (ed.) (Scottsdale, Penn.: Herald Press).

Millham, Douglas
1986 *Lake Wales Consultation Reference Manual* (Monrovia: World Vision).

Moberg, David O.
1972 *The Great Reversal: Evangelism Versus Social Concern* (Philadelphia: Lippincott).

Moffitt, Robert
1987 "The Local Church and Development," in Vinay Samuel and Christopher Sugden (eds.) *The Church in Response to Human Need* (Grand Rapids: Eerdmans, pp. 234–253).

Montgomery, James and Donald A. McGavran
1980 *The Discipling of a Whole Nation* (Santa Clara, Calif: Global Church Growth Bulletin).

Montgomery, John
1970 "Evangelical Social Responsibility," in Gary Collins (ed.) *Our Society in Turmoil* (Carol Stream, Ill.: Creation House).

Moore, Duane and Ramona Smith Moore
1980 *Ending World Hunger: A Four Season Study on Hunger for Christians* (North Manchester, In.: Mennonite Central Committee).

Moran, Robert T. and Philip R. Harris
1981 *Managing Cultural Differences* (Houston: Gulf).
1982 *Managing Cultural Synergy* (Houston: Gulf).

Morrison, James H.
1976 "Determining Training Needs," in Robert L. Craig (ed.) *Training and Development Handbook* (New York: McGraw Hill, pp. 9-1–9-17).

Myers, Bryant
1982 "The Development Process for People, By People," *World Vision* 26 (November):12–15.
1987 "Teach by Showing; Learn by Doing," *Together* 15 (July-September):16.

Naisbitt, John
1982 *Megatrends* (New York: Warner Books).

Nee, Watchman
1969 *Changed Into His Likeness* (New York: Christian Literature Crusade).
1972 *Spiritual Authority* (New York: Christian Fellowship Publishers, Inc.).
1980 *The Normal Christian Church Life* (Anaheim: Living Stream Ministry).

Niehoff, Arthur H. (ed.)
1966 "Theravada Buddhism: A Vehicle for Technical Change," *A Casebook of Social Change* (Chicago: Aldine).

Neill, Stephen
    1964   A History of Christian Missions (Baltimore: Penguin Books).
Nemer, Larry
    1983   "Spirituality and the Missionary Vocation," Missiology (11:4:419–
           434, October).
New English Bible
    1976   (New York: Oxford University Press).
New Road Bulletin
    1987   "The Scientific Imperative of Conservation" (Gland, Switzerland:
           World Wildlife Federation Network on Conservation and Religion).
Newbigin, Leslie
    1978   The Open Secret: Sketches for a Missionary Theology (Grand Rapids:
           Eerdmans).
Newsweek
    1981   "The Vanishing Tribes" (October 12, pp. 92–97).
Novak, Michael
    1982   The Spirit of Democratic Capitalism (New York: Simon and Schus-
           ter Publishers).
O'Gorman, Francis
    1978   Roles of Change Agents in Development (Occassional Paper No. 3)
           (East Lansing: Michigan State University, Institute for International
           Studies in Education, Non-Formal Education Information Center).
    1979   Participatory Development: The Socio-kinetics of Praxis (Ph.D. dis-
           sertation, Michigan State University).
Olsen, C. M.
    1973   The Base Church: Creating Community Through Multiple Forms
           (Atlanta: Forman House).
Pagliuso, Susan
    1976   Understanding Stages of Moral Development: A Programmed Learn-
           ing Workbook (New York: Paulist Press).
Pannenberger, W.
    1968   Jesus—God and Man (Philadelphia: Westminister Press).
Paredes, Tito
    1987   "Culture and Social Change," in Vinay Samuel and Christopher
           Sugden (eds.) The Church in Response to Human Need (Grand
           Rapids: Eerdmans, pp. 62–84).
Parshall, Phil
    1983   Bridges to Islam: A Christian Perspective on Folk Islam (Grand
           Rapids: Baker).
Patterson, George
    1981   Church Planting Through Obedience-Oriented Teaching (Pasadena:
           William Carey Library).
Paul, B. D.
    1955   Health, Culture and Community (New York: Russell Sage Foun-
           dation).

Pearson, Richard B.
  1976 "Organization and Management of Training," in Robert L. Craig
        (ed.) *Training and Development Handbook* (New York: McGraw
        Hill, pp. 2-1-2-17).
Pierson, Paul
  1974 *A Younger Church in Search of Maturity* (San Antonio: Trinity
        University Press).
Popham, W. James
  1973 *The Uses of Instructional Objectives* (Belmont: Fearon Press).
Popham, W. James, et al.
  1970 *Establishing Instructional Goals* (Trenton, N.J.: Prentice-Hall).
Prozesky, M.
  1987 "Christology and Cultural Relativity," *Journal of Theology for
        Southern Africa* (35:44-67).
Rabben, Linda
  1988 "Land, Debt, and Democracy," *The Nation* (246:601-606, April 30).
Rao, Arunasharee P.
  1985 "Gender and Development: Some Strategic Issues," *Women's Stud-
        ies Quarterly* (13:1:18-22, Spring).
Rayburn, William O.
  1960 "Identification and the Missionary Task," *Practical Anthropology*
        (7: Jan.-Feb.).
Ramirez, Anthony
  1988 "A Warming World: What It Will Mean," *Fortune* (July,
        102-107).
Raspberry, William
  1988 "Values: Curse of Low Expectations Hampers Black Underclass,"
        in *The Arizona Republic* (March 12, A31).
Rauschenbaush, Walter
  1917 *A Theology for the Social Gospel* (New York: Abingdon).
Rensberger, Boyce
  1977 "14 Million Acres a Year Vanishing as Deserts Spread around the
        Globe," *New York Times* (August 28).
Riew, Yong K.
  1983 *Biblical Principles Regarding the Missionary Role Found in the
        Gospel of Matthew* (Master of Missiology Thesis, Fuller Theological
        Seminary).
Riley, Maria
  1986 "Essential to the Society: Invisible to the Economy," *Concern*
        (28:1:12-15, January).
Robinson, J. A. T.
  1973 *The Human Face of God* (Philadelphia: Westminister).
Rogan, R. G.
  1981 *Evaluation of the Needs Assessment Phase in a Community Devel-
        opment Project* (Ph.D. dissertation, Michigan State University).

Rogers, Everett
   1983   *Diffusion of Innovations* (3rd ed.) (New York: Free Press).
Rogers, Everett, with Shoemaker, F.
   1971   *Communication of Innovations: A Cultural Approach* (New York: Free Press).
Rooy, Sidney H.
   1965   *The Theology of Missions in the Puritan Tradition* (Grand Rapids: Eerdmans).
Ruiz-Garcia, S.
   1973   "The Incarnation of the Church in Indigenous Cultures," *Missiology* (1:1:21–30).
Ryrie, Charles C.
   1977   "Christ's Teaching on Social Ethics," *Bibliotheca Sacra* (134:535:223–224, July/September).
Samuel, Vinay and Christopher Sugden (eds.)
   1987   *The Church in Response to Human Need* (Grand Rapids: Eerdmans/ Regnum).
Sanders, I. T.
   1970   "The Concept of Community Development," in C. G. Cary (ed.) *The Community Development Process* (Columbia: University of Missouri Press).
Santa Ana, J. de.
   1979   *Good News to the Poor: The Challenge of the Poor in the History of the Church* (Maryknoll: Orbis).
Sargent, Douglas A.
   1960   *The Making of a Missionary* (London: Hodder and Stoughton).
Sattler, Gary
   1982   *God's Glory, Neighbor's Good* (Chicago: Covenant Press).
   1986   Interview with Lynn Samaan, August 28.
Schell, C. Stevens
   1984   *New Covenant Fellowship: A Strategy for Developing the Spiritual Health of the Congregation* (Pasadena: Fuller Theological Seminary, School of World Mission).
Schon, Donald A.
   1983   *The Reflective Practitioner* (New York: Basic Books).
Schrotenboer, Paul G.
   1972   "Theological Education on the Mission Field in Kingdom Perspective," *Nederduitse Gereformeerde Theologiese Tydskrif* (13:3:193–200).
Schuh, L. H.
   David Zeisberger (Columbus: The Book Concern).
Schumacher, E. F.
   1973   *Small is Beautiful: Economics as if People Mattered* (New York: Harper and Row).

Shaeffer, John R. and Raymond H. Brand
 1980 *Whatever Happened to Eden?* (Wheaton: Tyndale House).
Sheldon, Joseph K.
 1984 "Christian Responsibility for Environmental Stewardship," *Eastern College Bulletin* (St. David's, Penn.: Eastern College, October).
Shenk, Wilbert R.
 1983 *Exploring Church Growth* (Grand Rapids: Eerdmans).
Shenk, Wilbert R. (ed.)
 1980 *Mission Focus: Current Issues* (Scottsdale, Penn.: Herald Press).
Sholoff, Stanley
 1969 "Presbyterians and Belgian Congo Exploitation, The Compagnie du Kasai R. Morrison and Sheppard," *Journal of Presbyterian History* (47:173-194).
Sider, Ronald J.
 1977 *Rich Christians in an Age of Hunger: A Biblical Study* (Downers Grove, Ill.: Inter Varsity Press).
 1980 "Resurrection and Liberation: An Evangelical Approach to Social Justice," in Robert Rankin (ed.) *The Recovery of Spirit in Higher Education: Christian and Jewish Ministries in Campus Life* (New York: Seabury).
 1980b Interview with Linda D. Smith, September 11.
Sider, Ronald (ed.)
 1982 *Lifestyle in the Eighties* (Philadelphia: Westminister).
Simkins, Tim
 1977 *Nonformal Education and Development* (Manchester: University of Manchester Press).
Sinclair, Maurice
 1987 "Development and Eschatology," in Vinay Samuel and Christopher Sugden (eds.) *The Church in Response to Human Need* (Grand Rapids: Eerdmans, pp. 161-174).
Sine, Tom
 1981 "Development: Its Secular Past and Its Uncertain Future," in Ronald J. Sider (ed.) *Evangelicals and Development* (Philadelphia: The Westminister Press, pp. 71-86).
 1987 "Development: Its Secular Past and Its Uncertain Future," in Vinay Samuel and Christopher Sugden (eds.) *The Church in Response to Human Needs* (Grand Rapids: Eerdmans, pp. 1-19).
 1985 *Taking Discipleship Seriously* (Valley Forge: Judson Press).
Sivard, Ruth Leger
 1985 *Women . . . A World Survey* (Washington, D.C.: World Priorities).
Smalley, William
 1967 *Readings in Missionary Anthropology* (New York: Practical Anthropology).

Smith, Linda D.
  1987   An Awakening of Conscience: The Changing Response of American
         Evangelicals Toward World Poverty (Ph.D. dissertation, Washing-
         ton University).
Sommer, J. G.
  197?   U.S. Voluntary Aid to the Third World: What is its Future? (Wash-
         ington, D.C.: Overseas Development Council).
Song, C. S.
  1977   Christian Mission in Reconstruction: An Asian Analysis (Mary-
         knoll: Orbis).
Spener, Philip Jacob
  1964   Dia Desideria (Translated by Theodore Tappart, Philadelphia:
         Fortress Press).
Spidlik, Tomas
  1986   The Spirituality of the Christian East (Kalamazoo: Cistercian Pub-
         lishers Inc.).
Srinivasan, Lyra
  1977   Perspectives on Nonformal Adult Learning (New York: World Edu-
         cation).
Staudt, Kathleen
  1986   "Women in Development: Courses and Curriculum Integration,"
         Women's Studies Quarterly (14:3, 4: 21–22).
Staudt, Kathleen and Jane Jaquette (eds.)
  1983   Women in Developing Countries: A Policy Focus (New York: Na-
         worth Press).
Steinaker, Norman W., and M. Robert Bell
  1975   "A Proposed Taxonomy of Educational Objectives: The Experien-
         tial Domain," Educational Technology (January).
  1976   "An Evaluation Design Based on the Experiential Taxonomy," in
         Educational Technology (February).
  1979   The Experiential Taxonomy: A New Approach To Teaching and
         Learning (New York: Academic Press).
Stewart, Doug
  1986   Personal letter to Lynn Samaan, December.
Stewart, Edward C.
  1972   American Cultural Patterns: A Cross-Cultural Perspective (La-
         Grange Park, Ill.: Intercultural Network).
Stewart, John
  1928   Nestorian Missionary Enterprise (Edinburgh: T. and T. Clark).
Stimson, Edward
  1979   Renewal in Christ (New York: Vantage Press).
Stitzel, Judith, Ed Pytlik, and Date Curtis
  1985   "On Connect: Developing a Course on Women in International
         Development," Women's Studies Quarterly (13:2:33–35).

Stockwell, Edward, et al.
  1981   *The Third World Development: Problems and Perspectives* (Chicago: Nelson Hall).
Stoesz, Edgar
  1977   *Thoughts on Development* (revised edition) (Akron: Mennonite Central Committee).
Stott, John R. W.
  1975   *Who is My Neighbor?* (Downers Grove, Ill.: Inter Varsity Press).
Stott, J. and R. T. Cotte
  1979   *Gospel and Culture* (Pasadena: William Carey Library).
Stravers, David
  1983   "World Views, Religious Conversion and Poverty" (Address given at Fuller Theological Seminary, March 8).
Stufflebeam, Daniel L.
  1973   "Evaluation As Enlightenment for Decision-Making," in Blaine R. Worthen and James R. Sanders (eds.) *Educational Evaluation: Theory and Practice* (Worthington, Ohio: Charles A. Jones Publishing Company, pp. 128–142).
Sunkel, Osvaldo
  1980   "Development Styles and the Environment: An Interpretation of the Latin American Case," in Heraldo Munoz (ed.) *From Dependency to Development: Strategies to Overcome Underdevelopment and Inequality* (Boulder: Westview Press).
Tate, M.
  1962   "The Sandwich Islands' Mission Create a Literature," *Church History* (31:182–202).
Taylor, John V.
  1975   *Enough is Enough: A Biblical Call for Moderation in a Consumer-Oriented Society* (Minnneapolis: Augsburg Press).
Teer, Fredrica
        Challenge—A Process Training Model for Learner-Centered Education (New York: World Education).
Thurow, Lester C.
  1980   *The Zero-Sum Society: Distribution and the Possibility of Economic Change* (New York: Basic Books).
Tienou, Tite
  1987   "Evangelism and Social Transformation," in Vinay Samuel and Christopher Sugden (eds.) *The Church in Response to Human Need* (Grand Rapids: Eerdmans, pp. 175–179).
Tinker, Irene, M. B. Bramsen and M. Buvinic (eds.)
  1976   *Women and World Development* (New York: Praeger).
Todaro, M.
  1977   *Economic Development in the Third World* (second edition) (New York: Longman).

Toffler, Alvin
  1970   *Future Shock* (New York: Random House).
Tongerson, Steve
  1982   "A Case Study and Evaluation of the Apprenticeship Model,"
         (Fuller Theological Seminary, School of World Mission).
United Nations High Commissioner for Refugees
  1984   *Report on UNHCR Assistance Activities in 1983-1984 and Proposed
         Voluntary Funds Programmes and Budget for 1985* (New York:
         United Nations High Commissioner for Refugees).
Voelkel, Alan
  1988   Interview with Darrow Miller, development worker, Food for the
         Hungry (March 12).
Von Mises, Ludwig
  1963   *Human Action: A Treatise on Economics* (Chicago: Contemporary
         Books Inc.).
Wagner, C. Peter
  1981   *Church Growth and the Whole Gospel* (New York: Harper and Row).
Ward, Barbara and Rene Dubos
  1972   *Only One Earth* (New York: W. W. Norton and Co.).
Ward, Ted
         "The Split-Rail Fence: Analogy for Professional Education," *Extension Seminary* (2:5).
         "Schooling as a Defective Approach to Education" (unpublished manuscript).
  1972   "The Rail Fence: An Analogy for the Education of Professionals"
         (Deerfield, IL: Associates of Urbanus).
  1977   "Steps Toward Increased Practicality and Relevance" (unpublished
         lecture notes, Michigan State University).
  1987   "Educational Preparation of Missionaries—A Look Ahead," *Evangelical Missions Quarterly* 23:4 (October):398-404.
  1981   *Church and Development* (Class lecture, Wheaton College).
Ward, Ted and John Dettoni
  1974   "Increasing Learning Effectiveness Through Evaluation," in Ted W.
         Ward and William A. Herzog, Jr. *Effective Learning in Non-formal
         Education* (East Lansing: Michigan State University, pp. 198-288).
Ward, Ted and William A. Herzog, Jr.
  1974   *Effective Learning in Non-formal Education* (East Lansing: Michigan State University).
Ward, Ted and Kathleen Graham
  1977   *Acts of Kindness: Motives and Relationships* (unpublished manuscript).
Ward, Ted and Bryan Truman, et al.
  1987   "Putting Nonformal Education to Work," *Together* (July-September, pp. 7-10).

Warren, M.
  1976 *I Believe in the Great Commission* (Grand Rapids: Eerdmans).
Weaver, Richard M.
  1984 *Ideas Have Consequences* (Chicago: The University of Chicago Press).
Webb, Joe
  1987 "Significant Trends Affecting World Evangelization" (unpublished paper).
Webber, Robert E.
  1979 *The Secular Saint: A Case for Evangelical Social Responsibility* (Grand Rapids: Zondervan).
  1979 *The Integrity of Mission: The Inner Life and Outreach of the Church* (San Francisco: Harper and Row).
  1981 "A Radical Evangelical Contribution From Latin America," in G. H. Anderson and T. F. Stransky (eds.) *Christ's Lordship and Religious Pluralism* (Maryknoll: Orbis).
  1982 "Christ Outside the Gate: Mission Beyond Christendom, A Wholistic Concept of Church Growth," in Wilbert Shenk, *Exploring Church Growth.*
Weber, Max
  1957 *The Theory of Social and Economic Organization* (New York: Free Press).
Weeks, William H.
  1979 *A Manual of Structured Experiences for Cross-Cultural Learning* (Washington, D.C.: Society for Intercultural Education, Training and Research).
Weissman, Myrna
  1986 "Epidemiology of Anxiety and Panic Disorders: An Update," in *Journal of Clinical Psychiatry* (47:6:11–17, June).
Williams, Emilio
  1967 *Followers of the New Faith* (Nashville: Vanderbilt University Press).
Willowbank Report
  1979 (Report on a consultation of gospel and culture held at Willowbank, Bermuda, Jan. 6–13, 1978) in J. Stott and R. T. Coote, (eds.) *Gospel and Culture* (Pasadena: William Carey Library).
Wilson, Robert H.
  1976 "Training in International Cultures," in Robert L. Craig (ed.) *Training and Development Handbook* (New York: McGraw-Hill, pp. 30-1—30-14).
Wimber, John
  1985 *Power Evangelism: Signs and Wonders Today* (London: Hodder and Soughton).
Wlodkowshi, Raymond
  1985 *Enhancing Adult Motivation to Learn* (San Francisco: Jossey Bass).

Wolterstorff, Nicholas
    1983   *Until Justice and Peace Embrace* (Grand Rapids: Eerdmans).
Wonderly, W. L.
    1973   "The Incarnation for the Church in the Culture of the People,"
            Missiology (1:1:23–38).
Woodbridge, John D., Mark A. Noll and Nathan O. Hatch
    1979   *The Gospel in America: Themes in the Story of America's Evangelicals* (Grand Rapids: Zondervan).
World Vision International
    1983   *Objectives of World Vision International* (Monrovia: World Vision International).
            Relief and Rehabilitation Manual (Monrovia: World Vision International).
Worthen, Blaine and James R. Sanders (eds.)
    1973   *Educational Evaluation: Theory and Practice* (Worthington, Ohio: Charles A. Jones Publishing Company).
World Wildlife Federation Network on Conservation and Religion
    1987   "The Scientific Imperative of Conservation," *The New Road Bulletin* (Gland, Switzerland).
Yamamori, Tetsunao
    1987   *God's New Envoys* (Portland: Multnomah Press).
Yankelovich, Daniel
    1981   *New Rules: Searching for Self-Fulfillment in a World Turned Upside Down* (New York: Random House).
Yost, Jim
    1984   "Development Can Hinder Church Growth," *Evangelical Missions Quarterly* (20:4:352–361).
Zaltman, Gerald and R. Duncan
    1977   *Strategies for Planned Change* (New York: John Wiley and Sons).

Index

LINCOLN CHRISTIAN COLLEGE AND SEMINARY